MOUNTAIN SISTERS

MOUNTAIN
SISTERS

*From Convent
to Community
in Appalachia*

Helen M. Lewis & Monica Appleby

Foreword by Rosemary Radford Ruether

THE UNIVERSITY PRESS OF KENTUCKY

Publication of this volume was made possible in part by
a grant from the National Endowment for the Humanities.

Scholarly publisher for the Commonwealth,
serving Bellarmine University, Berea College, Centre
College of Kentucky, Eastern Kentucky University,
The Filson Historical Society, Georgetown College,
Kentucky Historical Society, Kentucky State University,
Morehead State University, Murray State University,
Northern Kentucky University, Transylvania University,
University of Kentucky, University of Louisville,
and Western Kentucky University.
All rights reserved.

Editorial and Sales Offices: The University Press of Kentucky
663 South Limestone Street, Lexington, Kentucky 40508-4008

07 06 05 04 03   5 4 3 2 1

Library of Congress Cataloging-in-Publication Data

Lewis, Helen M., 1924–
    Mountain sisters : from convent to community in Appalachia /
Helen M. Lewis and Monica Appleby ; foreword by Rosemary Radford Ruether.
        p.   cm.
    Includes bibliographical references and index.
    ISBN 0-8131-2268-6 (alk. paper)
    ISBN 0-8131-9090-8 (pbk. – alk. paper)
    1. Federation of Communities in Service—History. 2. Women in church work—
Appalachian Region—History. 3. Glenmary Sisters—History. I. Appleby, Monica,
1937– II. Title.
BV4420.L48   2003
267'.44273—dc21   2003007041

This book is printed on acid-free recycled paper meeting
the requirements of the American National Standard
for Permanence in Paper for Printed Library Materials.

Manufactured in the United States of America.

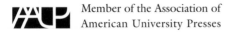
Member of the Association of
American University Presses

Dedicated to the mountains of Appalachia and the people who live here. Thank you for your energy, hospitality, and wisdom.
And to
Mother Mary Catherine, who led the Glenmary Sisters to "walk on water."

CONTENTS

FOREWORD

Rosemary Radford Ruether

This book by Helen Lewis and Monica Appleby about the Glenmary Sisters' journey from religious order to community organization is both fascinating and historically important. It is a story that tells us a great deal about Catholic women in the last fifty years of the twentieth century and into the twenty-first century. It is simultaneously a Catholic story, an American story, and a women's story. It illustrates the extraordinary encounter between these three realities of Catholicism, women, and American society in the context of the Appalachian Region and its people, culture, and struggle for dignity and economic well-being.

As a Catholic story this is a case study of the exciting promise and sad failure of reform in the Catholic Church after the Second Vatican Council. The Council unleashed enormous energy for new theology and pastoral initiatives in a church that had languished under Counter-Reformation repression for four hundred years. The Council suggested a new openness to the modern world that the Catholic Church had tried to shut out for many centuries. It suggested a reform of social structures that would allow democratic collaboration between laity and religious women, religious women and priests, and people and bishops—rather than a church ruled from the top as a feudal monarchy. It suggested a new theology that took into account the whole people of God, particularly women and marginalized groups, rather than privileging the celibate male as normative subject and agent of theology and ministry. It suggested a church truly engaged in justice and the building of the Kingdom of God within history.

The energies released by the Second Vatican Council resounded throughout the Catholic Church, particularly in the United States of America, where Catholics readily identified the church's "people of God" with "We the people." Women in religious orders particularly were inspired to break their traditional boundaries, which had tied them to a monastic life of prayer, penitence, and strict obedience to superiors and divided them from lay people as part of an impure world to be shunned. The Glenmary Sisters responded to the challenge to be with the people. As missionaries to a mostly poor and Protestant area, the Glenmary Sisters quickly found it necessary to improve their education in order to understand the economic and social structures of the region where they were to minister. The traditional long habit was an impediment to real communication with the people already suspicious of Catholics in general and nuns in particular.

But the real impediment to their ministry was the traditional concept of obedience that sought to stifle personal initiative and democratic decision-making among religious women. As the Glenmary Sisters became more and more knowledgeable about what was necessary to carry out effective ministry, they increasingly clashed with hierarchical authority. There were efforts to reimpose a more traditional habit and put them under male clerical administration. The hierarchy's endlessly repressive response to what the Sisters had discerned as the right direction for their Christian service development finally came to a breaking point. There was no option but to leave the order. Many of the former Sisters then created an alternative service community that could function with the kind of freedom and commitment that expressed their calling.

The failure here was clearly that of the hierarchy, not the Sisters, who had made every effort to function in harmony with the bishops—and would have, had they been allowed the appropriate space for their ministry as they had come to understand it. Ultimately this failure of hierarchical authority testifies to the Catholic Church's unwillingness to trust "the people of God"—especially women—to define what God is calling them to do. External regulations, cultural forms, and systems of top-down control were more important than real life inspired by the gospel of love and service to others, particularly the poor and oppressed.

This story of the church hierarchy's failure to allow freedom for real reform illustrates a pattern of continual reassertion of pre–Vatican II models of authority and theology evident since the closing sessions of the Council itself. Catholics caught by the spirit of reform and renewal would leave religious orders, the priesthood, and the Catholic Church itself in droves to find new forms of community—sometimes in other churches, sometimes in new lay communities of their own devising. While enormous creative energy has flowed into these alternative movements, the official church has grown increasingly narrow and stifling, systematically cutting off its most creative offspring. This is sad.

This book is also an American story. It is a story of a region, culture, and people of Appalachia, long exploited and impoverished by outside corporations, neglect of social infrastructure, and abuse of land. The Glenmary Sisters came into the region at a time when coal mining was being mechanized, creating new unemployment and flight to urban areas. They found themselves ministering to Appalachian people both in the rural areas of their original homelands and the urban ghettos to which they had been driven.

As the Glenmary Sisters departed from the religious order to found a new community, the Federation of Communities in Service (FOCIS), they tested the limits of American tolerance for community organizing, which sought to debunk the basic trends of modern state and global centralization. Everything the new community organization stood for went against the grain of the dominant political, economic, and cultural models. It aspired to create community-based educational, cultural, health, legal, and economic development in a national and global society that, in contrast, worked everywhere to replace local control with centralized domination.

Their accomplishments in creating these community-controlled alternatives have been impressive. Even more impressive has been the tireless energy with which they continually picked themselves up after failures and even outright repression by corporate power. But their failures are also illustrative of the extent to which their direction flew in the face of the corporate, political, and economic systems of the American elite, which seem bent on destroying such community-based ways of living and making a living.

Finally this is very much a women's story in the context of the women's movement in American society and in the churches in the 1960s to the present. Most Glenmary Sisters were young women in their teens when they entered the order. Few had finished or even begun a college education. It was assumed that they should be strictly subordinate to male authority and not think for themselves on any subject. Initially they were even treated as servants of the male Glenmary priests and Brothers, spending much of their time cooking, cleaning, and doing laundry for the men. They were seen as a "women's auxiliary" to the male order and the hierarchy, not a real missionary community in their own right.

Their story is one of continual consciousness-raising about their own status and potential as women. They began by realizing their need for better education, finding their way to college and graduate programs to give themselves knowledge of the society to which they were called to minister and the skills to do so. But this education also changed their understanding of who they were as women. They began to reject, piece by piece and layer by layer, the restrictions under which they were told to live and discover their own capacity for autonomy and leadership.

As they moved from religious order to community organization, they began to form new relationships with each other as a women's community. Then they realized the need to form new relations with the people to whom they ministered, moving from charity to community, from paternalism to equal partnership. They also moved from a culture of repressed emotions and sexuality to a discovery of their wholeness as persons in relationships. They moved from dependency to autonomy in organizational relations and economic maintenance. As one Sister put it, "first to go was obedience, then chastity, and then poverty."

Some of the Sisters married, some remained single, and some formed lesbian relations. Their discovery of their sexuality caused some to leave the new community, while others brought their new spouses and partners into it. The community itself expanded, became ecumenical, and included men and children. As a living process, FOCIS itself was continually rethought and reorganized to fit the evolving new patterns of their lives. It moved from being a secular organization—similar to a women's religious order, but no longer under hierarchical authority—to becoming a dispersed network with many centers that animated local projects and communities.

As their sense of their own capacities as women expanded, their understanding of theology and church also was transformed. They began to connect with contextual and liberation forms of theology. They began to shape their own liturgy and celebrations. They realized that some of them were priests, called to create and lead liturgy. They began to realize that they were living a new theology, a feminist liberative theology, and a new church, a women-church, as a discipleship of equals. Alleluia.

Rosemary Radford Ruether is Georgia Harkness Professor of Applied Theology at Garrett Evangelical Theological Seminary in Evanston, Illinois. She is author of many books, including *Women-Church* and *Gaia & God*. She is also co-editor of the documentary history *Women and Religion in America*.

PREFACE

Why and How We Produced This Book

Twelve years of research, reflection, and writing have produced this book, a collective participatory process led by Monica Kelly Appleby, a Glenmary Sister from 1955 to 1967 and the first president of the Federation of Communities in Service (FOCIS). Monica had returned to Blacksburg, Virginia, from working in southern Africa (Botswana, Zimbabwe, and South Africa) in 1987 and was convinced that reflection on the lives and experiences of the former Glenmary Sisters would be a valuable theological process.

Monica understood the power of storytelling to create and maintain community. She explains her motivation:

Storytelling is at the interactive core of community life. In a sense it creates life in community. I felt that to tell this particular story of the Federation of Communities in Service and its origin in the Home Mission Sisters of America would give voice to the personal stories of all of us and create a community story from different perspectives of similar experiences—joining, going on mission, leaving, dispersing, celebrating. Somewhere I read that community is the place where people you would never dream of living and working with come together for a common purpose. We did that as Glenmary Sisters and FOCIS with the purpose of living and working in rural America, although we did not know in the beginning that it was to make a home here in rural Appalachia. Storytelling is interactive in that the person's story creates the community story and the community has its story, too, which is still unfolding.

Several members of FOCIS formed a study group in 1991 and began telling their stories. That same year, Rachel Anne Goodman, a radio producer with WMMT, the community radio of Appalshop Media Center in Whitesburg, Kentucky, became interested in these former Glenmary Sisters who had left the order in 1967 to continue their work in the mountains without the encumbrances of the church hierarchy. She carried out interviews and developed a radio program, *Changing Habits: Catholic Sisters and Social Change in Appalachia*, which was aired by Horizons of Public Radio International (PRI) in 1992 on 140 stations.

Monica Appleby, fellow FOCIS member Anne Leibig, and Appalachian sociologist and activist Helen Lewis began to talk about publishing the stories in a book, believing it was important to document the history of Glenmary/FOCIS and the group of women who had played very important roles in the social movements in the Appalachian Region. The original theology study group became the FOCIS History Book Committee, and they decided to collect oral histories from the members. The committee included Monica Appleby, Helen Lewis, Anne Leibig, Catherine Rumschlag, Jean Luce, and Margaret Gregg. Helen encouraged using oral history since it is a simple tool that provides a way of reclaiming the past and passing it on. The committee decided the history should be told by the people who lived it. Since the voices of the former Sisters became central to the book, the format and presentation as oral history have been preserved. Some stories were so profound and illustrative of important experiences they are presented at length. Later reflections on the interviews were also included. As such, the narrative is not straightforward; it goes back and forth in time. To the reader we ask you to persevere, listen to the voices (most have never been heard in public before), and simply and hopefully join us in community storytelling.

In 1992 interviews with about twenty members of the group were carried out by Jean Luce. Most of the stories were told individually, transcribed, and edited for publication. The History Book Committee then began to collect other interviews, photographs, videos, music, poetry, journals, archival material, and magazine and newspaper articles. The committee reviewed the material that was developed, extracted themes, and developed lists of questions for research.

FOCIS celebrated its twenty-five years in Appalachia with a Festival of Friends in 1993. The festival's storytelling sessions and reflections on their quarter-century together allowed the book to become a collective FOCIS project. Margaret Gregg collected photographs from FOCIS members and made collages and photo-scrapbooks. She also made a more systematic collection of her art through the years and developed a chronology of her work. Monica wrote two articles from the interviews and from her own files and experience. She read a paper at the Appalachian Studies Conference in Cincinnati in 1997.[1]

In 1996, Helen Lewis took on the task of compiling the material and writing the book. By 1998 rough drafts of thirteen chapters were sent to all FOCIS members who had been interviewed and who were willing to read them and come together to reflect on their experiences and the stories of their colleagues. The working title was "Changing Habits." On October 24–26, 1998, fourteen members participated in a weekend workshop at the Highlander Center in New Market, Tennessee. It was in part a dialogue between the group and the writer-compiler, who presented some questions and challenges to the group. They were asked to reflect on what FOCIS had accomplished, what they had learned, and what impact their lives and work had made on the communities and people they had encountered. As the discussion progressed small groups were formed to further discuss certain issues that emerged as more important: Theology, Grieving, Generation Gap, the Future. Suzanna O'Donnell, a writer and librarian, joined the group and agreed to help with the book. All discussions at the workshop were transcribed and edited by Suzanna, who followed through on the many corrections and suggestions from the group.

By reading one another's stories, sharing their experiences, and reflecting on the meaning and impact of their work, the FOCIS women composed a collective story that helped them understand what they had experienced, what was important, and what they could now ignore. The book became a structure for their perceptions and a way to make sense out of the facts and events of their lives.

The year 2000 was a year of rewriting, revising, and reorganizing. Monica and Helen worked closely together to rewrite and reorganize the chapters. They felt at times as if they were snipping lives apart and piecing them together again, selecting from all the stories to make a collective story. John Zeigler of the University Press of Kentucky read the manuscript and made valuable suggestions, recommending making extensive cuts and adding more interpretation. Mary Belenky, author of *Women's Ways of Knowing* and *A Tradition With No Name*, read the manuscript and suggested that we had a good "in house" book, but we needed more context and clarification for the "out house" book.

Suzanna took all these suggestions and did the final editing and cutting to make the manuscript ready for the publisher, while Helen added introductions for each chapter to place the story in context.

It has been an interesting and transforming process as FOCIS members have shared their stories and reflected together about their experiences. It has been a way to come "out of the closet" literally and figuratively. In 1989 Anne Leibig and Monica Appleby discovered their religious survey files in a closet at the Peace and Justice Office in Saint Paul, Virginia. These were brought to Berea College in Berea, Kentucky, where they were discussed with the staff of Appalachian Ministries Research Center and deposited in the Berea College Archives. This was the beginning of a process of sorting lost boxes of files and bringing both papers and memories "out of hiding."

Initially many Sisters were resistant to the process of remembering and reflecting on their experiences. In the discussions, both guilt for leaving Glenmary and anger at the church's actions surfaced. The metaphor of divorce was used. The twelve years of writing and meeting have offered some the opportunity to express their feeling and hopefully to come to peace. The project has also allowed FOCIS members to document their contributions to Appalachia and understand more fully the influence they have had in the region—and the impact the region has had on their lives and work. For the History Book Committee, which had begun as a theology study group, the writing of the book has been part of a deliberate and intense effort to understand and express their own local theology, which is based on their experiences in community, in their relationships, and in their personal life experiences. It has been a way to come "out of hiding" in the mountains and make contact with each other and those who have had similar experiences, adding to the "her story" of Roman Catholicism in the United States.

Many other people helped with the development of this book. Financial assistance for transcribing, research, editing, photo reproductions, etc., was provided over the twelve-year period by a number of people and groups: The Virginia Foundation for the Humanities funded the radio program and Berea College's Center for Appalachian Studies funded some research. Additional money was made available from the FOCIS Development Committee; the Tennessee and Virginia FOCIS groups; and some individual FOCIS members and friends: Anne Leibig, Dick Austin, Kathy Hutson, Margaret Gregg, Ginny Remedi-Brown, Dene Peterson, Ellen Browne, and Jean Luce. Other contributions were made by Clinch River Education Center, Stephen Rhodes, Bishop Walter Sullivan of the Diocese of Richmond, the Glenmary Fathers, Andy and Alan Rabinowitz through the Tides Foundation, and the University Press of Kentucky. The Lyndhurst Foundation donated funds for the Festival of Friends, which provided valuable material for the book.

In addition to the members of FOCIS and former Glenmary Sisters, other friends and colleagues were interviewed or wrote contributions for the book. We especially thank John Gaventa, Patricia Ronan, Carol Honeycutt, Shelby York, Rich Kirby, Frankie Taylor, and Teri Vautrin for their remembrances; Jack Wright for his great story of the High Knob Festival; Sara Friedman for her description of a FOCIS meeting; Kathy McCarthy for her letter and articles about her ordination; Jean Gibb for her letter; Sister Nancy Sylvester for the use of her Presidential Speech to the Leadership Conference of Women Religious; and Rosemary Radford Ruether, who encouraged us to produce the book and took time from her busy teaching schedule to write the foreword.

Our special thanks to colleagues, students, neighbors, and friends who helped us develop this book: Sandy Reagle, who transcribed the first interviews; Rachel Goodman, who helped edit the interviews and wrote a sample chapter; Ginger Nickerson, an intern at Highlander who did interviews in Clairfield, Tennessee, and research in the Notre Dame University Archives and helped organize all the material for writing; Susan Helton, friend, colleague, and social worker/therapist, who helped facilitate the Highlander workshop; Suzanna O'Donnell, who transcribed and edited the discussion at the Highlander workshop and edited and re-edited the manuscript to cut one hundred pages and pull it all together into a coherent story; Lori Briscoe and Erica Collins, students at Appalachian State University, who transcribed some later and difficult-to-understand interviews; Kathy Wager, writer and friend in Blacksburg, Virginia, who helped edit and format the first draft of the book; Lynn Barrett, friend and neighbor, who helped format the final manuscript; Cynthia Maude, writer and editor with the Blue Ridge, Georgia, *News Observer*, who did a final reading and made some editing suggestions; graphic designer Dan Pruitt and photographer Ronald B. Henry, who prepared the pictures for publication; Joe Finacane, husband of FOCIS member Chris Griffin, who moved boxes of material from Georgia to Tennessee; Matt Servaites, graduate student at Virginia Tech, who created the network map of FOCIS connected organizations; André Abecassis, who provided us with photographs from Glenmary days; Nellie Appleby, artist, photographer, and Monica's daughter, who took photos of the 2000 FOCIS meeting; Marie Tedesco, East Tennessee State University faculty member, who arranged with that university's archives to receive the interviews and material collected for the book. She also wrote and presented a paper from the archived material.[2]

Chris Valley, a former Catholic seminarian in Atlanta, provided us with some of his files of Glenmary Sisters, helped prepare the glossary, and read and made editorial suggestions. He later proposed to the Bishop of Cincinnati that the church should apologize to the former Glenmary group. The bishop declined, responding that he believes "the best thing for me to do at this time would be let things alone."[3] That decision was doubly unfortunate, as an apology would have provided a fitting closing to the book.

INTRODUCTION

This story is part of several larger stories. It is part of the history of the post–Vatican II revolution in Catholic religious life in America. It is part of the story of the sweeping change in private and public values that occurred in the 1960s. It is part of the story of what is now called the women's movement. It is part of the history of American movements for social change and part of the history of a troubled region. But above all in these pages is the story of one remarkable group of individuals who came together, first as members of the Glenmary Home Mission Sisters of America, and later as creators of a new community to support their continued service to the people of Appalachia. They are veterans of many struggles, marked and changed first by belief, then by place, and finally by circumstance. What special qualities of the Glenmary Sisters first drew them to choose the congregation as their home for life? What forces later impelled them to abandon the spiritual dwelling they had furnished with hopes and dreams and years of service? And what then happened to the women, their new organization, and their vision for it and for themselves? After more than thirty years, what are their achievements and what have they learned?

This group of creative, dedicated women has lived and worked primarily in the mountains of central Appalachia since the 1960s. There they have upheld their motto: "Honor and Trespass Boundaries as Love and Justice Demand." Although they live in different communities, they maintain a remarkable network of communication and support. In 1966 they were part of a group of one hundred Glenmary Sisters living a communal life under the directives of the church. Today they are wives, mothers, educators, artists, and community workers living independent of church control but still following their commitment to service.

The Glenmary Sisters were a distinctive religious order from their beginning. Father William Howard Bishop established the order to work with the poor in rural regions and to help rural people survive and maintain rural values so they might reinvigorate the church. Glenmary Sisters were not the traditional nurses or teachers but "visitors" and friends to families in Appalachian communities such as Big Stone Gap, Virginia, and McDowell County, West Virginia. As such they became deeply involved in the lives and problems of the Appalachian poor—marginalized people in a marginalized region, trying to survive, to have control over their lives, and to resist the destruction of their communities and their land.

The more the Sisters became involved in the lives of the mountain people, the more they felt impeded by the rules of the church. Long habits, cloistered living, and rules against eating and working with seculars were great barriers to "visiting the poor" in rural Appalachia and the urban ghettos. The Sisters gradually began to make changes in their habits and the rules and regulations they considered unsuitable and outmoded.

Pope John XXIII's historic 1962 proclamation was revolutionary for all religious orders in the United States. The decree endorsed sweeping changes in traditional practices and rules once considered written in stone. While some changes were endorsed by Rome, the hierarchy of priests over nuns remained intact. Although they outranked priests in numbers and education, Sisters had little power within the church even in the post–Vatican II world. Even so, the Second Vatican Council (1962–1965) resulted in dramatic changes in all aspects of Catholic life. In particular, the changes enacted by the Council had significant effects on the lives of women religious,[1] who were encouraged to reexamine all aspects of their constitution and practices in light of contemporary needs and issues.[2] The Glenmary Sisters took the directives to modernize and renew the church seriously, and they began to make changes to better serve the poor. With the permission of local bishops they became an experimental community, and they believed the directives of the Second Vatican Council condoned and encouraged their attempts to make their order fit the modern world.

However, their efforts to modernize their order's governing rules were not universally accepted in the institutional church, and their negotiations with the bishops, cardinals, and priests went without success. The changes in the habit became a hot issue in the church, and their struggle with the male hierarchy over their experimental short habit led to an impasse. Discouraged, some Sisters began to "slip away" from the Home Mission Sisters of America.

In 1967 seventy Glenmary Sisters left the order. Of these, forty-four decided to form a secular, non-profit organization, the Federation of Communities in Service (FOCIS). These young women chose to continue their work with Appalachian families in rural Appalachia and in the urban centers with Appalachian migrants.

The forty-four Glenmary Sisters who left to form FOCIS and the thirty women who left individually were at the forefront of the exodus of women from religious orders in the United States in the 1960s. The effects of that exodus are still reverberating through the religious world.

The 1960s were a time of turbulence and self-questioning for Sisters all over the U.S. There were 180,015 Sisters in religious orders in 1964, the height of religious Sisterhood in the U.S. There are currently about 82,693.[3] There are records of what has happened to Catholic orders of Sisters and some stories of Sisters who left convents. Because FOCIS was an organized effort to maintain the mission and vision of women in ministry it provides stories of transition, of changes over a fifty-year period and the transformative process for FOCIS people and for many whose lives they share within Appalachian communities.

A year after the Glenmary Sisters lost three quarters of their members, 550 members of the Sisters of the Immaculate Heart of Mary from Los Angeles asked for dispensation of their vows in defiance of their cardinal, who wanted them to retract their post–Vatican II reforms. Four hundred of them established a new, non-canonical community. On Christmas Day, 1996, in an article in the *Washington Post* entitled "The Revolutionary Mary," Coleman McCarthy wrote, "In the 1960's, both the Immaculate Heart of Mary Sisters of Los Angeles and the Glenmary Sisters of Cincinnati came up against the male-centered conservatism of local bishops. Empowered by the renewals of the Second Vatican Council, large numbers of Sisters in both these orders left to form their own communities and directly serve those of low degree. They would discover truth in the powerless while rejecting the false dictums of the powerful."[4]

Living and working in the Appalachian Mountains, where they had "sided" with the poor, greatly influenced the Glenmary Sisters. They visited and listened to the people up the hollows of West Virginia, Tennessee, and southwest Virginia. They interviewed the families who became refugees to Detroit, Chicago, and Cincinnati. Instead of converting the mountain people to Catholicism, the Sisters were evangelized by the mountain families. The Sisters had carried out a "religious survey" asking questions of mountain men and women about their beliefs and their faith. They were reeducated by mountain theologians and were "baptized" in the mountains, "converted" by Appalachia.[5] Theirs is a story about a change from missionaries to community. In it they describe how they influenced and were influenced by the incredible economic and social changes that are part of the Appalachian story.

The 1960s were also a time of turbulence and self-questioning by the young adults of the nation. The young women who entered the order in the 1960s were influenced by the national social movements of the times: the women's movement, the Civil Rights movement, and the anti–Vietnam War demonstrations. They began to take public stands on social issues as well as experiment with new liturgies and reinterpret their vows of "obedience, poverty, and chastity."

As FOCIS women, the former Sisters developed a new way of working in communities, in partnership with the poor. In 1968 they stated their mission: "FOCIS members live in local communities as inside-outsiders, residents of Appalachia who have come from other places. With this identity they live as neighbor, friend, interested citizen, professional worker, and community participant."

Through FOCIS these former Catholic Sisters have lived out their original purpose outside of the institutional hierarchy of the church. Their presence, their network of resources, their creativity and spiritual energy have been the organizing force for over a hundred different community projects in six states, from health clinics in Tennessee to community-based factories in Virginia, from arts in the schools, to town water systems and homeless shelters. FOCIS now includes men and members with Protestant backgrounds, who joined the group after its break from the Catholic Church. Some of these had been volunteers and friends of the Sisters, others became colleagues in development work, marriage partners, or secular friends who shared the women's vision and goals. Although the original members share a rich history as religious women, each FOCIS member has a unique story to tell. Their stories document the evolution of women religious (Catholic Sisters), the development of Appalachian communities, and the tenacity of relationships between women committed to a region and to one another.

Part 1: The Glenmary Years tells the stories of the Sisters' first years in the Glenmary Order—their joining the Home Missioners and their training and formation into Glenmary Sisters. Their later reflections on why they joined and the impact of the formation process are included. They tell of their mission experiences and how they dealt with the contradictions between their training, the rules of the order, and the work in the rural mountain communities. From these experiences came their ideas and proposals to renew the church and make their work fit the context in which they were serving. This led to major conflicts with the church, several years of struggle with the hierarchy, and, finally, their painful decision to leave the order, after which some moved to the mountains of Virginia, Tennessee, and West Virginia while others stayed in the Appalachian ghettos of Chicago and Cincinnati.

Part 2: Forming FOCIS begins with the founding members' ceremony of commitment to their newly formed organization and their dreams and plans for a secular organization in which they could continue their missionary work unhampered by the rules and regulations of the patriarchal church. FOCIS moved from an organization with a central staff and community centers to a dispersed community, a federation of friends. FOCIS became a network and a community of mutual support centered on and bound together by their work in the various communities in which they lived and shared values. In their first major region-wide project, FOCIS ARTS, described in chapter 9, they not only brought to the region a new model of community development, but they also learned how to work with communities in a different way.

Part 3: Working in Communities details forty years of work in the region, which has included the formation of health clinics, cooperatives, arts programs, educational programs, legal services, and community development corporations. As FOCIS became a dispersed community, its members utilized their close network to bring and share resources throughout the region and help encourage other work for social justice. They were advocates, social change agents, activists, teachers. As they empowered other women in the communities, they grew and developed their own ways of working and their own understanding of the causes of the region's poverty and inequalities.

Part 4: Honoring and Trespassing Boundaries closes the book with reflections on the FOCIS members' work and an account of their own spiritual growth and theological development. They reflect on how FOCIS developed and changed and how it has served as support, community, and church for the membership. Their evolving feminism and methodology as community workers is explored. They deal with what lessons they have learned and what impact they have made on the church and on the region. They also consider whether they provide a model from which other groups can learn, especially groups who break from hierarchical, authoritarian organizations yet wish to maintain a way of working together and sharing skills and resources. As they reach retirement age, a group of the FOCIS members are now creating an ecumenical retirement community that can provide physical and spiritual support for the closing of their lives in the mountains.

PROLOGUE

A small middle-aged woman dressed in green, purple, and blue and wearing a purple hat steps onto the stage, carrying a split oak basket filled with bones.

To the people assembled in front of her, she says, "I brought some Dungannon bones just to let you know I did get there." She holds the basket of bones above her head and then lays them out on the stage, saying, "These are from the back of Chestnut Ridge Farm. If you walk on Chestnut Ridge Farm you will find bones. Here are some bones to set the scene."

Behind her hangs a blue, yellow, and green Log Cabin friendship quilt designed by one of the women in the room and pieced from squares containing symbols of their lives, which were created by many of those present. Another woman here made the bright quilted banner in front of the podium that repeats the word "Meaning." At the back of the stage a dozen of the same woman's posters silently shout a history of events and issues in the mountains where they are gathered.

It is a Sunday morning in June 1993 in Cumberland Falls, Kentucky, and the final event of the Festival of Friends, marking the twenty-fifth anniversary of the Federation of Communities in Service (FOCIS). More than a hundred members and friends are together in this room.

They are a diverse group: mostly women, from a variety of lifestyles—single, engaged, married, divorced, celibate, heterosexual, lesbian—along with some men, husbands, sons, and friends, and their children. The core are the former Glenmary Sisters who started FOCIS. There are also other ex-Sisters, non-Catholics, friends and colleagues, and current priests and religious from various orders. Most live and work in Appalachia or share a past here.

Having arranged the bones, Anne Leibig stands in front of the altar and raises her arms in celebration. Once a Glenmary Sister and now a

Gestalt therapist living on a farm in Dungannon, Virginia, Anne is married to a Presbyterian theologian who is also a member of FOCIS. She begins the morning ritual with the story of her life journey.

July 26, 1967, twenty-six years earlier—

Mary Catherine Rumschlag, Glenmary Sisters Mother General, issued this press release:

> The Glenmary Sisters have announced that a number of their members plan to move into a new form of life and work. They are asking for a dispensation from their vows and plan to work as a lay, Church-affiliated organization.
>
> The new group will be a lay organization living in community, committed to service for human development with a focus on religious and social needs. For the present, this group will continue to serve particularly the people of Appalachia. . . .
>
> Glenmary Sisters were founded by Father William Howard Bishop in 1941 to work in rural America where Christian influence is minimal.[1]

The *National Catholic Reporter* carried the following account:

Glenmary Down to 15; 50 Leave for Lay Work

by Art Winter

The once-102 member Glenmary order will dwindle to about 15 sisters this month when 50 nuns leave together as lay women. Leading the move into the new organization will be Mother Mary Catherine Rumschlag, superior for the past 14 years; Sister Marie Cirillo, number two in command, and all four sisters on the governing council. It was believed to be the largest departure of nuns from a U.S. religious order since Vatican II. The major exodus in the Glenmary order—one of the youngest and liveliest in the U.S.—was described last week by three members of the order who are joining the new group, to be called the Federation of Communities in Service. . . .

The Sisters said the new group plans to support itself largely from salaries earned by some members.[2]

PART 1

The Glenmary Years

Chapter 1

CHOOSING A LIFE

Glenmary was new, it was young, they were doing something different.

The story begins with very young women choosing a life, as we all do, before they are ready. In 1967 they chose to leave the Home Mission Sisters of America (Glenmary) and the life of service and dedication they had chosen, some five, some ten, some as much as twenty-five years earlier. They chose another life in a secular, non-profit organization, which they created in order to continue the work they had chosen when they joined the Glenmary Sisters. Who were these young women? Why did they join Glenmary in the first place, and why did they leave?

Glenmary was founded by a priest who was involved in the rural renewal movement. He recruited young women to form a missionary movement in poor, largely non-Catholic, rural areas: Appalachia and the South. After World War II, these were areas with immense social and economic problems that became recognized nationally as depressed regions in dire need of help.

Why did young women decide to join an order and leave friends and family forever? Becoming a nun was an accepted, even prestigious career for young Catholic women in the 1940s, '50s and early '60s. It was an alternative to early marriage, going to college, or working in a factory. It was, paradoxically, a secure way to leave home, travel, and have an adventure, yet still be of service and answer the call to a religious vocation. Before 1960 young Catholic women felt they should have a vocation, and many followed the role models of their teachers whom they saw as powerful women. For many it was a way to escape the domestic life lived by their mothers: raising big families and struggling to make ends meet.

As non-Catholic young women went shopping for a college to attend, these young women went convent shopping. Some of them chose Glenmary, which was a new, exciting, and different order. The majority of the women entering Glenmary were very young—most in their late teens, just finishing

high school. Typically they came from Midwestern backgrounds. Many be-
lieved this youthful organization would prove more exciting and interesting
than the older, established orders that traditionally specialized in either teach-
ing or nursing. Glenmary's mission was open-ended. Some were attracted by
the recruitment picture of a young woman on a tractor and a romantic idea
of rural living. In Glenmary, they could be a missionary and not go overseas
or have to learn a foreign language.

The Glenmary Sisters were organized in 1941 by William Howard Bishop, a priest in the Archdioceses of Baltimore-Washington who had founded the Glenmary order of priests and Brothers (Home Missioners of America) in 1937. He envisioned a complementary group of Sisters going out on mission to rural communities "to work for the extension of the Catholic faith and the spiritual advancement of the people in sections of America where there are few or no Catholics by means of Christian education, nursing, and social service, carried on by Sisters who, for the most part, are natives of the countries in which they work."[1]

Father Bishop expressed his vision of their ministry in an article in the *Glenmary Home Missioners* magazine:

> You must acquire Christian-like love for the poor and a great desire to minister to them. You must win them by your kindness in relieving their suffering. You must be careful that you never make them feel inferior by flaunting your superiority or by an unkindness in any way. They must see your love for Christ and your sincerity in trying to help them. You will see suffering of every kind among these people and your hearts will go out to them. You will minister to their bodily needs and win their confidence. Then you can speak to them about Jesus, Mary, and Joseph, the ideal family who were poor and who suffered.[2]

The order (Home Mission Sisters of America)[3] was based in Glendale, Ohio, on a farm bought by Father Bishop in 1940. After fourteen years of experience as a rural pastor and director of the Rural Life Conference in Baltimore, Father Bishop became president of the National Rural Life Conference, serving from 1938 to 1944. He was part of a larger movement interested in rural revitalization. Among more secular young people it became known as the "Back to the Land Movement." The publicity used to recruit the young women to Glenmary prominently played upon this social interest, showing a photograph of a young Sister driving a tractor.

Newport, Kentucky, native Gertrude Kimmich was Glenmary's first member, and Dorothy Hendershot, a nurse from Grand Rapids, Michigan, soon joined her. The early work of the new group was quite limiting, as they were asked to devote much time and effort to cooking, cleaning, and laundering for the men's community. Kimmich served as Father Bishop's secretary. Their first organizational name, "Home Missioners' Women's Auxiliary," adopted in 1942, aptly reflects the type of work the women did in those early years. They did begin some missionary work in the summer of 1944, teaching Bible classes and helping the poor who needed assistance in black and white communities in western Kentucky.[4] However, Gertrude Kimmich left the community in the fall of 1945 because she felt that the original plan for the group was being thwarted. She wanted a group of Sisters who would function incognito in the missions and who would have the necessary independence of action to satisfy needs of the frontier. She moved to work in the diocese of Raleigh, North Carolina.[5]

Catherine Rumschlag was the first of the women highlighted in this history (i.e., those who would eventually form FOCIS) to join Glenmary. She came to Glendale in 1944 and replaced Kimmich as secretary to Father Bishop. Drawn to Glenmary because of its rural outreach, Catherine talked about her decision to join: "I grew up on a farm in a Catholic atmosphere, very Catholic, went to Catholic school, same Catholic school for all twelve grades. I liked the advantages of farm life and the idea of mission work. . . . I heard about Glenmary and it sounded good. I graduated from high school in 1944. I visited the Glenmary Sisters in June and entered in September 1944. When I visited there were five in the community, and when I entered there were three more coming in, so that made eight, and one more came in October." The women at Glendale lived in an old farmhouse. The men lived in a new dormitory, sometimes called "the barracks." Later the men moved into a new seminary and the Sisters moved into the barracks.

Other FOCIS members tell how and why they joined Glenmary. Inspired by the patriotism of the time, Marie Cirillo viewed the order as a chance to serve her own country:

I heard about Glenmary and it was very appealing because at the time I was thinking about foreign missions, [but] I was very conscious of the fact I was terrible in foreign languages . . . and I thought, "Here I can do the same thing only in our own country." Also, it was a period right after World War II, and it was a time of a lot of patriotism. It was sort of "our country" and "victory" and "the flag." So Glenmary . . . was advertised as a call to battle. By joining Glenmary I could do my part to save America.

Mother Mary Catherine (Rumschlag) with picture of Father William Bishop, 1953. Cincinnati, Ohio. Glenmary Home Missioners photo.

Sister Mary Jogues on tractor at the Glenmary Farm, Glendale, Ohio. Glenmary Home Missioners photo.

Several of the FOCIS women mentioned how compelling they found the image of the young sister on the tractor. Monica Appleby was "attracted because I liked riding a tractor and [the thought of] being a missionary, and Glenmary was closer to home than China."

Evelyn Eaton Whitehead was drawn to the energy and unconventionality of the new order, which she sensed during her first meeting with a Glenmary Sister:

There was a big national meeting at the University of Notre Dame and this group of young people and Glenmary had a booth. It was the first time I had ever met [any Sister] as energetic. . . . The next year when I was a senior and looking over applications I decided I wanted to try religious life, and I knew for sure I didn't want to be a Mercy Sister. Not because of bad experiences, but they were way too ordinary. Glenmary was new, it was young, there were only a few of them, and they were doing something different and it was adventurous.

The third of six children in a very Catholic family, Beth Busam Ronan recalled that the atmosphere of the Motherhouse helped her choose Glenmary: "I had been convent shopping in high school actually. Some went to colleges to see them and I went to convents! I interviewed their recruiters, and decided whether I liked their parlors or their facilities. I was actually not attracted to Glenmary from their literature. But when I went out to the Motherhouse, I was attracted to the familiarity of the people and to the peace and the spirit."

Most of these young recruits were also looking for a life different from that of their mothers and other women they knew. Typically new members had been influenced by Catholic nuns in school and admired their independence and power. Beth Ronan responded to that sense of authority:

I really wanted to be a religious. It meant being a woman of power. . . . My only figures of women were my mother, aunts, Sisters, and my teachers. Sisters always had something important to do. They were important people, important to the church; people showed them respect, they talked about important things . . . . They were broader than my world.

Mary Schweitzer was attracted to Glenmary's atmosphere of liberalism and its spirituality: "It was a more liberal community even though in retrospect it doesn't look it. But in 1954 it was really quite liberal. . . . The work really appealed to me: smaller numbers, not huge communities, Sisters in the Southland doing religious education, doing home visiting, and visiting the sick. The spirituality appealed to me, too."

Monica Appleby felt the pull of women religious but was ambivalent about their role in the church:

I was always fascinated by the Sisters who taught us. They were strict and mysterious. Early on I would stay after school and help with the blackboards and pound the erasers for my classroom Sister. I would much rather work for the

Sisters than at my family home. I also spent my quiet time reading the *Lives of the Saints*. I was fascinated by the missionaries and especially those sent to China. Early on I learned about women's and girls' place in the church and in society. I would visit the Blessed Virgin Mary altar and pray that I could become a priest some day. I think I instinctively knew that I didn't want to be a Sister's helper and subsequently a priest's helper all my life.

Not all families were happy with their daughter's decision to become a nun. Margaret Gregg's father opposed her choice even though older sister Joan had already joined Glenmary:

My father was very upset. I was sort of the pet of the family, more so than my sister. So it was hard for him to let go—so he would drink and scream about not wanting me to go, and I wasn't fulfilling his dream. My mother didn't put up blocks. She was just there letting whatever happened happen. She drove me to the airport and she visited me. He wouldn't verbalize his feelings. It reinforced my determination to go.

Escaping the uncertainties of courtship or the drudgery of early marriage and frequent childbearing helped motivate some of the joiners. Maureen Linneman, for example, saw Glenmary as her sole alternative to imminent matrimony:

I hadn't really thought about being a Sister. I did not have an affinity to the nuns that taught me; it was that particular community [Glenmary] that attracted me. They were young, vital women, a community that was religious and spiritual. I did have a developing spirituality at that point and I think I saw it as a great alternative to going right into a marriage, which was really the only other option, and I really didn't want that. My parents didn't really talk to me about college. I didn't want to go and get a job at seventeen. . . . I liked the idea of working with the poor and being in this country and not having to go far away. The Sister on the tractor and all those false images of what life was, were very attractive. . . . I entered on September 8, 1962.

Similarly, Jean Luce welcomed the release from relationship pressures that came with joining the order:

I am glad I went to college for a year. I think I grew up, and it was a really neat college where they gave us a lot of responsibility. . . . I dated and went to football games and worried about one thing . . . crossing that line into mortal sin. I was sure if you went to bed with somebody that was the line, but you know even a thought was wrong. . . . I remember being french kissed when I was in college and I was sure that was a sin, and then somebody touched me in a place that I thought probably would lead to sin, and I remember talking to these girls about it. We were all in conflict about it. So anyway, there was a lot of sexual tension going on, plus this lingering thought about going into the convent. Then I heard about Glenmary and it seemed exciting. I think it directed some of that sexual energy to excitement in serving the Lord. I wouldn't have to worry about these mortal sins. I think there was a guy, he told me he was in love with me, but I wasn't ready to get married, so going to the convent sounded like a better idea to me.

Reluctant to adopt the "conventional" family lifestyle, Ginny Remedi felt that she had been called to celibacy and service:

I entered the convent in 1965 at the age of twenty-one; I had just graduated from college. I felt I had a calling; I felt like I really wanted to serve God, that a life of prayer and dedication made sense to me. I felt like I was called to a lifestyle of celibacy and prayer. I see now that one of the things I did not want to do was more of a conventional lifestyle of getting married and having children. And, I liked being with women. I wasn't aware of these other elements when I entered the convent, but they were there—I see now as I look back.

When a rough draft of this book was completed it was sent to all the FOCIS members who agreed to read it and come to a weekend workshop to reflect on the book and their experiences. Fourteen members met at the Highlander Center in Tennessee on the weekend of October 24–26, 1998, to discuss the book. We transcribed the conversations and included their responses from the interviews. Although the group knew each other well and had met often over the years, they had never shared some of their individual stories about what led them to join the order. In reading the others' accounts they learned more about themselves and each other. Some were surprised by what they read, and some were upset by the nonreligious reasons people gave for joining the order.

At the workshop Maureen Linneman expressed her surprise at the responses: "I felt that I heard other people saying the same thing I was saying. And I was surprised. I thought I was the only one." Kathy Hutson felt the non-religious motivations expressed by the women in their oral history interviews in the early 1990s (which comprise the bulk of quotations in this book) didn't represent their true feelings on joining but were the product of revisionist hindsight. Kathy had applied to join Glenmary Sisters in 1965 and had been denied membership. Instead, she continued as a volunteer with the Glenmary Holy Cross Center in Big Stone Gap, Virginia, and joined FOCIS at the time of the breakup.

KATHY HUTSON: [T]hinking about my own wanting to join Glenmary . . . what I experienced when I read that chapter was not that [sense] of a group of young women who were dedicated to finding out who they were in relationship to God, to being willing to lay down their life for that and for the work of the church, to reaching out and changing people's lives. Now that sounds a little naive, but I think that is why people were so attracted to what they saw at Glenmary. It wasn't boring. . . . I think they saw that religious life wouldn't really have to be a drag, people are having fun. This did not come out in that chapter. I heard people saying it was better than getting married and having kids, you know. . . . [You] saw it as an alternative, and not the idea of saving the world.

During the workshop the other participants shared their feelings in response to her objections. In the lively conversation that followed, the ex-Sisters reflected on how their own assessment of their motivations had changed:

JOAN WEINGARTNER: I could have said the same thing, Kathy. Because when I joined I remember . . . I went to the Motherhouse and it was so neat, and I wanted to do that, and I wanted to go to Appalachia, and I wanted to make a lifetime commitment, all that stuff. That was what I thought then. But when I gave the interview, thinking back, I think really I was just trying to run away from home. You know, I said all those good things, you know. And I really believed them in my heart; but when I look back, it was like a transition.

MARIE CIRILLO: And it seems to me, what we believed at that time was that the call was important, that you followed vocation. I remember specifically looking out and finding Glenmary, and then those of us that knew Father Bishop—there was one thing that he said that really hooked me, and it still has hooked me, and I wonder if that would be true of others, the older people that knew Father Bishop? It was that rural people were moving to cities, and that rural people had such inherent values because of their way of life, that if we would bring them into the church before they moved to the city, that they would be this wonderful gift to the city. And I still believe that, and am still living that.

MONICA APPLEBY: We had this mythology—had this great kind of brainwashing, maybe you could call it—growing up as young Catholic women, the best thing to be was a Sister, and more than that, the best thing would be a missionary. That's how I felt.

MARGARET GREGG: I was not getting a lot of emotional affirmation from my parents, I was getting it from the nuns. They were role models for me. And that helped me move where I moved.

JOAN: Until about thirty years ago, the convent was the only place a woman could be an executive. I mean she could be a college president, she could be the head of a . . . hospital, she could be a school principal. . . . In the Roman Catholic world access to formal power was limited except if you were a nun.

MARGARET: There was also a lot of reference to escape. To go do something to get away from something else, and I think that has a relationship to creating an alternative. You know?

JOAN: I went to the convent to run away from home. I know that. I was running away from home.

ANNE LEIBIG: I think I was, too. One of the psychological categories that I'm working on now and which I think fits, is it's a holding space of safety. Glenmary was that for us, and then FOCIS. . . . I think that in Glenmary we had safety. Like our parents couldn't come and get us, because God had called us.

GERALDINE ("DENE") PETERSON: I felt when I read the first chapter, and Kathy and I talked about it, I felt that if someone had said to me, "Why did you go to the convent?," you would have gotten a very different answer than if they had asked me why I went to Glenmary. . . . I felt like why I went to the convent was more generic. I mean it was why I left home: I had a vocation. I had three older sisters, none of whom thought they had a vocation. So I thought, well—I'm really a practical person—if I go to the convent and don't like it I can leave. If I get married and I don't like it, I'm really stuck. And the Glenmary piece was like I wasn't going to a teaching order because I didn't want to teach school, didn't want to be a nurse, didn't want to be a housekeeper; those were the three options as a nun. . . . Well if I said why, I really was following the will of God. That's what having a vocation meant. You [did] what God wanted you to do. Now this is very spiritual and deep, even though it was all a lot of practical other things going on in the midst of that. . . . And [later] when I went to Chicago and studied unconscious motivation, I realized God probably didn't care whether I was a nun or not. That's when I made the decision, if God didn't want me here, I don't want to be here. . . . But that is a terrible confession, but here it is, folks. I mean I felt like my motivations were really more practical than anything very high.

In reflecting on their reasons for joining Glenmary, the ex-Sisters confronted the contradictions in their own motivations. They reflected on the possibilities open to them and the choices they made. Glenmary was a choice that offered a somewhat unconventional life of service—more adventurous than the traditional teaching or nursing orders. Because of that it attracted a group of young women who were ambitious, creative, restless, seeking to serve God in a more exciting way. In Glenmary they thought they would be leaving the city and going to the backwoods, driving a tractor in no-priest land. It was an opportunity to serve God and have an adventure, too. These young women became the "new nuns" of the 1960s, who almost reformed the church.

Chapter 2

TRAINING TO BE
A SISTER

Part of our formation was to learn to act like children—to obey blindly, to do dumb things.

These Sisters entered the order at a time when the Catholic Church was changing and the country was changing. They became part of those changes although their early formation, or training, ill prepared them for the problems these rural families were facing. In the early days they spent much of their time cooking, cleaning, and doing laundry for the Glenmary priests and Brothers—work some of them resented since they had come to do missionary work and felt they could do it as well as the young men for whom they were servants.

Much of their early formation was carried out in the traditional way by the Dominican Sisters, who were brought in to help form the Glenmary Sisters. With its rules, prayers, venias, forced silence, and bans on discussing vocations or problems, the formation period was designed to humiliate the new Sisters, erasing all pride and ambition. Obedience meant following all rules set by superiors without question. Some described it as a process of mortification, humiliation, and demolition of sense of self. Despite the rigors and painful experiences, the convent provided a safe all-women's community where the young Sisters found shared values and lasting friendships and were mentored and challenged to grow.

When the Glenmary Sisters took charge of the formation in 1955, they followed much of the Dominican protocol, but the Sister Formation Movement in the 1950s and, later, Vatican II in the 1960s greatly influenced the training program. Glenmary superior Mary Catherine Rumschlag attended the 1954 Sister Formation Conference, where they were enjoined "to hasten and improve the education of young Sisters."[1] After that she sent many of the young Sisters off to finish college and encouraged the study and discussion of theology. Sisters were sent to Brussels, Belgium, for a one-year course on catechetics. This program was considered the cutting edge of catechetical re-

*newal. These Sisters brought these new ideas back to the Glenmary Sisters'
General Council, and they were influential in the development of their constitution and recommendations for changes in their rules and practices.*

*The Glenmary Sisters were ready for the big changes that came in the
1960s when Pope John XXIII convened the Second Vatican Council. When
the Catholic Sisters were asked to reassess their ways of being in the world and
find new ways to serve and minister to the world,[2] the Glenmary Sisters were
ahead of the game. The decrees stated that the church was to be in solidarity
with the world, actively working for and with the people. They had already
defined their ministry—to be with the rural poor in Appalachia and the
South. And they were ready to help in the renewal of the church.*

In the early days of the Glenmary Sisters, the training was both informal
and sporadic. Their dreams of serving the poor were almost lost in the
daily routine of housekeeping for the Glenmary priests. Their early training was developed by Father William Howard Bishop, who, at first, was
the Sisters' sole mentor and formation leader. He taught occasional classes
and organized conferences. However, Archbishop McNicholas of the Archdiocese of Cincinnati, who was a Dominican, intervened and asked the
Dominican Sisters to develop a training program for the new order. It was
his right to oversee the group since it was headquartered in the archdiocese and hadn't yet been officially recognized by the Vatican. The Dominican Sisters of Saint Mary of the Springs from Columbus, Ohio, worked
with the new recruits for eighteen months between 1942 and 1944. They
developed some of the schedule of prayers and readings for the women.[3]

The formation process remained relatively unstructured until 1946
when the Dominican Sisters took charge. When Catherine Rumschlag
joined the group in September 1944, she found the training very limited
and the legitimacy of the order in limbo. Three more young women entered that year, bringing the total to nine. They wore black skirts and gray
blouses, and later added a small black veil and white headband. Some of
the Sister-candidates enrolled in a nurse's aide class at Saint Mary's Hospital as part of their training. Father Bishop occasionally taught classes.
Catherine remembered that Father Bishop taught a class on cooperatives:
"I was impressed and thought that was something I would like to be involved in." (In 1971 Catherine would found the Bread and Chicken House,
a workers' cooperative in Big Stone Gap.)[4] In this early period, Catherine
was greatly concerned that they had not yet been approved as a religious
community. This required the archbishop to sponsor the group as a canonical community and get approval from Rome. Only then could they

Glenmary Sisters: Aspirants, Postulants, and Sisters in first habit with Sisters Kevin and Immaculata, Adrian Dominicans, 1953. Glenmary Home Missioners photo.

have a novitiate (an established training period) and make their public vows and become legitimate Sisters.

Adrian Dominican Sisters Kevin Campbell and Immaculata Ebbitt arrived August 16, 1946, to train the Glenmary women.[5] Sister Kevin was in charge, and Sister Immaculata, who was retired, came as her companion. On August 17, 1946, Sister Kevin wrote to her mother general, expressing amazement at the patience of the young women in the difficulties surrounding them—patience she deemed almost unbelievable when she learned that three of the four women had been there for as long as five years with very little in-depth spiritual or educational formation. She could see that very little was going to be done. In letter after letter Sister Kevin tells how the women cleaned chickens, cooked meals, and washed clothes for the "men members." Father Bishop also required the services of one of the group for secretarial and office work, as well as that of all the women when the Glenmary magazine was to be prepared for mailing. (Catherine Rumschlag remembers that their rigorous schedule of work and prayer required awakening daily at 5:30 A.M., "except on Sunday we had a late sleep: we got up at six.") In one letter to Mother General Mary Gerald Barry, Sister Kevin wrote: "Father Bishop ordered these young Sisters around so long at a minute's notice that he feels free to change all programs, conferences, classes and plans of ours: he expects things to click to his wishes. Thank God we are not dominated by men in Adrian."

As she poured out her doubts to Mother Gerald, she asked many questions: "How can I direct a new foundation with Father Bishop's constant interference? Must he, as founder, be consulted on every detail? Is he supposed to give permissions for coming and going? How can I form Sisters for a rural apostolate when I am not free to be there with them? Is the apostolate of these Sisters little more than a convenience for the seminary: a group of women to cook, wash, and mend for the men?" In response, Mother Gerald urged Sister Kevin to "dwell on the beauty of the souls of the young women and their call from God to do a great work for Him." Father Bishop had to be a holy man to give his life for the dispossessed of the land, so she should be patient with him and considerate even in disagreement, "gently taking the reins from him—and not yielding under stress."[6]

Thus began several years of conflict over the order's future between Archbishop McNicholas and Sister Kevin on one side and Father Bishop on the other. The archbishop, who was Dominican, wanted them formed as Dominicans, free to go anywhere in the country where the rural poor beckoned them. Father Bishop wanted a new order—under his control—with public vows, community life, and a gray habit. The question of adopting the white habit of the Dominicans became a lightning rod in the clash of wills. Catherine Rumschlag commented: "When I look at it now there was confusion about authority and a lack of clarification of issues. . . . I felt a lack of leadership in the community."

As the conflict escalated, the archbishop sent instructions ending Father Bishop's jurisdiction over the Sisters and revoking the regulations the priest had imposed upon them. The archbishop transferred authority to Sister Kevin, who promptly began to reduce her charges' tasks. The washing and mending of the men's clothes were the first to go.

Later Sister Catherine, at Sister Kevin's direction, wrote a letter to the Sisters on mission asking for their input: "Does our group sincerely wish to become a community of Dominican Sisters? If so, are we prepared to accept conditions which may be laid down? You realize that one point on which we may expect disagreement is on adoption of a habit" (Sister Mary Philip Ryan, "Glenmary and Adrian Paper," Glenmary Papers, 8). Asked to vote on the issue, the Sisters expressed the wish to be Dominican Sisters in the gray habit, as were the Maryknoll Sisters in Maryknoll, New York. The majority, especially the pioneer Sisters, preferred gray because it was more practical and because Father Bishop had wanted it. In late December 1948, the archbishop met with the Sisters. In her report to Mother Gerald, Sister Kevin quoted him as saying: "Sisters, I am now ready to plead your cause in Rome. You have proven yourselves. You will be Dominicans and wear the white habit in the Motherhouse, but if you wish to wear something else for street wear and the mission fields you may—even overalls if your work demands it."

The white habit was traditional for Dominican Sisters. But before this could be established, Archbishop McNicholas died, in April 1950. According to a distressed Sister Kevin, Father Bishop began working covertly to thwart the dead prelate's plans. Father Edward McCarthy, the archbishop's secretary, believed that a diocesan status as a distinct Glenmary Institute would be feasible and advised Father Bishop to bide his time until Karl Alter was installed as McNicholas's successor (9).

Sister Kevin believed Father Bishop tried to influence Alter even before the newly appointed archbishop assumed office. Late in June 1950, Father Bishop announced to Sister Kevin that the Sisters were not to be Dominicans and they were not to wear a white habit.

Although she continued to work with the Glenmary Sisters, Sister Kevin had suffered a heart attack in April 1949. In deference to Sister Kevin's ailing health and to avoid further rancor between the antagonists, Mother Gerald reluctantly agreed to send a replacement to Glenmary if the new assignee would be free to direct the women's formation without Father Bishop's interference. In September 1950, after having been at Glenmary only a week, Sister John Joseph O'Connor wrote to Mother Gerald to inform her that she did not feel wanted. Sister John Joseph was "convinced that the Sisters would have to be gotten away from Glenmary." She reported that she had angered Father Bishop because she had visited the Glenmary Sisters on their mission in Russellville, Kentucky. He felt she was an intruder, a trespasser on his territory. She felt she could not form Sisters for places and people and ministry she did not know (12, 13–15).

Mother Gerald decided to find a way to get the group out of the "trap" and offered the Saint Catherine Siena Center on Madison Road in Cincinnati, Ohio, to the Glenmary Sisters (14). It was the convent of Adrian Sisters who were doing parish visiting. Archbishop Alter met with Sister John Joseph and Mary Catherine Rumschlag in what Sister John

Joseph reported as "a most wonderful conference." John Joseph wrote to Mother Gerald:

[Archbishop Alter] stated that he had been purposely waiting until he had an opportunity to study all sides of the present difficulties. . . . The Sisters will not be Dominicans; they will be an entirely individual community. They will have absolutely no connection with the Glenmary Fathers, except in prayer and unified interest in the Home Missions. All power of governing is invested in the superioress of the Sisters, who is subject only to the Ordinary [bishop] of the Diocese. . . . He said that he would make this emphatic to the Sisters and to Father Bishop for he considered this a great stumbling block. The Sisters must not be located on the Fathers' property. . . . The habit, which he said he considered so incidental, could be the present gray one. He said he would speak with Father Bishop, and though he knew that Father would not like the complete separation, it was necessary in view of things. The Sisters should be of service for the Fathers whenever possible . . . . He stressed the full authority of the Sister superioress both at the present time and when a Glenmary will be elected.

She concluded, "I feel relieved. . . . If Father Bishop is out of the picture one can at least feel more harmony (16)."

As soon as the Adrian Sisters moved out in June, the Glenmary Sisters took possession of the house on Madison Road, and the farmhouse was moved to the extreme end of Glendale and used for the postulants (the probationary candidates).[7] Father Bishop had trouble accepting the separation; Sister John Joseph was conscious of his hostility each time she visited the three Sisters living in the farmhouse or brought them to Madison Road for relaxation. Mother Gerald spoke candidly with Father Bishop and pointed out that he must learn, as the seed, to die to himself and his idea so that the good tree he had brought to birth would live in robust health and bear fruit in abundance. It was, Mother Gerald recalled, a conciliatory encounter: "The result has been an understanding talk. He said that he was not saintly, nor was he heroic, therefore he did not think it possible for him to stand by and merely watch a work that he himself had started. He seems to have a terrible fear that the Sisters will forget him, or not be interested enough in him."[8] Understanding his inner suffering at losing his own cherished idea, Mother Gerald urged Sister John Joseph to bear patiently with him and try to work their problems out through dialogue.

Catherine Rumschlag, Geraldine Peterson, and Marie Cirillo were at Glenmary during these early days. Although Catherine was quite involved in the workings of the order, as she was Father Bishop's secretary and assisted Sister Kevin, she said, "The Dominicans did not discuss with me the conflict with Father Bishop." She felt the controversy was out of the control of the younger Sisters:

I remember Sister Kevin asking me if I wanted to become a Dominican, and I said, "I don't know, I never thought about it." I felt, what difference did it make if we had to be Dominicans to be recognized by the church? Most of the conversations were between the superior,[9] Father Bishop, and the archbishop. The younger Sisters weren't involved. I think Geraldine and Catherine Duval went to Father Bishop and said they didn't want to be Dominicans and wear white habits. I had the idea that we needed to get the recognition of the church and we needed to get going, so we could make our vows.

By the time Geraldine ("Dene") Peterson joined in 1947, there were thirteen Sisters, all still living in the old farmhouse. She remembered the conflict about the path they might take: "Early in Glenmary we knew we were allowed to take sides. You were either with the founder or you were with the institutional church. We were always allowed to make up our own minds on things, and we had people on both sides. [We argued about] whether to have a gray habit or a white habit. We did have the Rule of Saint Augustine, and that stayed with Glenmary—the Dominican Rule. I would have preferred the Benedictine. I thought it had a lot more humaneness rather than discipline, which I really liked better."

Marie Cirillo entered with two other newcomers in 1948, the year after Dene Peterson arrived. She remembered that the Glenmary women were still doing the cooking and cleaning for the priests and Brothers on the farm:

There was a lot of canning, and that first six months we took turns, the three of us, one month cooking, one month laundry, and one month housekeeping. We didn't have dryers and we used wringer washers so it took all week to wash for the group. Hanging the clothes out to dry, mending, and folding were part of the process. . . . Sisters Margaret Mary and Mary Thomas did secretarial work for Father Bishop so they would have a half a day in the office, but I would cook the whole time. There were some low moments that first year. . . . I am not sure why I didn't think about quitting and going home, it was so awful. At the seminary it wasn't that I minded cooking, I just didn't feel I should be cooking for the men . . . so that they could get out to mission. I thought I could do as well on mission as some of them. . . . The novitiate was pretty awful too.

Yet even in her role of servant to the Glenmary men, Marie felt no hesitation about choosing sides in the conflict between Father Bishop and the Dominicans. "Though I did not know how the sides came about, I knew immediately that I was on the side of Father Bishop." She was treated capriciously by the Adrians. "My first Christmas there, Sister Kevin called me into her office . . . and asked me if I would rather be a nurse or a school teacher. I said, 'If those are my choices I would rather be a nurse.' Then the next year they sent me off to teachers' college."

In the summer of 1952, permission was received from Rome to set up the order. In July 1952, at the feast of Our Lady of Mount Carmel, Archbishop Alter read the decree of canonical erection for the Congregation of the Home Mission Sisters of America, which became a diocesan community under his jurisdiction. Fifteen senior members began their novitiate in September, with Dominicans still in charge of the training.

Father Bishop had participated in the celebration. Sister John Joseph reported his change of attitude: "He wanted me to know that he considered the Sisters in good hands and complimented our Congregation highly for its good balance of religious spirit and efficiency in many matters." He spoke freely to Sister John Joseph of what he called his jealousy of her and the other Adrian Dominicans, of the two archbishops, and indeed anyone who might have won the devotion and loyalty of the Glenmarians. Father Bishop died in June 1953, only months after these conversations with Sister John Joseph.[10]

Sister Mary Catherine Rumschlag was appointed mother general of the Glenmary Sisters in 1953. Archbishop Alter asked the Adrians to remain longer to help with training. Sister Elinor Patrice, postulant mistress at the Glendale farmhouse, who had come in 1952, stayed until August 1954; Sister John Joseph stayed until 1955.

When Lenore Mullarney entered in 1952, she became the oldest woman in Glenmary. Born in 1917, she had worked for fifteen years with the Alcoa Company in bookkeeping and office management prior to joining. Lenore found Sister John Joseph's regime a tough one:

Sister John Joseph got Sister Mary Ann (Rita Strehle) and me and said, "You two are so smart, you can show how smart you are by being in charge of the dinner to be served to the novices and their families when they take their vows." That would be over eighty people. We had never complained that we could "do anything"; all we ever did was try to keep our noses clean and run around and answer bells and say "Yes, Sister" and "No, Sister." I'm not that kind of person [a smart aleck] and Rita wasn't either. Just tell me what to do and I will do it.

Mary Schweitzer, who entered in 1954, agreed. The will of Sister John Joseph, like that of a drill sergeant, reigned supreme in their lives. Instead of push-ups as punishment, the candidates did venias.

Sister John Joseph could be icy, icy, icy. Never once in those two years did I ever see one drop of human kindness toward us. We had venias all over the place. That is what Dominicans are good at. They are good at the profound venia. The venia was when one gets down and lies prostrate on the floor, and our lives were really peppered with them, every place you went. For example, in chapel when you came in the morning, you made the profound bow and then you made venia. It was a sign of humility. Then you went to your assigned place. Always at night you were expected to make the venia again. Then there were other times in chapel you were expected or told to make venia. Some of us didn't have a very good ear. If you forgot if you were hebdomadarian [leader for divine office or singing the psalms] or first cantor, or if somehow you forgot to intone properly, you would be tapped on the shoulder, and then you would get out in the aisle and do the venia.[11] She knew how to humiliate people. Before we would have our instruction in the morning she would walk around when we were supposed to be doing our cleaning. That was the time of silence and the whole house was quiet and she would start with her yelling. She would yell and scream, and she would tell people they were lazy; she would really just berate them. She had a certain way she wanted her coffee. You had to put the cream in before you put the coffee in. I remember once when I didn't do that and she said she could tell the difference and threw it at me. She broke the cup and broke the saucer.

In her last letter from Glenmary in August 1955, Sister John Joseph wrote to Mother Gerald:

Five years ago when you told me to go to Glenmary and to teach these little ones to love God in one another, the assignment seemed incredible. . . . At first it was so difficult, so lonely, perhaps because the emphasis was on my efforts, forgetting that He would do the work, using me only as an instrument and mouthpiece. . . . I must say that these little ones to whom you sent me have become very dear to me; they have played a big part in weaving the fabric of my own spiritual life during these last few years. . . . It hardly seems possible to me now that I likened Glenmary to a concentration camp, when I first arrived—and Father B. (with all respect to him now) seemed harsh as any Russian officer. But now Father is a real

Novices playing volleyball on Madison Road, Cincinnati, Ohio. First Novitiate, 1952. Glemary Home Missioners photo.

intercessor in heaven I am sure, and Glenmary today with God's help is a place of concentration upon the one thing necessary—God's honor and glory.[12]

By the mid-1950s the training protocol had been taken over by Glenmary Sisters and was more established and organized. Monica Kelly (Appleby) was a postulant, the stage preparatory to becoming a novice, in which she had one year's training to prepare her to profess her vows. Sister Mary John (Deborah Prenger) was both postulant and novice mistress. Trained under Sister John Joseph of the Dominican Sisters, Mary John followed the training she had received. Monica detailed the schedule they followed:

[The postulant] training consisted of experiencing religious life: prayer life from dawn until dusk; silence except for two periods of recreation; grand silence after night prayers until wake-up at 5:30 A.M.; reading from the *Lives of the Saints*, the Rule of Saint Augustine, and spiritual writers during meals; learning Gregorian chant; cleaning, preparing, and serving meals; entertaining ourselves—creating plays and skits, volleyball; [and] working outdoors. (I liked this part a lot.)

During the postulant time we could go out on the enclosure to pick apples from the ground orchards, or to movie theaters that had special showings for Sisters, or to the Motherhouse in Glendale. We were preparing for the big step of becoming a novice, in which we chose a new name and received the habit of the community. We also sewed our new habit.

In May 1956, I received the habit of the Glenmary Sisters and a new name— Sister Mary Monica.[13] During the novitiate, which lasted one year, we were not allowed to see our family. . . . We did much the same things every day as the postulants. We ate meals, worked, and prayed together. Humiliation was the key to losing one's self.

In 1959 the number in the order approached one hundred, and their quarters had become crowded. That year the Glenmary Sisters were offered a building at an unused boarding school in Fayetteville, Ohio, that had been run by the Sisters of Charity. Sisters Marie and Elizabeth (now

Sister Mary Eileen (Maureen Linneman) and Bill Sweeney at the Fayetteville training center, 1966. Glenmary Home Missioners photo.

Patsy Taylor McMahon) were sent to Fayetteville to get the place opened. After much hard work on their part the renovation was completed at a cost of one hundred thousand dollars.

Fayetteville became the Glenmary training center. It was close to a junior college run by the Ursuline Sisters for their new members, and they agreed to share the classes with new Glenmarians.

Anne Leibig, Jean Luce, and Margaret Gregg entered in September 1959, when Sister Gerald (Geraldine "Dene" Peterson) was the postulant mistress. In 1960 as novices they moved to Fayetteville, where Sister Mary John was the novice mistress and Sister Marie was the superior of the house she had previously worked to renovate. Geraldine remembered the young women entering at that time being less traditional than the earlier recruits. "As postulant mistress, it was kind of wonderful. I got to rethink all those principles of religious life. The new group of postulants thought the word 'obedience' was the most far-out and crazy thing they ever heard of in their lives. They grew up after World War II. . . . They were different persons; they had grown up with a very different set of values than I had."

Beth Ronan joined in 1963 and went to Fayetteville. She remembered "an excruciating entry for candidates. . . . Everyone was carted into Cincinnati for dental and physical exams, and then we met with psychiatrists in groups. And then if you were special or weird or something you had to meet with the psychiatrist yourself. I didn't have that privilege, thank God. After that we went home and waited for a letter. I think about fifteen to twenty were accepted. I wanted to pass, and I wanted to be a Glenmary Sister."

The years leading up to the final vows were a probationary period. Some postulants and novices might decide to leave on their own, while others might be asked to leave by those in charge. A fraught silence surrounded the entire subject. Beth Ronan recalled that the young Sisters were forbidden to talk with one another about their feelings:

The sacred rules were you couldn't talk to anyone about their vocation. If [you] felt [you] should leave, you [didn't] talk to your peers, you only [talked] to the postulant mistress. But she was an unapproachable person. And I remember one night, Joanie [Weingartner] and I stayed up, and Joan was talking about leaving. . . . We were up past curfew and Joan didn't care. . . . The postulant mistress had been waiting for us, because she knew we weren't in our rooms. . . . We had broken the rules of talking about vocation after lights out. Oh, my God, that was a terrible sin, and it hung with me for a long time. I heard [the postulant mistress] come out of her room and go to Joanie's room and I jumped into bed fully clad, like I would sleep that way. . . . She came to my room and said, "This isn't a mature way of acting. I will see you in the morning." You can imagine I got very little sleep that night, none as a matter of fact. I thought, "Tomorrow morning I am gone, I am dead, and my life is over." I had done the unforgivable sin of talking with someone after lights out about their vocation. She never said anything so I just hung on to this guilt.

Jean Luce had a similar forbidden encounter:

I remember one night both Anne [Leibig] and I broke silence. . . . Something was really bothering her, something to do with her novice mistress, so we decided the greater thing to do would be to talk. . . . I think we even rationalized that this was not wrong, it was probably what God wanted us to do. You were really aware when you did things like that, [that] if you were caught [you] might have to go to the Chapter of Faults, things like that. [The Chapter of Faults was held monthly, and everyone confessed to the rules they had broken. The superior then gave them penance.] We never fessed up to it.

Many women recalled that the silence magnified their feelings of sadness and hurt when a peer abruptly vanished. For Jean Luce, the missed opportunity to say good-bye left a lingering sense of loss:

People started leaving, and it was weird because you never knew when somebody was going to leave. Like the first time somebody left, people in the chapel noticed she wasn't there, but we just thought she had overslept or something. Then we go to breakfast and she still isn't there, then we go to class and Sister Gerald tells us that Sister Judy has left. Doesn't tell us anything else and said, "This is the way it is here, you leave freely, you don't talk about it and you don't say good-bye." I didn't like that. . . . I didn't know what happened, even. A few years later I began to process it, and it really is one of the worst things that can happen if somebody disappears and you don't get to say good-bye or what it means to you.

Like Jean, Ginny Remedi found the secrecy troubling:

[T]here were parts that were hard and scary, and not very kind. There was fear of being rejected, of not being good enough. . . . And there was the secrecy element around those who were in training and those who were in authority. Who was gonna stay and who was gonna go and who was gonna be asked to leave. One day your friend was there, and the next day your friend was gone and you didn't have time to say good-bye. That was real strange and real hard to take. . . . [I]t felt like you just couldn't know and you couldn't ask.

In hindsight Jean Luce perceived a *Wizard of Oz*–like quality in the process.

By the time I was a novice several had left; twenty-six of us came and eighteen of us took the veil. . . . You get really nervous about what the screening process is. We had such young superiors. They were only two or three years older than we were, and they didn't have any experience doing it, so they were just trying to imitate what they had learned. And I suppose that is what life is all about with bosses. But the difference was, we were trained that it was interpreted . . . as God's will. When you go to [secular] work and don't like your boss, you can say, "This is a real jerk." But if you don't like your superior . . . it was a real conflict. You didn't have enough sense to know she didn't know what she was doing, you just looked at it that it meant something. It was God's will layered on top of it that made it weird.

For some of the new postulants, the promise of adventure, hope for independence, and expectations of travel seemed lost in the daily chores and rigorous training of formation. Monica coped with the stresses and restrictions by clowning around and "acting crazy."

When I was a postulant I started doing all these dumb things. . . . When I made the postulant outfit I put the pockets in backwards, I had all my possessions on my backside. I became known as the clown of the class. It wasn't as if I didn't know how to accept responsibility; it was the environment and that acting crazy was a way to get attention. Sister Mary John told my parents that I was ambitious, and we used to get clobbered for being proud. We had to learn to keep silent and say prayers and do chants, come in at the right time. I remember it as a time to lose yourself and find Jesus and become a worthy bride of Christ. So a lot of it was about mortification. I remember being real lonely and homesick.

Yet the formation process of this period also offered the women a close-knit community, which supported them and challenged them to grow. As Ginny Remedi explained:

There were times when I felt very close to people; I felt very blessed by being there and have wonderful memories of being around campfires and working in the kitchen, talking with someone late at night when you weren't supposed to be,

Sister Ruth (Margaret Gregg) in art studio at
Mount Saint Joseph College, Cincinnati, 1964.

. . . walks, and saying the rosary with the group, Mass under a big tree, and boat
rides on the lake, taking care of horses. It was very upholding and communal.

In addition to providing a solid sense of community, Glenmary gave
many of the young women an opportunity for an education that they
otherwise may not have had. The order supported Margaret Gregg, for
instance, in becoming an artist:

I was encouraged to do things in visual arts, and had opportunities to participate in making a drama or making a celebration . . . right from the beginning. I

also peeled potatoes, cleaned the johns, swept the floors, decorated for liturgies and parties, made beds, [and] worked on layouts for publications.

I was one of the few Sisters given the opportunity to go to school, while others went right to missions. Several people in the community were prominent in saying, "Yes, she should go to school. Let's keep her doing these things, give her these opportunities." Why was I given the opportunity? It was what I did best. Today I am very grateful.

Maureen Linneman discovered her musical voice through her experiences in Glenmary and later in FOCIS.

I was just learning to play the guitar during my first year [in Glenmary] at Fayetteville. I wanted music to be part of my life and it became my way of artistic expression, which was appreciated and encouraged by the women of this community. We were there learning the songs of peace and freedom and connecting their message with our work of justice and peace in rural and Appalachian America. In our ritual and liturgies the movement of the Spirit was embodied in us and the music was a vehicle for experiencing the awe, mystery, and presence of the holy.

Beth Ronan remembers being greatly challenged by the creative members, a process engendering both anxiety and joy:

I came from the west side of Cincinnati, a pretty secure Catholic area, to this outrageous group of women who were thinking other things. I was learning new theology, new words. And they were arty—I wasn't exposed much to people who were arty. My dad was a mailman, my mother made applesauce; we didn't have art in our background, or people who thought about philosophy [or] got excited about liberal thinking. I was also more geared toward science. Glenmary didn't have a predominance of people who looked at science or math, objective things. It was a creative organization with many creative people. I was sort of a fish out of water because I was not all that creative. I was expanded; I was challenged: it was great, but it was also insecure. . . . But, daily I thought about where is my suitcase, and how long it would take to get packed. There were challenges, heartaches, and homesickness, and periodically I visualized my suitcase and I was out the door. I used to call it "getting my grip," and the other postulates would laugh and say, "There's Beth getting her grip."

In this formation period, the closed world of the convent provided protection and security along with warm fellowship in a women's community. It was a disciplined life and the training was rigorous and constant. Based on the requirement of unquestioning obedience, it produced a dependency on an authority whose power came from God. Some forms of growth and creativity were encouraged, while other faculties were repressed. The closed community encouraged closed minds.

In reflecting on the tenor of her 1950s-style formation, Monica Appleby finds a subtext of retrogression.

I attended the Glenmary Sisters' anniversary event in Cincinnati with about eighty other Sisters and former Sisters in 1991. As part of the reunion we got together with our "class" to tell stories about our early days of formation in religious life. I realized, then, that part of our formation was to learn to act like children—to obey blindly, to do dumb things . . . to put on plays and to sing songs for company. Our group's theme song was "I Won't Grow Up!" from the musical *Peter Pan*. Looking back, we could laugh. After all, we lived through it and are doing O.K.

Chapter 3

GOING ON MISSION

Going on mission was the ultimate of what it meant to be in Glenmary.

The Glenmary Sisters' experiences in mission changed them and their ways of working in community. It was in mission that the women began to confront the contradictions between their training and their work, between the rules of the institutional church and the needs of the community. It was also out of the mission experience that they began to devise new ways of ministry and new ideas and practices of community development. In 1964 they developed their own training program, the Appalachian Field Study Center, to train themselves for mission work in Appalachia. The Center was located in Chicago in collaboration with a professor at Loyola University and Marquette University.

As they became influenced by the social and theological movements of their time and immersed in the practical demands of their ministry, the idealistic young order quietly but persistently negotiated with the male church hierarchy to change the rules they felt were impeding their work in the modern world. They modernized their habit and became more flexible with many of the rules related to cloister, relationships with seculars, attendance at secular meetings, and prescribed prayer times and places. They were supported by local bishops who understood the difficulties of working in rural Appalachia. Moreover, they were backed up by the Vatican II decrees that asked them to reassess their relations with one another, their church, and the wider world.

Vatican II had a profound influence on all Sisters. Lumen Gentium, "Light of All Nations," stated that all Christians are called "to the fullness of the Christian life and the perfection of charity." Sisters were no longer closer to God than the laity; they were no longer "special," as everyone had the potential and the obligation to be holy. So why live separately, in isolation from seculars? The Decree on the Appropriate Renewal of Religious Life stated that "The manner of living, praying, and working should be suitably adapted everywhere, but especially in mission territories."[1] *This is what the Glenmary Sisters were doing.*

Many Glenmary Sisters went as missionaries to central Appalachia, a region that proved to have an enormous impact on the young Sisters who lived and worked there. In Appalachia they did not find happy yeomen farmers or rural families living self-sufficient lives. Rather they found poverty, hunger, and unemployed industrial workers. Mechanization had arrived in the coal mines of central Appalachia, resulting in massive unemployment. Thousands were leaving the coal communities for northern industrial cities seeking work. Surface mining had developed as a new technology, adopting the methods of giant earth-moving machines, which had originated in World War II to build air strips in the South Pacific. In Appalachia, however, the earth movers' role was one of destruction: Strip mining destroyed entire communities, mountainsides, rivers, and streams and produced incredible damage to the environment and the health of the people. Other new machines used in underground coal mining, known as "mechanical miners," were producing more coal with less labor force. Yet those who remained underground were now breathing more coal dust in poorly ventilated mines. Lack of dust controls and proper ventilation brought more death and disabilities to the miners. The United Mine Workers cooperated with the coal operators to mechanize the mines, but neither union nor companies provided alternative employment or help in relocation to displaced and disabled miners.

In response to the problems plaguing the region, many social movements emerged in the 1950s and 1960s to control or outlaw strip mining, reform the union, develop health and safety legislation to protect the workers, compensate for black lung disease, and develop health care for miners and their families. All the while, the Sisters were visiting and listening to families dealing with these multiple problems. The region's economic and social problems captured the attention of national media and politicians, who defined the area a "poverty pocket." Widely circulated images of poor and pitiful children added to the sense of hopelessness surrounding many of the families caught in this new phase of the industrial revolution. The Sisters sought to understand and analyze what was happening and why. They were caught up with contradictory explanations of causes and solutions. Giving out old clothes was helpful, but it was not enough. Eager to address some of the underlying sources of the region's poverty and exploitation, they began to study the history of the region, take courses at local colleges, and join social movements and organizations working to change the destructive, exploitative system that had burdened Appalachia for so long.

The Glenmary Sisters working in the coalfields and in the city ghettos where the Appalachian refugees lived began to transform their mission from being charity-driven to development-oriented, from organizing donation boxes to working for social change.

Their experiences in mission are an example of reverse evangelization. Early on the Sisters were excited to be working in what was termed "no-priest land." As missionaries their ultimate goal, as envisioned by Father Bishop, was to befriend and bring the rural poor into the Catholic Church, which would be enriched by their wholesome rural values. They found themselves in a very different rural environment from the romantic rural farm they had anticipated. They also found a very different culture from that of their Midwest working-class or middle-class Catholic families and communities. As they visited and listened, they found themselves converted by the mountains.[2]

For most of the women, desire to become a missionary was the reason they had joined Glenmary. The idea of going on mission sustained many of them through the difficult formation process. At the completion of the novitiate the Sisters took their vows. Subsequently the order would send some to obtain degrees in nursing, social work, or other disciplines related to their work, while routing others directly to mission sites. A few Sisters had some mission experience as postulants, but most did not go until after the novitiate.

Some of Glenmary's first mission sites were in parishes whose priests requested the Sisters' help in catechetical programs, summer Bible schools, or as parish school teachers. Russellville, Kentucky, and Georgetown and Eaton, Ohio, were among these. The order also started missions in southwest Virginia, south Georgia, and southern Ohio.

Decades before the War on Poverty was a gleam in Lyndon Johnson's eye, Glenmary began sending missionaries to the central Appalachian coalfields, which featured some of the highest rates of poverty, unemployment, and out-migration in America. In 1947 the Sisters first came to southwest Virginia to work with Glenmary Fathers' missions in Norton, Appalachia,[3] Big Stone Gap, Keokee, and Saint Paul—all in Wise County—and Dungannon in Scott County. Geraldine ("Dene") Peterson recalled the depressed state of southwestern Virginia in the summer of 1948:

[W]e lived in the back of the church in Appalachia, Catherine [Rumschlag], Dorothy [Hendershot], and Rosemary [Esterkamp] and I. Dorothy was an amazing person. She could find people that no one else even knew lived. One day we parked the car by a railroad track and then we walked down the track to this dirt path away from that through a field and we came to this house. There were children working in the corn and the mother and father came out. They weren't used to visitors. None of the children were wearing clothes, but they went to the back of the house and . . . all of them, boys and girls alike, came out wearing the same

Sister Mary Philip (Anne Leibig) with Bible school children at the trailer behind the Saint Therese Church in Saint Paul, Virginia, 1962–1963.

smocks. And another family lived in a cave where they built a room onto the front of the cave. Appalachia was very primitive at that time.

Among the first Catholic relief workers in the region, the women had an uphill battle to convince local people they were trustworthy. Anne Leibig remembered walking up a muddy road in her full-length black and gray habit in the 1950s. The family she had come to visit, while polite, later told her they thought she was a witch in her dark robes. How many families would let their children go to Bible school with a woman who veiled her hair and dressed like a witch? Countless similar instances led the Sisters to feel that wearing a traditional habit—while completely unremarkable to Northerners—imposed a barrier to their work among Appalachian people.

The Sisters in the Appalachian coalfields began to talk with the Appalachian bishop and priests about changing the traditional habit and some of the rules that were difficult to follow in cramped living conditions. They found support from the bishop and local priests who understood the conditions under which they worked, and they began to experiment with their costumes and their practices.

Marie Cirillo commented on the contradictions between their life experiences, their training, and their mission work:

One of the things that really bothered me was we were mostly city girls who came to the convent. We were there to give our life to rural service and nobody knew how to prepare us or teach us how to live a rural life, we were just taught how to live a convent life. So as we were struggling with outmoded forms of convent life we were not being prepared to support rural life that had become outmoded in American society.

Monica Appleby's first mission was teaching in tiny Saint Paul, Virginia:

I lived in a trailer with one other woman behind Saint Therese Church. . . . We began doing Bible schools in the summer in Wise County. . . . We would visit in coal camps such as Straight Holler, Bear Wallow, Saw Mill Holler, Artesian Well Holler, Stonega, Bonny Blue, and Derby. Most often we taught under trees or at

Sister Mary Rose with Bible School, Statesboro, Georgia, in 1951. Glenmary Home Missioners photo.

the mouth of an abandoned coal mine or on someone's front porch. We were a traveling show, in many ways, teaching in one place in the morning and another in the afternoon. At the end of two weeks of learning, singing, playing games, and sharing refreshments, [there was] a community celebration to which all the families of the children were invited.

From their Bible school experiences, the Sisters learned how to use community celebrations to mobilize community participation. The Bible school model was later used in organizing residents around community problems. Monica Appleby recalled that the realities of mission life made it difficult for the women to follow the demanding schedule of spiritual observances set forth in the congregation's constitution, modeled on that of the Dominican Sisters.

We rose early in the morning, chanted the hours of the divine office, meditated for thirty minutes, drove to Appalachia to the parish church for Mass, at which we sang the Latin responses and songs (practiced the night before). During the day we often recited the office while driving in the car. We read from inspirational literature during our meals, we kept silence in our home during the prescribed times, when we weren't interrupted by callers. We prayed the divine office again in the evening, read for fifteen minutes, and kept the grand silence until bedtime. We also had special Glenmary prayers that we said together every morning and evening. We recited the rosary, which was an easy prayer to say in the car while driving. We had a special prayer we said before we started a trip in the car. We had a day of recollection every month and a week-long retreat every year.

The idea of keeping grand silence for several hours each evening in "a very small trailer" now seems comic. Monica said, "We would pass each other and we were always bumping into each other, but we . . . wouldn't talk until the following morning."

The first mission where Marie Cirillo served as superior was in Pond Creek, Ohio. Marie's experience led her toward a vision of mission work in which Sisters might function as something other than priests' helpers:

We were in the country, we had this little house. . . . [T]here was a small Catholic community, and they were very friendly, wholesome people. A farm family, the Roths, and the Catholic church were across the road and creek. Father Pat O'Donnell was there when we first came. He was an artist so I enjoyed doing art stuff with him. We made a film together about the Glenmary Sisters. . . . Mr. Roth, Sister Joan's father, had a woodwork shop where we could work, and he would come over and play poker with us. . . .[4]

We got a little building and put it behind our house to keep donated clothes. We involved some of the women in the church to run the thrift shop. The money we made we saved to rehab some houses. I remember we bought our first house and put this family into it . . . everybody in the community helped to fix it up. We didn't know to call it community development or recycling, but that is what we were doing.

I was trying to figure out how to do mission. We had to go out on missions in fours and we were sort of intended to be the priest's helpers. Poor Father [Pat] O'Donnell, with a congregation of twenty families, would have to support four of us as well, which he couldn't do. So these priests would sell your services to other parishes, and then you spent all your life running from church to church to church and missed the community you lived in and missed the poor, missed the relationships you wanted to have. So that sort of being there to feed the Catholic thing was not very appealing at all. So that is when I began to dream up the scheme to become community developers.

After four years at the Pond Creek mission, Marie Cirillo's next mission work was in Chicago, where she was sent in 1964 to finish college. She soon found ways to work in the Appalachian ghetto of Uptown, which became a Glenmary mission site and, soon after, a training center to prepare Sisters for work with Appalachian people in both urban areas and the mountains.

Marie did not want to go to Chicago to college. She wanted to be on mission. But she followed orders, and once in Chicago, she found a way to work with Appalachian migrants in the area and get college credit for the mission work. She recalled how she sought out the Appalachian migrants and designed her studies around working with them:

From Monica and the Sisters in Big Stone Gap, [Virginia], I knew the history of the migration of Appalachians to the cities, and I started calling around to see if there was a particular neighborhood where the Appalachians had landed. I was looking for them. I couldn't understand why mountain people, who loved the land more than anything else, were forced to move into dirty, industrial cities to make a living. Why did they have to leave? I wanted to find out the answer, and thirty years later I am just beginning to get a grasp on it.

My search . . . led me to Father Jack Egan, who became a life-long friend. With his help I moved into Saint Mary's Convent on Kenmore Street [in] Uptown, where some forty thousand Appalachians lived.[5] There was nothing the church was doing for them. I realized that living in the convent was still a real barrier to the people. . . . I recruited Geraldine [Peterson] to come up and go to school and Evelyn [Eaton Whitehead], who had just gotten her degree in philosophy. I thought it would be a good experience for her to live in the city area and do nitty-gritty stuff. We found an apartment on Kenmore, and I liked everything but the roaches.

Sisters Evelyn and Juliana in Uptown Chicago, 1966. Photo by André Abecassis.

I had met Dr. Martin Corcoran [at Loyola].[6] I kept looking for teachers that would let me do field work. He was the only one I could find, so I took every class he was teaching. Then before I knew it there was more field work than I could do. . . . [W]e started a training center, the Appalachian Field Study Center.

Evelyn Whitehead reflected fondly on the rich education she gained during the Chicago experience Marie called her to:

I came then as a budding philosopher into an experience of incredible poverty in a city that had all its layers of maybe help, maybe hindrance to these people. One of the earliest lessons I learned was that everything I had spent the last five years of my life with was absolutely useless to me. . . . I went into a period of anti-intellectualism and a sense or feeling that I had been betrayed, because nothing that I had learned in philosophy gave me the sensitivity or skills on what to do here. And so basically we would go out and knock on doors and meet people. The three of us lived there for probably three years. . . . We were trying to locate natural leaders . . . trying to encourage them and perhaps form them to take greater responsibility to become spokespeople for the Appalachian community, to make some claims on the urban infrastructure. None of these people were Catholic. . . . I was doing something on the edge, very adventurous, learning very much from the Appalachian people.

Evelyn was the administrator of the Appalachian Field Study Center. She worked with Dr. Corcoran of Loyola to develop the curriculum, arranged academic credits for Sisters in degree programs through Marquette University, and found housing for each crop of new students. She credited Marie Cirillo with the center's genesis: "I attribute all these ideas as originating with Marie. . . . We were talking about the two-pronged Glenmary Sisters' presence, rural Appalachia and Appalachian communities in larger cities. We thought we could provide some sort of training for people who were going to be serving urban Appalachians, including helping professionals . . . in Chicago or Detroit as well as Glenmary Sisters. . . . Lots of good process things happened in the Appalachian community that we called the Glenmary Event in Uptown."

Monica Appleby, who was living and working in Big Stone Gap, Virginia, went to Chicago in January 1966 for four months of training:

This was when I learned the importance of in-depth interviewing and multidisciplinary, self-directed learning. It was a connecting of the inward and outward, the personal and the social. . . . We spent most mornings in small groups discussing the books we read, which included sociology, psychology, anthropology, philosophy, and drama. We took heavy tape recorders with ten-inch reels into people's apartments and interviewed them for at least an hour about their lives in Chicago and back home. [In the interviews] each class was concentrating on one of the social institutions. Our group's focus was around family. [Subsequent] classes talked with [Uptown residents] about education, recreation, and religion. I realized that home visiting was a powerful environment when relationships could be developed that would lead to organized events and personal . . . reflection and growth.

It was revealing to experience life in another place, reflect about it on almost a daily basis, and think about the implications for our work on mission and in our religious life.

Some recruits to the study program did not rate it highly. Maureen Linneman had hoped the Chicago training would prepare her for mission, but she felt it was only partly successful in readying her for her work in Virginia:

When the Chicago training period started I was in my third year, and I signed up for it right away. . . . I thought some of the sessions were long and tedious to a point of being contrived with Corcoran's stuff. . . . I planned to go to Big Stone Gap and I went to Chicago to train to go to the mission. I signed up for it so I could educate myself enough to know what to do when I got there. It did that to some degree, but when I actually got to the missions I still felt untrained.

Mary Jo Leygraaf went reluctantly, leaving other Sisters at Georgetown, where she was superior, because Catherine Rumschlag asked her to. She remembered: "Dr. [Martin] Corcoran would just let you sit for five or six hours and no one made a move! (I didn't mind doing the interviews and stuff. I liked the people.) . . . And then we'd end up having a discussion in the discussion, discussing a paragraph or a page that somebody found one thing they felt was meaningful to them—that's where we'd spend all our time. And all I could think of was, 'Home! When do we get out of here and go back home?'" Ultimately, though Mary Jo resisted the academics, she continued with the interviewing and later worked with the religious surveys in southwest Virginia, which grew out of the Chicago research.

Marie Cirillo asked Elizabeth Roth Turner (Sister Mary Joan) to come to Chicago to set up files and do administrative work for the Appalachian Study Center. Elizabeth recounted her transition to Chicago and how she developed her work with Appalachian migrants:

I arrived [in the fall of 1966] with one medium-sized suitcase—my total wardrobe and possessions. I did not unpack for three weeks, not sure I was staying. . . . I had come from the Glenmary training center in Fayetteville. . . . Fayetteville had been immaculate, the driveway strewn with autumn leaves as the car pulled away. Chicago was gray, dusty, with broken bottles, garbage and litter, rodent control posted on the alley telephone poles, fire trucks speeding at night to a fire that lit up the sky when I looked out the window. . . .

I met Lula Couch one day as I was coming through the alley on my way home. She was from Hazard, Kentucky. . . . I was quick to recognize that she was someone who could teach me about the how and why of my mission there. This encounter was the beginning of nine years of service to the Appalachian community of Uptown.

Upon my request I was admitted to the Appalachian training program and [did the bookkeeping for] the Study Center. . . . One of the persons who stayed on after training was Gail Addy. Gail and I connected with our strong interest in relating to our neighbors. This developed into an extensive practice of home visitation and activities around rummage sales, birthday celebrations, introducing newcomers and finding them apartments, going to second-hand stores for furniture and appliances, finding strong bodies to move the stuff, [and] outings to Grant Park concerts. I attended my first funeral parlor wake in Uptown. Underlying all this was music. Gail soothed with her soft singing and healing guitar playing. Lula Couch and Georgia Adkins and her sons played. Always there was music and just about any evening we could stop by someone's apartment for music and reminisce about life back home. . . .

People knew us as Glenmary Sisters whose names they often recalled with the fervor of a litany of saints: Sisters Marie, Geraldine, Anna Marie, Evelyn, Grace, . . . Eileen—and the names went on.

An influential mission experience very different from Chicago was in south Georgia. Here the Sisters were involved in the early integration of schools and health services. Mary Schweitzer (Sister Mary Paul) was assigned to enroll at Georgia Southern University as integration was beginning there. Sister Anna (Shirley Gallahon) was in a similar situation as a nurse's aide in the Bulloch County Hospital in Statesboro.[7] She wrote to the order's *Community Bulletin* in 1966, "I believe that one of the important tasks of the Church in the South today is to help the poor white person adjust to and accept willingly the integration of the Negro into the total community."[8] Mary Schweitzer praised the mission work developed in Statesboro by Kathleen (Kay) Kaercher Barnett and Jane Schulte: "Kay Kaercher was a fantastic superior. She was a real encourager and she was a truster and yet she was always there when you needed her. The worthwhile project [1961–1962] I got into was a radio program, *Together Toward God*, which we did once a week . . . for [parents and religious educators of] preschool children. . . . We had to develop our ingenuity and creativity and we were rewarded for that."

During their mission work in the South, many of the Sisters encountered their first instances of racism. One event still haunts Kay Kaercher Barnett:

I had my first firsthand experience of racial prejudice and hatred when a young black girl, who was helping me prepare a store-front chapel, was cursed and had her very life threatened because she used a "white only" restroom. I had told her to since there were none labeled "colored" in that small town. What a sickening and helpless feeling that was. I felt those words cut through me like knives into Lydia, who was cowering behind me. And to think this was and still is a common type of experience for many. . . . This episode . . . [gave] me a deep sense of compassion and love for my black friends and students. They surely must be among the last who will be first in the Kingdom.[9]

Much of the mission work that provided the model for the group's later community development in Appalachia evolved in experiments in Big Stone Gap, Virginia. There, the Sisters had established the Holy Cross Center in 1955. It grew from their earlier Virginia mission work, which mostly comprised emergency relief and vacation Bible schools in the coal camps and hollers. But, eventually, the Big Stone Gap work moved in a different direction and became the model for experimental ministry.

Monica Appleby was assigned to Big Stone Gap in 1959 and stayed until 1970. When she arrived Sister Mary Joseph was superior. Monica said of her: "I had a great admiration for her openness to all kinds of people and [her] sharing our household with them. . . . It was an encounter with a larger world, with another culture, with another way of life." Under Monica's leadership the center became a gathering place for community people, social activists, and students.

Monica became the superior of Holy Cross Center at a time when community action and social movements were emerging in the region. As such, she was poised to move the mission in a different direction. Monica had visited Marie Cirillo at the mission in Pond Creek and was later missioned there. This work and her earlier experiences in Virginia led her to a conclusion about the need for community development:

People were laid off and they were really trying to survive . . . or [they] had to move to urban areas to find work. And in the past they had moved and always came back to the mines. We did clothing drives, gave out food and gave a . . . party and toys at Christmas, but the same people kept coming back. So we tried to figure out why the situation was the way it was. And that was when the [idea of] community development first came to me on how to get groups together to help solve their own problems, more than the relief sort of approach.

Under Monica's leadership the Sisters in Big Stone Gap became involved with the Council of Southern Mountains[10] and the beginning of the federally sponsored local programs of the War on Poverty. The first VISTA (Volunteers in Service to America) workers in the nation came to the area and Sister Eileen (Maureen Linneman) joined VISTA as an Appalachian Volunteer.[11] Monica recalled their role as innovators in service to the region: "We were on the first committees to begin community action in Wise [County], the start of the Community Action Program."

Monica and Anne Leibig, also in Big Stone Gap, formed a leadership team. Monica said they "were a synergistic pair." Anne was a good organizer and introduced the idea of a catechetical coordinator who would work with all the Glenmary pastors in southwest Virginia and not just those in a single parish. Later, Bishop Joseph Hodges in the Wheeling, West Virginia, Diocese approved a broader social ministry, and Monica became the coordinator of community development and then the field coordinator of the Office of Appalachian Ministry, which extended the Sisters' reach to West Virginia.[12]

The two women developed a new type of missionary approach that included community development, political advocacy, and social services. Anne coordinated the religious education programs for four parishes, while Maureen Linneman and other Glenmary Sisters and volunteers worked in rural coal camps, schools, and community programs such as Headstart. Monica had taken classes at Clinch Valley College in Wise, Virginia,[13] in sociology and history and became very involved in the development of the Office of Economic Opportunity (OEO) programs in southwest Virginia. She was often called on to speak at conferences for clergy and social workers about how to work with Appalachians, and she became known for her knowledge and understanding of Appalachian problems and culture. The Holy Cross Center was now a gathering place for the young activists of

Sister Mary Juliana (Ellen Burbach Browne) with young people at Holy Cross Center in Big Stone Gap, Virginia, discussing race relations, 1962.

the region, VISTAs, Appalachian Volunteers, and lots of visiting students from colleges and universities seeking an "Appalachian experience." The center provided food, clothing, and sometimes shelter and advocacy for people who were inadequately served by agencies such as welfare and health departments. The entire group in Big Stone Gap was active in the Council of Southern Mountains. Most had been trained in Chicago at the Appalachian Field Study Center.

Maureen Linneman came to Big Stone Gap fresh from the Chicago experience:

I began to see a purpose, I knew I was to help create a community organization in that community. But that was very difficult for me. I was out there by myself. It was a lot of organization and hard, lonely work. People wouldn't show up, and if they did show up they would be late, and it was cold, the building was cold and damp. I remember walking up dirt roads in the mud and being cold, and that was when I loved the potbelly stove—I could stand around it. That was my real introduction to real poverty, real isolation, and the people were very kind to me. I was Sister Eileen. I was in a contemporary habit, and I was to be self-employed, and I was told it would be good for me to become an Appalachian Volunteer [so that's how I was supported].

Monica remembered those halcyon days as the high point in her life: "I miss those high-energy days. I loved being a Glenmary Sister in Big Stone Gap. I loved the house and the places where so many people's lives and movements for change converged. I had a name and a voice and a recognized role. I was part of a group of women who did significant things. My lifelong friendships were made during this time."

Bishop Joseph Hodges of Wheeling, West Virginia, was a strong supporter of the Sisters and their new form of ministry. As the women became more involved with community action they began experimenting with changes: wearing the short habit and being more flexible with rules. Maureen Linneman attributed the experimental environment to Monica's influence: "Monica was the mission voice that was asked about things and Big Stone was the trial place for the contemporary habit and new work involvement. . . . Monica wanted to do something different. I was the VISTA in a habit and I didn't wear the veil."

An important piece in the reeducation of the Sisters was the religious survey that grew out of the interviewing projects developed by Dr. Martin Corcoran for the Appalachian Field Study Center. Sisters used the survey in the coal camps as another way of entering the community. The Sisters were even trained to query the transactions of the interview itself: Who says what to whom? In what manner? Under what circumstances? For what reasons? With what effect?

Monica got the support of the Office of Appalachian Ministry in the Diocese of Wheeling to continue the project in Virginia and West Virginia, interviewing people there about their religious values and practices. The main focus was to learn from Appalachian people. The interviews were an important tool in learning about the people they were serving, Monica explained: "By this time we realized that our views were different from theirs and that we had to learn to listen. We also believed that the interviews themselves would help both persons involved learn something they didn't know about what they thought and felt."

The experience of interviewing and talking to mountain people about their religious beliefs—and the friendships that evolved from the visits—had a big impact on the missionaries. The ideas and approach to religion expressed by people in the coal camps, up the hollers, or in the city ghetto were quite different from those the young Sisters had grown up with and embraced in their theological education. The following excerpts from various interviews indicate what they were hearing:

"One thing I think makes a real good preacher is stand [*sic*] firm to his word. Now I don't like these preachers that'll tell you one thing and then turn around and tell somebody else another one."[14]

"A preacher should live a good life. . . . Some preachers really know the Bible and live a good life, and these other preachers that don't know the Bible say these preachers ain't living a good life. The Bible tells you what's a good life, honey, and what ain't a good life; and then you can make up your own mind" (Anne Leibig, "Excerpts from Interview Material on Religion in Appalachia," 2).

"I do read the Bible quite a lot, and I know when they preach the truth, and if they don't preach the truth I don't hear 'em a second time. . . . I think it's the Lord that preaches in the man that's saved cause the Bible says a man opens his mouth and he'll feel it. I don't think a man has to sit down here and read and read and read and then go start writing down notes. . . . If you makin' a speech, you have to make notes, but when you're preachin' you're supposed to be talkin', tellin' people of God, and you don't have to make notes. I think that's the way I feel about it, because God preaches you; and if you don't preach within the Spirit, you're not preaching anyway (3)."

As Anne Leibig deepened her relationship with the people around her, she felt her consciousness of the institutional and abstract (i.e., relating as a nun and representative of the church) give way to the personal aspects Appalachians valued:

[M]y first impression was excitement and the openness of people even though we were strangely dressed. And I also began to realize they saw me as a person more than a connection to the costume and the institution. That was a good experience. I think it was in 1968 or '69 I wrote an article, "Appalachia Converts Sisters."[15] I had that experience, [of being] changed around to them instead of changing them to where I felt they needed to be. It was Reverse Evangelism.

From the Roman Catholic viewpoint and being a missionary it was very important to bring the Catholic message and faith to everybody in the world, and to do that you went to where there weren't Catholics. . . . Today, I realize the institutional things aren't as important as I thought they were, but the personal, and the choice, and the . . . availability of what's going on in the present is what *is* important—and to be in dialogue with those around you, create the meaning and not to bring meaning from another place.

Monica, too, felt changed by the Appalachian people and described the transformation worked on the Sisters by their new home: "The conversion was not an instant conversion like Saint Paul. No outside flash of lightning. It was a slow following of what was close up before us and in us. It was people and place oriented and not ideological or dogmatic."

As they became influenced by the social and theological movements of their time and immersed in the practical demands of their ministry, the idealistic young order quietly but persistently negotiated with the male church hierarchy for the rule changes they saw as necessary. Sometimes they felt supported, as by Bishop Joseph Hodges of Wheeling. Archbishop Alter, who was their legal "protector" since they were a diocesan community, also approved changes such as the experimental habit modified for mission wear. He was also a real protector of the Sisters until the mid-1960s when he began to receive complaints from Rome and from the community that the Glenmary Sisters were becoming too modern.

But they were still hampered by many of the inherited rules of their congregation, which had been originally designed for cloistered nuns (stemming from Archbishop McNicholas's earlier choice to model the new group on the Dominicans). The Sisters had an eight o'clock curfew that prevented them from attending organizing meetings in the evening—the only time miners' families could come. They had to travel in pairs. Monica explained another major hindrance to neighborliness and trust: "[W]hen we did home visits we were often asked if we would like a cup of coffee or tea and a snack. According to the constitution of our Glenmary community . . . we were not allowed to eat with the 'seculars.' Now in the context of our relationships with people in mountain communities, this rule did not fit. It was just not polite to refuse to eat with a family when it was offered."

If, as Evelyn Whitehead believes, the congregation had "stayed South," perhaps it could have continued working through its differences over the next decade with the hierarchy, which would see rapid change among American religious. But in Chicago the women stumbled suddenly into a national spotlight they had not sought, when the mainstream media discovered them in Uptown.

While Monica Appleby was in Chicago, the *Saturday Evening Post* featured the Sisters in an article by Michael Novak titled "The New Nuns." Photographs showed Monica in the short habit, "walking down an alleyway with a suitcase," and joyously at play with a child.[16]

Under the header, "What Sisters Are Meant to Be," Novak wrote glowingly:

The Glenmary Sisters are warm and living symbols of reform and reinvigoration in the Roman Catholic Church. Compared to the old-style nuns, who cling to the cloister and follow a strict rule under the eye of stern superiors, the Glenmarys are a new breed altogether. Their small order—not quite 100 strong—works throughout the South and also in Chicago with hill people who have come north for jobs. In Chicago slum apartments the Sisters live informally, in intimate touch with the neighborhood and its woes. They shop at the chain store or pick up a hamburger or eat with a family down the block. They roughhouse with children and never mind the small grubby hands. They tease one another, argue, laugh readily. From the "railroad flats" they go out into the alleys to teach the migrants how to cope with city living at the same time conducting a study of the migrants' problems so that the insights may be applied elsewhere in the nation. They are quietly experimenting with practical new garments and accessories; instead of a cross, one Glenmary wears a pin showing a group of people—people, the focus of Christian concern. If the American Sisterhoods are changing, many in the church hope it is in the direction of the Glenmarys.

Elsewhere in the article Novak quoted ominously and at length from a bishop's recent sermon:

Some people are shocked by the manner of dress of the "new nuns." Some [of the Sisters] can hardly be distinguished from the laity—knee length dresses, a lot of color, almost no headdress. The reason their superiors give for such is that it brings them closer to the laity. Is this desirable? If they dress like lay people, will they not be treated like lay people? The Sister's habit not only protects her, but is a source of inspiration and veneration to the people. What is more alarming, we find nuns more and more out of the convent and appearing in public. They appear at evening meetings with the laity; give lectures to the public; eat in public restaurants; march in picket lines and demonstrations for social justice; travel alone from one end of the nation to the other and live alone on the campuses of universities, because they have been offered a scholarship or grant. One sometimes wonders, "Why did they go to the convent?"[17]

Monica commented on the article's effect: "To us it was normal, but to the outside world it was a dramatic viewing. As a community we started getting a lot of media attention, and that brought the eyes of the institutional church upon us. Before this, we were a small community [who] . . . had permission from the Archbishop of Cincinnati . . . to experiment with our mission work and religious practices. 'Experimental' had been our way for quite a long time so what we were doing in Chicago did not seem that unusual."

Glenmary's new notoriety would inaugurate a period of increased turbulence with an outcome few could have foreseen.

Chapter 4

CONFLICT WITH THE HIERARCHY

The Glenmary Sisters were a moment of threat for many bishops.

The Glenmary Sisters' failed negotiations with the male hierarchy of the Catholic Church left them feeling betrayed and, ultimately, led them to leave the order altogether. Although Vatican II asked for renewal and change, there were still many cardinals, bishops, archbishops, and priests who were not progressive thinkers. The struggle and the confrontation with the church ended when the Sisters were ordered to stop their experimentations. Much of the struggle centered around their modified, short habit. The habit has always been a symbol of the sanctity of the person, signifying preferential treatment and privilege. In the habit the nun is no longer a woman, and she must therefore hide all feminine characteristics. This was clearly articulated by the cardinal who said their new habit showed "too much bosom" and failed in its purpose to emphasize the religious more than the woman. When Rome assigned a priest to take charge of the order, as one of the Sisters said, "that was the last straw." As one Sister concluded, the church's real problem with the Sisters was not the habit but their lack of obedience, their struggle against hierarchical control and management, and their demand for community autonomy.

Sister Evelyn (Evelyn Eaton Whitehead) was interviewed by Studs Terkel in Chicago in 1966, and she talked about the Sisters' growing conflicts with the church. Evelyn concluded:

> *Any person who attempts to shake an institution has to be willing to take the consequences. We certainly don't look upon ourselves as prophets. We look upon ourselves as people who are testing a situation. But in the testing, we have to infringe on certain notions that have become traditionally the way Sisters do things.[1]*

Mother Superior Mary Catherine Rumschlag led the group through the most difficult part of the conflict and through innumerable negotiations with the institutional church with incredible patience and unwavering resolve.[2]

What the Glenmarys were doing in Chicago and Appalachia seemed decidedly unusual and threatening to the church hierarchy, which would mainly reveal itself to be of like mind with the bishop quoted in Michael Novak's *Saturday Evening Post* article in chapter 3. The ears and eyes of Rome were vigilant. Reaction by the Sacred Congregation of Religious to the article prompted the U.S. apostolic delegate, Archbishop Vagnozzi, to write the archbishop several tart letters urging him to admonish the upstart congregation.[3] First, the delegate insisted that the women should "observe the directives that have been given with regard to their habit." Next, he instructed the archbishop to "ask them to adopt a more humble attitude. . . . [and emphasized that] they should understand that there are in America luminous examples of goodness, sacrifice and dedication given before them and better than them by so many Sisters of different Institutes."[4]

But tensions had begun to emerge—both among the Sisters themselves and between the congregation and the hierarchy—as early as 1964. In addition to the important new perspectives they were gaining on mission, many were pursuing further education, attending international conferences and educational programs, and doing a lot of reading and thinking about mission and theology.

The great majority of the Sisters embraced their increasing opportunities to grow and change. For some, their most dramatic encounter with the New Theology came through Lumen Vitae in the city of Louvain, Belgium. An international catechetical center for the training of teachers and pastors, Lumen Vitae featured noted theologians like Bernard Haring and Edward Schillebeeckx.[5] Kay Kaercher Barnett remembered the thrill of going there:

That summer in 1959, Sister Dolores and I received a new assignment—to attend Lumen Vitae. . . . The eight-day journey over on the *Queen Mary* was only the beginning of the excitement. The students were priests, Brothers, Sisters, and lay people from twenty-six different countries. The studies themselves opened up a whole new vision of our faith. We had wonderful professors . . . some of whom were helping to prepare the bishops for the Second Vatican Council. Never before had scripture, the liturgy, and theology come together with so much meaning. We felt like those people who heard Peter on the first Pentecost—Wow! What are we to do about this?[6]

The sexual content of the 1960s revolution could hardly have failed to touch the community as well, along with the New Theology and heightened concern for social justice. Jean Luce observed: "We were also young and experimentation was going on. There were people falling in love with men, with priests, and in Cincinnati especially, that became a real threat."

It was in this atmosphere that in 1964 a small minority of five to seven dissident Sisters complained to the archbishop that they believed the order was interpreting the role of Sisters too liberally in the post–Vatican II age. They felt that Glenmary was in danger of losing its religious spirit. Toward the end of July, Archbishop Alter made known to the General Council certain criticisms and complaints that had come to him about the community from internal and external sources. At the 1964 summer institute, which was held annually to plan their year's work, develop policies, and deal with problems and issues, they sought to reconcile their differences and answer the archbishop's request to reach a common understanding concerning their mission and lifestyle. They formed interest groups, which met throughout the year, to deal with these problems.

The Sisters were eventually refused permission to send any more members to attend courses at Lumen Vitae. According to the *National Catholic Reporter*, the dissident Sisters blamed the school as a source of radical ideas.[7]

Lenore Mullarney attributed some of the order's internal division to differences in education and experience: "I feel sure some of the division in the community was due to [those] who did not have the opportunity for advanced education where they would be broadened and better understand the new theological insights and movement in society and church. It makes me think of children going off to college and learning all kinds of things and not understanding the ones at home who are thought of many times as 'narrow' or 'behind the times.'" Lenore summarized the problems the congregation was experiencing:

[The Glenmary General] Council[8] was trying to administer the organization in light of Vatican II and to be open to the reports from the missions; to understand the needs of the Sisters in college; to work with the archbishop; to live with the tensions occasioned by some Sisters who maintained extremely strong ties with the Glenmary Fathers (and these were not always at one with our efforts); to respond to the extremely . . . large number of Sisters who seemed to be in need of psychological counseling; and at the same time attempt to keep the community solvent with very little income and large expenses. . . . The Motherhouse was like the hub of a wheel and all the vibrations and stresses reached it.

The "new nuns" had not only outgrown some of their Sisters, they

IT'S A BAD SIGN: MOTHER SUPERIOR HAS STARTED TO REFER TO SOCIAL WITNESS AS "GLENMARIOLATRY".

Joe Noonan cartoon in *National Catholic Reporter*, December 6, 1967.

had also outgrown their male spiritual advisors. Marie Cirillo chafed at their limitations and refused to take their spiritual direction:

The two critical spiritual directors we had were . . . still very much of what we call now the 'old school.' They encouraged the sense of submission and obedience and obeying the rules of canon law. There were the kind of self-imposed penances and mortifications and fastings. On the other hand, we had Sisters going to Louvain in Belgium, and we had the liturgical movement going, and we had Sisters in Chicago and Cincinnati seeing a whole other world. So there really were very personal tensions, because here we were, fifteen to twenty years, getting spiritual direction from these guys, and the other ideas became stronger. I remember at a point saying I could no longer take spiritual direction from Father because I can't live in both worlds.

The differences in ideologies increased, and the divisions in the group became more apparent. Jean Luce described the different groups that formed within the order:

Glenmary was no longer one big group; there were little groups forming that were differing, with different ideologies. One was that we were Sisters and we were supposed to be religious and do what [the] pope and bishop told us. . . . Being part of the church was a very important thing for this group, and they worked very hard to do that. They were trained by the Dominican Sisters to be a helper to the priests: we were "the auxiliary." Other people were talking about being a more autonomous group, not so dependent on what the priest said and fearful of the church and archbishop. These were the younger ones where experimentation was going on. Then a lot of people didn't feel so bound to religious life, [in] that they wanted to do new things. One group wanted to be religious in the broader sense and not focus on any region. The other group wanted to concentrate on Appalachia.

Again their habit became a symbol of the growing alienation and discontent between the church and the Sisters. The experimental habit was the focus of the conflict, and just as the Sisters' habit was a dominant symbol in the contest of wills between Father Bishop and two archbishops over the early direction of Glenmary, so did it rise to visibility again in the congregation's struggle with the hierarchy over the authority to direct its own affairs.

Beginning in 1961, the Glenmarys were one of the first orders to request changes in the design of their habit.[9] With the local bishops' sanction, Sisters in Georgetown, Chicago, and Big Stone Gap began experimenting with a shorter contemporary habit in 1963. The congregation endorsed the proposed new habit in a Special Chapter, which was held in June 1965. (Special Chapter's are meetings called outside the time of the regularly scheduled General Chapter with an important or urgent agenda.) This meeting was requested for Vatican II Renewal of Religious Life. Formal approval for the new habit had to come from the Sacred Congregation of Religious in the Vatican. Rather like the interminable lawsuit in Charles Dickens's *Great Expectations*, the approval process was not finally concluded until years after most members had left the congregation. The following letter from Monsignor Edward McCarthy, Archbishop Alter's secretary, reveals the efforts Monsignor McCarthy made to negotiate with

Sister Dolores Meyer in Chicago wearing the experimental short habit. Photo by André Abecassis, 1966.

the authorities in Rome for approval of the new habit. He and Archbishop Alter were trying to deal with a slow moving and intransigent church hierarchy in Rome, conservative colleagues and lay members in the States, the disgruntled conservative Glenmary Sisters, and the "new nuns" in the Order. They showed respect for Mother Mary Catherine and admiration for the work of the creative and modernizing Sisters. They had been "protectors" of the Order as they worked in the mission fields, and early on they had allowed them to make changes in their practice to enable their work. But they also were caught in the rules requiring "obedience," often to rigid officials in their petty exercise of power.

October 13, 1965

Dear Mother Catherine,

My sincere thanks for the kind feast day greetings!

It was quite coincidental that I found your letter last Saturday morning, just after Bishop Leibold and I had returned from the Sacred Congregation of Religious offices to inquire, among other things, whether the new Glenmary habit had been approved.

We talked to Father Ransing, whom I think you know. He is the American Holy Cross priest who works at the Sacred Congregation. He told us off the record that he heard there was difficulty about approval of the Glenmary habit, that it had been sort of a test case on which several other approvals of similar habits depended. He said he was not in a position to get into the matter since it is not his department and the information he had was confidential. He said that it is actually the Cardinal who personally approves habits. I then asked to see the Cardinal and Father Ransing made an appointment for me for Tuesday of this week (October 12).

When I met the Cardinal, I explained to him the reasons for the change in the habit—the fact that you work among Protestants and how the strangeness to them is a barrier to your work; the fact that you have given this a great deal of study and found this particular habit proposed quite suitable for your needs and acceptable to the people; the fact that the bishops of the dioceses where you work approve the habit.

The Cardinal replied that the Sacred Congregation has letters from Protestants indicating they prefer the conventional type of habit. I answered that this could be among Protestants in Catholic areas who know religious but the people in your mission area are quite different. Later the Cardinal referred to the dress of the Salvation Army and of nurses in America that he felt indicated Americans didn't expect an ultra modern dress. He spoke of the necessary protection of the Sisters. His main point was that the new scheme on religious says that the habit, while being changed, must first of all indicate that the wearer is one consecrated to God. (Father Ransing had said that the feeling at the Congregation is that the habit must emphasize the religious more than the woman.) The Cardinal made a point of telling that the Congregation has sent back designs for not being changed enough, as well as for being too much changed.

As to your habit, the Cardinal said that the Congregation will approve the use of the two colors (summer and winter); it will approve the veil; it will approve the collar arrangement and it will approve the part from the waist down but wants it "a little longer."

He is however not satisfied with the upper part of it. His main objection is that the bosom is too noticeable. He says there should be a sort of cape arrangement (something like the bishop's mozetta). The area from the waist line up to the cape should also be of the same habit material (I assume he meant by this that a blouse should not show).

I hope that I have been clear in explaining the above.

The Cardinal asked me to communicate all of this to you. Apparently you will not receive an official reply. He asks that the modifications be made and that new photographs be submitted.

If you are able to have anything ready before I leave Rome (I suppose in mid November) I will be pleased to take it over to the Congregation for you. I think you should talk it over with His Grace [Archbishop Alter] however before sending anything else over.

It occurs to me that perhaps the photographs which you sent originally were taken under wrong light conditions—that shadows were cast which emphasize the form. If this were true, and it could be proven without doubt by new photos, I might perhaps represent the new photos as your first choice (if that were indeed so) when I present the revised photos. The Cardinal however seemed adamant in his position and said it was not his alone but also that of his advisors.

If there are further questions, don't hesitate to write. With greetings, and prayer for a blessing for all of you, I am,

Devotedly yours in Christ,
Edward McCarthy

P.S. Nothing should be announced at this stage even of the partial approval that was granted.

P.P.S. The Cardinal asked how many professed Sisters there are. When I told him, he said there would have to be at least 200 before you could think of becoming of pontifical right.[10]

Monica Appleby suggested that the habit showing too much bosom was hardly the only problem the Glenmary women presented to the male hierarchy:

The decision to change our habit to the experimental design that we had been wearing in Big Stone, Chicago, and later in other places was critical and symbolic of the decisions about our religious life and mission work.

[But] the key area of discussion at the August '65 Chapter had been about how decisions would be made. We voted on decentralizing our organizational structure based on the Vatican II–articulated principle of "subsidiarity."[11] We revised the constitution and sent it to the archbishop.

Men had more access to the place where decisions were made. They were the clergy, and when we started getting out and deciding things for ourselves, they didn't like it. We wanted to make it [so] that the women stationed in West Virginia could make more decisions without checking with our Motherhouse in Cincinnati. That was more threatening and scary than changing our habits.

Glenmary priest Les Schmidt recalled: "The Glenmary Sisters were one of the most prophetic elements in the church during the 1960s. They were [also] a moment of threat for many bishops."[12]

In September 1965 Archbishop Alter issued sixteen directives to try to correct what he saw as "discrepancies" in the Sisters' practices. The directives belied the autonomy the group felt it should have to be flexible in responding to mission needs and modernizing its rules and spirit in response to Vatican II. Among other restrictions, the archbishop's directives ordered all Sisters to be in bed and observe profound silence at 10:00 P.M.; not to be absent from their houses for meetings or classes after that hour; to keep cloister (bar laypeople from most of their dwelling area); and not to disturb the order's religious spirit by "excessive absences," especially for "attending workshops or conferences outside the diocese where they live." He limited their professional training to areas related to "health, clinics or service, catechetics, and approved apostolic activity" and decreed that he himself would approve all course enrollment at the beginning of every semester. The women were further enjoined from engaging with lay people in "particular friendships" or "recreation inconsistent with the reserve" of "their religious state." Regulation even pursued them to the dining table: they were forbidden to invite lay people (except female relatives) to eat with them, while the material they read aloud during meals was to be from an approved list and not "offensive to virtue and the vow of chastity."

Foreshadowing some of the themes expressed by the bishop quoted in Novak's article "The New Nuns," after enumerating the directives in a letter to Mother Mary Catherine, the archbishop concluded:

These directives are intended to be of help in guiding the Community through not only the difficulties naturally associated with reaching maturity, but also through a difficult period in the history of religious life in general, when the new spirit in the Church, on the one hand is opening new avenues for perfecting the religious life and developing fully adult religious personalities, but which on the other hand, is introducing many dangerous, novel, and unbalanced ideas that are disapproved by the Holy Father and by the authorities of the Church and which dangerously threaten to lead the religious astray.

The Home Mission Sisters have reached a period in their development when they need to settle down to a consistent, ordered program and way of life. . . . A community suffers from too much change, too much restless seeking after new approaches, the confusion of attempting to assimilate too many new ideas at once, the dissipation of energy of engaging in too many movements, attendance at conventions, workshops, etc., with the result that a sense of uncertainty, insecurity and unrest develops almost unconsciously.[13]

As tensions increased, Mother Mary Catherine took leave from the Motherhouse in early 1966 and spent four months in Chicago taking courses and living with Marie Cirillo, Evelyn Eaton Whitehead, and Geraldine Peterson. She said, "The stress of this time really got to me, and I decided to take a break from governing the community." While there she met with Dr. Martin Corcoran and engaged him to develop an image study of the community to help with planning. His survey brought to light many differing opinions of what the community's life should be. The order held workshops in the spring of 1966 to follow up on his findings.

At the end of August 1966, ninety-seven members signed a letter and "Statement Concerning Goals of the Glenmary Sisters Community" addressed to Archbishop Alter. This was the group's attempt to clarify the community's mission and its right to govern and renew itself. They were forthright in defending the authority they felt Vatican II had vested in the congregation. In their letter they stated:

We feel that the issues can be most profitably dealt with in the light of the recently issued, "Instructions Implementing the Conciliar Decree Perfectae Caritatis." This instruction was presented by Father Ransing of the Sacred Congregation of Religious at the National Conference of Major Superiors of Women of the United States held in Milwaukee. We refer in particular to the statement in the instruction that the chief role in renewing and adapting religious life belongs to the Institute itself, especially through the General Chapter. . . .

We are encouraged by the fact that the Holy See has given to the Institute itself the primary authority and responsibility for its own renewal, planning, and experimentation.

The archbishop had recently suggested that they consider leaving the archdiocese. They took up this gauntlet:

We would like to remain in the Archdiocese, and would appreciate knowing whether Your Grace would find acceptable the approach described here, namely, that the Special Chapter, in response to the new Instruction, have the freedom to initiate and carry out programs for renewal and adaptation; or whether, on the contrary, we should pursue the suggestion made by Your Grace that we seriously consider finding another Bishop, in whose diocese we may locate our novitiate and Motherhouse.[14]

In their "Statement Concerning the Goals of the Glenmary Sisters Community," the Sisters started by grounding themselves in the goals and vision of their founder, Father Bishop, who enjoined them to improve people's lives through works of mercy, "regardless of their beliefs or lack of beliefs; regardless, even, of whether they will ever accept the Faith or not." While remaining true to the tradition of the church's missionary response to the world, they felt it was necessary to respond to the particular circumstances in which they found themselves. "It is in consideration of time, place and the cultural background of the people who are being served that Glenmary's particular response to these needs are [*sic*] determined."

In their statement, the Sisters argued that the congregation's unity of purpose could be expressed through a diversity of both works and roles: "We do not see this diversity of expression as detrimental to unity and understanding in the total community but rather as an aid toward deepening of a true religious spirit." In creative contrast to the archbishop's attempt to limit their apostolate to a few activities, the women envisioned it as including "parish work, social work, nursing, catechetical-worship activities, ecumenism, community action, education, arts and humanities, and other works which would fulfill the needs of the mission people who suffer especially from the lack of qualified professional workers."

The statement ended with a defense of subsidiarity, and thus of their right to control their affairs: "[I]t is only with mutual understanding and recognition of respective areas of authority that there can be life and growth in the apostolate. In order that the principle of subsidiarity can function, it is necessary that individuals, local houses and the congregation itself exercise responsibility in the spheres of their respective jurisdiction and in relationship to those authorities above them."[15]

Community members invested a lot of emotion in the letter and statement, hoping against hope that it could mark a turning point in their relations with the archbishop. But it was also meant to draw a line in the sand. Anne Leibig wrote excitedly in her journal:

Wow—things have happened! The Archbishop wrote Mother a letter asking us to leave the diocese. The way we responded was a sign of the Spirit. We could have been humbler but yet there are many things I do not know. Mother is leading and we are gladly with her. All but six people signed the letter and statement. I have been sensing we are a part of Salvation History. I am grateful to be here now, not doing much, just being a part. I am glad for being in the mountains for I know that what we are working toward . . . will be a Christian response to service and will not lessen us religiously. I feel privileged to be making final vows at a time when they can be a sign of trust—Hope![16]

Mary Schweitzer's feelings mirrored the intense frustration of many: "I remember a lot of the pain, a lot of the hurt, of my own and other people's. Anger, lots of anger I certainly did not want. If the archbishop did not respond favorably to the letter we wrote and one hundred of us signed about the changes, I knew I would not stay. I was dead serious about that."

Mother Mary Catherine had the following telephone conversation with Secretary McCarthy about the community's letter of August 26, 1966, which he termed "inappropriate." Archbishop Alter insisted on obedience to the directives and an apology from the Glenmary Sisters, whom he felt wanted to set their own terms. With dignity and determination Mother Mary Catherine upheld the community's prerogative to govern itself:

MOTHER MARY CATHERINE: I am sorry things are the way they are.

SECRETARY MCCARTHY: Not as sorry as I am!

M.M.C.: Do you plan to give us some indication of His Grace's attitude toward the developments we discussed on your last visit?

S.M.: Well, the proposal can only be considered if it comes from the community as a whole; secondly, it is necessary to have other matters cleared up before such business can be handled.

M.M.C.: I am not sure what you are referring to . . . .

S.M.: I am speaking of the letter members of your community signed last August. This letter was totally inappropriate, and we will only open communications if the Sisters apologize for the attitude apparent in the letter. It was insulting!

M.M.C.: The letter was not intended to be insulting. What specifically did you object to?

S.M.: You didn't answer His Grace's question concerning your willingness to be obedient to his directives. You seem to want to set your own terms for staying in the diocese.

M.M.C.: It seems to me that the alternatives offered are not reasonable—to obey His Grace in all things spiritual and temporal or ask for dispensation from vows.

S.M.: Well, he did use the word "canonical authority," which limits the obedience that is requested of you. Are there things in the directives which you think go beyond the power of the bishop?

M.M.C.: It seems that the bishop would not have power to impose proscriptions on internal matters that aren't part of our rules, for example, seculars eating with the community.

S.M.: Are you conscious that there are abuses that result from eating with seculars, such as improper relationships?

M.M.C.: I think such abuses would result from prohibiting the practice, rather than allowing it. If the letter signed by the community and all the other letters don't make sense to you and the other bishops, I have little hope we can come to an understanding. It's necessary for the community to act according to the convictions of its members, and we just can't consider some of the points taken up in the directives as important. They're just not the sort of answers that fit the problems of the community, and in fact they hamper our working at the real problems.

S.M.: I think you are making the Archbishop a scapegoat for your problems.

M.M.C.: There may be some truth in that.

S.M.: Can you give me specific examples of things that hamper your work?

M.M.C.: Living on exceptions is hampering. Also, not being able to work under secular auspices is hampering.

S.M.: You're picking out little things and magnifying them all out of proportion to their seriousness. The only solution I see is to start out by apologizing to the Archbishop for your actions. If you think there is nothing to apologize for, I think we are at an impasse.[17]

Marie Cirillo believed one source of the Sisters' institutional problems was their increased visibility in the urban North, where some traditionalist Catholics objected to their missionary methods:

Basically, we were a new group, which meant we were all young. We were going into places in the South where there were no Catholics to see us, there were no Catholics expecting us to behave certain ways; and I think we were very good at responding to the needs and in time fitting in and trying to be adaptable to the ways of the people. . . . [But when we moved to] Cincinnati, and Chicago, and

Detroit, we were shocking the Catholic community. Because, number one, we were young, and because Sisters didn't do those things in those days. We were out at night in meetings and we were walking the streets with all kinds of people. And I think when the word got back to the bishop he just felt that was not appropriate behavior, and because this was the time when the church was asking for change, he thought we were doing this just to try to change.

Evelyn echoed Marie's analysis that their increased visibility in the Catholic bastions of the North provoked the harsh reaction:

We were doing things Sisters don't do. We were young and naive, thinking Vatican II was enough approval for this. We angered and stepped on some toes because we were different than some, and began to draw some institutional wrath. They said: "You can do this work, but you took religious vows, and you have to act like Sisters."

That is when the pressure started. The demands of institutional religious life suddenly for the first time in Glenmary were being seen as antagonistic to the work we were doing. Before, we all saw religious life as helping the work happen. But new rules were made. We were given a list of "must do's." . . . We had to reestablish cloister—I mean, what does cloister mean in Big Stone Gap, Virginia? It meant we tried to keep people out of the second floor so we had some privacy in the bedrooms, that is what that meant. But cloister? So that was insisted on, as a sign of good will: basically on our part, [to] capitulate, and Glenmary respectfully refused to do that. Based on all the Vatican II principles, based on what our mission was, this was appropriate accommodation.

Beyond the bounds of the Glenmary community, even people outside the order reacted strongly to news of the directives.[18] In October Mother Mary Catherine wrote to her community:

The publicity concerning the archbishop's directives has brought us many letters expressing concern and prayerful support. I would have preferred that this information be kept from the public but since it is out, I think we must consider the effect of so much publicity and discussion on the community and its future.

One effect is surely good, namely, that many people are praying for us and our work. Another effect can be for good or ill, depending on the response of Glenmary Sisters. I refer to this, that our words and actions are noticed by others much more than they were before. Comments will be made, conclusions will be drawn, and the effects may go far beyond the immediate scene of the action.

I am not sure what this means, but I think we must recognize that the national publicity places upon us a greater responsibility to speak and act with prudence and courage, charity and justice. . . . We need to increase our striving to become the Christian community that will be a sign of faith and hope and love to the increased numbers who are, for one reason or another, now looking our way. . . . It is a time of opportunity and a time of responsibility for each and every Sister.[19]

During this unsettled period, members and some of their leaders began to leave Glenmary. Monica noted that changes in the larger world were also pulling women in new directions. "Individuals were leaving because this was the time of the peace movement, the marches, Martin Luther King, and people wanted to be involved in it so they were leaving." The political climate, along with the Sisters' increased education and mission experience, had opened many other opportunities for service: the Peace Corps, VISTA, Community Action programs. A number of the Sisters left, frustrated that the archbishop had vetoed many of the order's attempts to have its members work in secular agencies—often as badly needed professionals.

While Catherine was on leave in Chicago, she put Sister Stephanie Fagan (now Stephanie Hemelings) in charge. Stephanie had to take on both dealing with the archbishop and the splits within the group. The pressure was too great. On May 21, 1966, Stephanie resigned as vicaress general and member of the Council. In her letter to the Sisters she wrote:

I feel that some of my views concerning religious life, concerning what may be essential or non-essential to it . . . are not always in harmony with [the archbishop's] thinking in the same matters. Since I have been increasingly unable to handle these conflicting ideas with any degree of grace or clarity (as has been evident in recent meetings with the Archbishop), it seems obvious to me that I do not belong in an administrative post within the community. I think I am unable to continue in a position where all one's movements must be measured and calculated—where the bulk of one's energies seem to be spent in proving one's case or point.[20]

Effective September 1, Marie Cirillo became vicaress general and a fourth councilor. Stephanie Hemelings was assigned another role, but she left the order entirely in October 1966. She felt a sense of overwhelming futility: "I had resigned from the [General] Council in May, and tried to tell the archbishop then that I felt totally out of sync with the direction he wished the community to move. I thought that, if I resign from office—if

I make that move—that might help "settle the waters." But then, after-wards, I could see it hadn't really made any difference. Things still weren't going anywhere. I was well aware of all the conflicting pulls within the community—aware that a powerful archbishop was also involved—and expecting it to all mesh together seemed impossible. I could see no reso-lution."

Stephanie was a strong leader and her leaving was a great shock to many of the Sisters. Marie recalled the after-effects:

When Stephanie left, the bottom fell out, and all these people just went home. As we would have Council meetings things would get worse instead of better. And we had the sense that everybody would go home. And I think I was the one that suggested maybe we think of creating a new group; that is the sociologist in me.

I wonder if Stephanie knows how her leaving impacted what happened. To me, she was the most interesting person in the community. If I had to choose a leader I would have chosen her. When she left, it was such a surprise to me. I thought she had leadership potential, and I probably presumed she had a way to fight this guy and win. I thought that if Stephanie were there she could take us on to this glori-ous something, but she wasn't. . . . And when she pulled out I thought, "My God, we are all going to go home." I couldn't imagine or assume leadership. I wasn't in that position.

In response to the Vatican II "Decree on Implementation"—the call to make recommendations on how religious life could fit into the modern world—the order had scheduled a special General Chapter for December 26, 1966, to plan for renewal. Preparation for the Chapter entailed months of research, reading, planning meetings, discussion sessions, and dissemi-nation of questionnaires. Working conscientiously in the face of mounting evidence of the hierarchy's opposition to their wishes and hopes, various committees produced position papers and recommendations for the fu-ture. On the eve of the Chapter meeting, Mother Mary Catherine sent a letter to all the Sisters. She wrote about their need and opportunity to develop a new form of religious life—to "walk on the water."

Walking On Water

When I think about the invitation of the bishops of the Church to re-think many things about religious life, and the unique position in which we find ourselves as Glenmary Sisters, I am filled with hope for the future, as well as awed by the responsibility which is ours. It seems of primary impor-tance that we recognize both our opportunities and our responsibility. . . .

I would like to suggest that we look upon this General Chapter as a new beginning in the life of the Glenmary Sisters. We are concerned about our goals and the means to reach them. These means include the works of the apostolate and our life in community. I think that in both these areas we can start new, in the sense that as a community we have not taken decisive action in these matters.

We are all convinced of the need for the services of dedicated women in the mission areas of our country. This General Chapter has the power to decide how we as Glenmary Sisters are going to respond to this need. It has more power than the General Council; it has more power than General Chapters have had in the past. As Father LeFebre put it in a talk given last year, Christ is inviting us to "walk on the water." Religious are called, as Peter was, to believe in the world of Our Lord. He has called us to a task in the Church; if we take the necessary step and trust in Him, the means will not be lacking. We must believe, we must take decisive action, we must keep our eyes on the Lord. If we "look at our feet," concerned with our own weakness and the weakness of our companions, with the possibility of failure, with all sorts of possible obstacles, we will surely begin to sink.

Our responsibility is increased because we have arrived at this stage of "starting new" sooner than many other communities. I feel sure that you all received in some way, as I did, the spirit that I think was evident in Father Bishop's attitude that the Glenmary Sisters were to have a new form of religious life. They were not to be "tied down" by outworn structures. What happened in regard to structures was not entirely satisfactory either to Father Bishop or to many members of the community, perhaps to most members. We did not know enough, and perhaps would not have been allowed, to develop new structures. We were introduced to religious life in the "old structures." I think we have proved that they were not taken on in a permanent and integral way.

Now the Church calls for new structures in religious life and in planning for the apostolate. In many ways it seems that Glenmary Sisters are ready, that their whole history has made them ready. I think it is a question of whether we have the faith, humility, the courage, and generosity. It is a question of whether we are willing to "walk on the water."[21]

A preparatory meeting was scheduled in November. Evelyn Eaton Whitehead was among the delegates elected to attend. Since the Chapter would address some of the community's differences, including where its primary focus would be, she had decided to take a strong stand in favor of missions. She had a definite sense of what was needed:

It had become clear to me that the Chapter or whatever decision-making crowd

[was] over us was waffling on whether we were going to stand up to make a decision to go in the direction of the mission statement or go in the direction of religious institutional life. I remember Rosemary [Esterkamp] and I deciding that we had to tell the Chapter that it was a judgment call, and we had to let them know what our judgment call was. Our judgment call was we were going to go with the mission. If the Chapter decided to return to religious life, we were leaving. We did not want this to be an ultimatum, we weren't saying come along, but these were the stakes. Rosemary and I decided we had to say that.

The representatives at the November meeting worked to come up with a structure that could somehow encompass the almost polar split in their convictions regarding life and work. Mother Mary Catherine wrote the Sisters on November 30, 1966:

In discussing the manner of living, working, and praying, which the Vatican documents ask us to consider in the light of conditions of today's world, we find that, while some common features are promoted by all Chapter members, we are able to identify several distinctive patterns. This led us to consider the possibility of the members of the community coming together in several units, which while seeking a common goal as religious, may have different secondary goals and different means to the goal. After working with this idea for some hours, in the general meeting and in smaller committee meetings, we found ourselves with three units, namely the experimental unit, the development unit, and the service unit. Any Sister or group of Sisters who cannot ascribe to one of these proposals is free to prepare a fourth or fifth proposal.[22]

At the December General Chapter the divided community managed to create a renewed statement of purpose and policies. As in their August statement of goals to the archbishop, they again tied their new vision of work and community to their founder's vision. Noting that Father Bishop had proposed a plan of action for the Glenmary Fathers but never for the Sisters, they now adopted one. Even though some members felt the focus was too narrow, the Chapter chose to align its ministry with the Appalachian people, whether as migrants in urban centers outside the region or at home in the mountains. They wanted their ministry to include a "diversity of works . . . intended to cut across existing lines and divisions—religious, class, racial, educational, cultural, political, etc.—to bring about an experience of social integration or community," in which "programs of social, cultural, and educational activities [would] predominate rather than specifically religious ones."

In charting the community's renewal, the Chapter saw "need to develop structures of religious life which will allow us the freedom to carry out the purpose and plans described," in which members would "live these norms on an experimental basis, to evaluate them [and] improve on them."

The community reinterpreted the meaning of living their religious vows. Poverty was "sharing with all our human and material resources"; chastity was "caring for others in their need"; while obedience meant "bearing responsibility for the self, religious community, [and] the non-Catholic community."

Under "Relation to the Church" the Chapter proposed that members would not necessarily work directly under a parish structure or under the supervision of diocesan Church offices. However, they would seek the permission and acceptance of a local ordinary for the work they do.

The community pledged to strive for a mutual understanding and respect among all Church persons and to make every effort to avoid conflict, confusion, or division among official Catholic Church representatives.

Assessing its problems, the Chapter decided that the community should leave the jurisdiction of the archbishop for another diocese, while also acknowledging ongoing internal differences and the possibility of further difficulties with the Sacred Congregation of Religious. They proposed three possible alternative resolutions of their dilemma: religious life, a secular group, or some members remaining religious while others cooperated as seculars.

Since the community felt Archbishop Alter would never ratify its vision for renewal, under "Conditions for Remaining Religious," they determined that they would have to relocate. If they were to carry out the decisions they had made in the Chapter, they must transfer the Motherhouse from Cincinnati.[23]

The Sisters duly notified the archbishop of their recommendations following the close of the Chapter in January 1967, and it was several months before they heard from the archbishop. He asked Mother Mary Catherine to come to his office with the members of the General Council. At the meeting he told her he had sent the results of the Chapter to the Sacred Congregation of Religious. Their response was that it seemed not like a religious community but more like a secular institute. The Sacred Congregation appointed a Franciscan priest to be a religious assistant to guide the government of the community.

The letter of appointment to the priest stated: "[I]t will be the function of the Religious Assistant . . . to assist in the work (affairs) of the general administration and to direct the government of the Congregation, especially in the accurate formation of its members, in the faithful observance of religious discipline, and also in the things which pertain to the economic administration."[24]

Catherine restated the message: "They had appointed a priest to be some kind of advisor. His title was Religious Assistant, and we tried to understand what this priest's position was. He was supposed to be in on all decisions. I asked, 'Is he in charge of the community?' And the bishop said, 'No, you're in charge of the community.' And I said, 'Well, I don't understand his position.' And the bishop said, 'You do as he says!' Well, we felt we'd had about as much of that as we could stand."

Evelyn Eaton Whitehead commented, "The Church responded. Basically the government of our religious congregation was taken away from Catherine and the Council and a Franciscan priest was made Religious Assistant of Glenmary Sisters, as a disciplinary action because Glenmary had not come in line. The humor of this was not appreciated that a male religious, this old Franciscan fellow [Father Sylvan Becker], was appointed as our superior. It became clear, at least by then, that this can't go on, or at least we thought it couldn't go on."

Marie Cirillo recalled, "As a member of the Council I remember my first words after learning about the appointment of a Franciscan priest to guide the community: 'If the Franciscan will first spend time in the missions, I will talk with him. If not, I'll not accept him.'"

Monica Appleby's response: "That was the last straw."

Chapter 5

LEAVING GLENMARY

You are not promised anything when you leave, except your dowry—that's kind of a joke from the Middle Ages.

Angry at the Catholic Church's refusal to grant them the autonomy they felt they needed to perform their mission work, many Sisters felt they had no other course but to leave. Their departure split the community into four groups: those who stayed, those who left to develop a non-Appalachian women's community, those who left to follow individual pursuits, and the forty-four who left to create a secular organization to continue work in the mountains and in the cities with Appalachian migrants. This later group, of course, would become FOCIS.

It was easy for some, especially the younger members, to think of leaving the heartache and turmoil behind. For them, the new organization appeared so similar to Glenmary (or the Glenmary they had wanted) that they would not grieve the passing of the old structure. But for others, decades of whole-hearted investment in religious life would be amputated in an instant through a simple procedure: dispensation from vows. Their feelings were deep and bittersweet; hope coexisted with loss and betrayal. Thirty-five years later, the ex-Sisters still speak of leaving Glenmary as if it had happened yesterday.

Following the March appointment of their "religious assistant," the General Council met in April (with Father Becker duly in attendance) and "proposed that the Sisters consider seeking a change of status, perhaps becoming a lay organization, to make needed adaptations without undue delays and complications." The large majority favored this plan.[1] The community conducted further consultation among its members, circulated a questionnaire, and held meetings to discuss the future and possible forms of an alternative organization with goals similar to those stated in the December General Chapter.[2]

Some Sisters felt deserted and betrayed by the institution to which they had committed their lives. And some, like Lenore Mullarney, were outraged:

Here we were, about a hundred of us, young people, eager to go and do. The archbishop once thought we were great, because we were alive and open to suggestion. We were really kind of the darlings for a while. But deciding the internal rules by which everyone will be governed, now that's the society's prerogative. When someone else comes in and starts telling you when to go to bed, that's too much. When you enter a society, that's the understanding that the Sisters control the living situation. You wouldn't do anything public contrary to the church. We finally felt we had done what we could.

The split of the community was painful, and the decision to leave religious life was most difficult for some. Kay Kaercher Barnett recalled the whirlwind that surrounded the move to split away from Glenmary: "It's impossible to describe any of this—I hardly know exactly what happened myself; but the end result was that we were a split community, some desiring to make little or no change and most of us deciding that to live the life we felt called to would require leaving religious life to become a lay community."[3]

By the time of their departure, the Glenmary Sisters had split into four different groups. One group wanted to remain as Glenmary Sisters, living the religious life in fidelity and obedience to the archbishop and Rome. Wanting to continue as obedient daughters of the church, they had resisted the changes that the other Sisters had instituted; they felt the group was losing its spirituality. The second group were women whose commitment was to live and continue their service work in a woman's community. They wanted more freedom to select the areas in which they worked, and they were not committed to and did not want to be limited to working in Appalachia. The third group left individually to pursue personal goals. The fourth group wanted to continue their mission with the Appalachian poor in the mountains and in the cities. They wanted to work with the non-Catholic populations, whom they had come to understand as deeply religious but with a different experience of the Christian message. This was the group which formed the Federation of Communities in Service (FOCIS).

There were some, though, who felt the real strength of Glenmary had been the combination of all of those interests and roles. Evelyn recalled that Dr. Martin Corcoran, for one, had encouraged the women to try to preserve the group: "I remember [when] Corcoran was working with us on the self-study, he was very strong on our staying together. He said as far as he was concerned, the group needed all three of those energies (the religious institutional, the mission, and the women's community). He said they would be a more mature group if they could work out and devise ways to stay in communication of one another."

In the meantime a number of Sisters who could not identify with the direction taken at the Chapter announced their intention to leave the community. Maureen O'Connor left in March 1967. In her April farewell letter she wrote: "I was in a way disappointed when . . . it seemed that Glenmary might be most effective by becoming totally involved with the Appalachian people. I felt that this would limit our vision . . . I felt that we could both serve the Appalachians and carry on what came to be defined as 'local community apostolates'—individuals using their talents as best they could for Church and world in inner city and town and country."[4]

O'Connor was also unhappy with what she considered Glenmary's still excessive centralism in prescribing the community's structure and process of religious formation. In preparing for the Chapter, she had proposed more radical reforms than the order had been willing to accept. "Because I have many doubts about institutionalized religious life and the structures that have evolved and are now seen as necessary, I wanted to start again with a group of dedicated women and see what forms of service, worship, community life evolved. . . . In time, I hoped that girls who wanted to join this type of community could simply [come] and live there."[5]

The Sisters gathered in Fayetteville in June 1967 to finalize plans for the change of status. They continued to struggle to create a structure to which all could adhere. Lenore Mullarney described the outcome: "It was at the last big community meeting at Fayetteville where one night it looked like we might come out with some sort of a federation of three different groups. But by the next morning the decision was that it would not work. So, the result was that some Sisters left individually, some remained, and some formed FOCIS."

Individual Glenmary Sisters perceived the situation differently depending on where they were located. Some, especially postulants and novices, were rather isolated (and perhaps intentionally shielded) from the conflict and were quite surprised when the final break occurred. Those most involved were the experimenters in Big Stone Gap, Chicago, and the Motherhouse.

Sister Mary Schweitzer felt largely sheltered from the tensions that had caused the split: "Life was really good and I wasn't personally chafing under the tensions like others. There were some things I did not like and thought ought to be changed such as the . . . night [curfew]. . . . But I was not chafing under the same stuff people were chafing under in Cincinnati and at Glendale."

Sister Mary McCann Thamann coped by simply blocking the situation from her mind: "That summer I had heard people talking about it, and I thought that it would never ever happen; it was the last thing in the world that would happen. I just think I blinded myself to a lot of things. I was happy and satisfied myself."

Sister Joan Weingartner staged a personal revolt, of sorts, when she heard the news:

When we went to these meetings in Fayetteville that summer, I remember people were crying and screaming, "What are we going to do?" I remember I got so upset, I skipped out. . . . I . . . went back to Georgetown . . . got lay people's clothes and put them on. Went into the drug store and bought some lipstick, put it on, then I went to see a movie. You know what I saw? Kind of a raunchy movie, *Alfie*. . . .

I was too new in Glenmary to understand the complexity of the political dynamics and how hard this was for Sisters with more time invested in the community. I didn't feel part of it, because it seemed to me to be between people who had much more seniority in the community.

By the summer of 1967, a total of seventy Glenmary Sisters had decided to leave the order. Among them, forty-four decided to stay together as a group, which expected to work for the same mission goals, unhampered by institutional conflicts. The new secular organization crystallized quickly, under pressure. Marie Cirillo recalled the situation surrounding the sudden impetus of the group:

I don't know how we got into the idea of forming a non-profit. But I do remember we had this idea, but didn't know how to start it. We were running out of time, so finally at one point I said to Catherine, "I am going to hand in my thing to the bishop to leave the convent, then I am going to ask to be accepted into this other group." I had figured out this commitment thing and did it. I remember Evelyn [Eaton Whitehead] was upset I did this before everybody had conferred, but I was looking at the clock and saw us running out of it and nobody knew how to take the first step. There was a point where we thought we would just fold up Glenmary and all become this other thing, but then some got real scared with that, so we had to have two groups. I also remember asking them if we could keep the name Glenmary because we felt we wanted to continue the work, and they were so upset with that we just got this other name.

In July 1967 representatives of the group forming the "Federation of Communities in Service" (FOCIS) met with representatives of those remaining in Glenmary to arrange division of mission responsibilities and property, along with publicity concerning the move. Father Sylvan Becker attended the meetings. The women sought Archbishop Alter's approval concerning the agreements they reached.

They sold Ohio Glenmary properties at Route 4 in Fairfield[6] and in Fayetteville. The Route 4 sale was completed on August 11, and the proceeds were placed in a special account to provide for Sisters leaving the community. Those intending to stay elected temporary officers who would became trustees for the corporation after the break.

In her letter of resignation to the archbishop, Catherine Rumschlag emphasized her wish to serve through membership in an ecumenical community: "The reason for my resignation is that I can no longer carry out effectively the duties of this office, and that I desire to leave the canonical religious life and become a member of the Federation of Communities in Service. I want to thank you for your many kindnesses to me personally and to the community through the years. I am sorry for whatever sorrow has come to you through failures of mine. I will always pray for Your Grace and the Archdiocese of Cincinnati."[7]

The leaders in the move to form FOCIS envisioned the new group as continuing their commitment to work in Appalachia and in urban areas with displaced Appalachians. Their ideas of mission included a community development approach rather than charity. Anne Leibig saw the move as a way to free them to concentrate fully on their work. "In the end we decided to . . . leave and form our own non-profit organization [to] continue in the work we wanted to do without having to dialogue with the rules. We switched into dialogue with the rural communities we were in, rather than put[ting] our energy into the Roman Catholic institution."

Many of the Sisters felt strongly that their vocation had shifted from Glenmary to the new organization, FOCIS. Beth Ronan remembered her sense of security in doing what she felt she'd been called to do:

The Sisters who stayed in Glenmary were good women, I cared for them, they were solid, they were the [same] solid I had met in those other religious communities. But they weren't the ones who "shook my boots"; the FOCIS group were the ones that made me think differently. [When] FOCIS came . . . I chose it. I didn't have anxiety about what my future would be like, I still had a sense and still have that sense that life is a vocation, and somehow we are constantly called to move on. . . . I thought I was following a call, so I didn't feel I was doing a bad thing, just that I was challenged by this group of women. . . .

I guess because we were young, we weren't as tied to the sense of security: [that idea that] "We better stay here and behave, because where would we go?" And also, we didn't have older Sisters, so we didn't have to say, "If we broke up what would happen to our older Sisters?" We were at the age where we were adventurous and pursuing our life's work.

FOCIS was the opportunity to stay in a committed community. It was a religious community and sort of paralleled the religious life and was much the same, just not having canonical things . . . so that seemed okay. . . . It was sorrowful but not terrible.

For some, FOCIS was growth, evolution, the inevitable move for those who were part of the new theology and modernization of the church. Maureen Linneman saw the change as part of a continuum:

I was influenced by the New Theology and the new work sort of automatically, and what I came to understand was if the work was to go on we had to change, and I was the one doing the contemporary work. So it was a normal progression to say we continue with this. It really wasn't much of a decision. I was sad to see a split come, but I was not tied to the old structures. I know I was sorry that people were not going to come along, and that a lot of people were leaving anyway. I remember having real feelings about the archbishop that this really didn't have to happen if he would get with it. I also know other people were dropping out for more personal reasons, too.

Others saw leaving as the result of the failure of the church. Lenore Mullarney reasoned that the church had shown bad faith in failing to fulfill its side of their contract: "[F]inally, and most importantly, the system and discipline under which religious societies functioned was no longer working. So I decided that if the system was not working as the church had intended then I need no longer be bound to be a part of it."

Continuing community and the appeal of staying with colleagues, friends, and a support system drew others to FOCIS. These women had lived and worked together for many years and shared both happy and painful experiences in training, in mission, and in conflict with the hierarchy. Going out in the world alone was frightening, but starting a new adventure with close, trusted friends was exciting and exhilarating.

Joan Weingartner chose FOCIS as a means of maintaining the personal connections she held dear:

I didn't take sides, you know; I liked everybody and it didn't matter the group or the affiliation. [But] I was not interested in staying, not when I saw who was staying and who was leaving. . . .

It was not because they were a FOCIS member but because they were a friend. There were many of us at that time who didn't think we were doing something significant—it was a way for us to stay friends and keep contact. We had a support system, not that we were creating an alternative social movement or a para-religious community. I think it was the next step in running away from home.

Jean Luce also felt a deeper personal kinship with the group members who decided to break away and form FOCIS: "I seemed to be more attuned to what the Chicago/Big Stone Gap idea was. I had always resented that I was in Eaton, [Ohio], all those years and didn't get to be a real Glenmary Sister in the Glenmary mission. . . . The thing that bothered me about saying I would do this [be a Glenmary] for the rest of my life was that the religious group, even though I liked those people and I admired them, I couldn't identify with them. . . . My close friends seemed to be excited about this idea with the Big Stone Gap/Chicago/Appalachian emphasis, so I didn't have any problem choosing the group I wanted to be with."

The archdiocese, in an act both public and gratuitous, actually banished the women who were leaving to form FOCIS. Beth Ronan recalled her pain and shock at the church's punitive response:

I was affronted by the fact that our vows weren't allowed to expire, but they banished us. Glenmary didn't do it, the chancery did it.[8] They sent a list out with our names on it. . . . Our names were posted on the door outside the auditorium in Fayetteville . . . before our vows ended, in June or July. FOCIS was started in August.

I didn't see any need for that. It was punitive—the chancery or the hierarchical church's last dig: "You're leaving so we are kicking you out." But I was in good company; I was angry at the list, but I enjoyed the company of sinners I was with. I was angry with the church for forcing these issues; I didn't think we needed the interference. . . . It seemed to me they were not helpful. The authority pushed within the group; pushing and pulling began to become malignant, and it did hurt the community a lot. There were unfulfilled expectations.

For many of the former Sisters, saying a final goodbye to the order was deeply painful. Lenore Mullarney recalled her last trip to the Motherhouse: "That was a lonely day when I walked up Cincinnati Street there and went up to the Motherhouse and picked up my stuff and I left. I felt pretty alone. I really hadn't wanted to leave, because I was in there for life and that was that. I really spent a long time deciding to go in."[9]

Kathy Hutson likened the separation to a marital divorce:

It was a divorce of a hundred people, a hundred women who were really close to each other, who had something that a lot of people looked at: there was energy, they were so positive, and they were doing good things and they were really on the forefront of a lot of things, communal kinds of things, new things. You can see the brokenness that would go through it. Losing friends, losing this lifestyle, and all these dreams, how many hours they'd put into, not just that house, but many houses. They had this house in Big Stone Gap, [Virginia]. They'd stripped every piece of the oak molding in this old house. Like you're starting a family, starting a home. All that stuff had been done by these young, energetic, bright people, and everything they'd put their energy into they were losing. If at thirty-two you would find your house burned down and your marriage in turmoil, that's the pain of what I saw these people living through. But it was lived through over a whole year of trying to reconcile.

The divorce metaphor was how Monica Appleby described the division of the group as well.

I just couldn't forget those feelings of what we had hoped for and how it was changed. The way we divided household goods was like divorce, with the bishop's representative there in a room at the house, and we talked about where we would go and where the Glenmary Sisters would go, and what would happen to the houses of training and formation and the headquarters. They sold them and we got part of the assets from them. We talked about cars, sheets, pots, and pans. It was a dividing up of a life.

Years of hindsight have given the women a different perspective on the role of the church in their ministry—and what they lost in breaking away. Anne Leibig came to acknowledge that the church's institutional structure was central to the work they'd hoped to accomplish: "We made the vows of chastity, obedience, and poverty when we became nuns. . . . I knew when I made the vows I wanted to be connected to women in a service ministry, and so I didn't feel like I was leaving, I felt like I was evolving. I think there was an excitement about creating our own institution and organization that would be guided out of our own process. Now as I take a look back I see I had a lot of naïveté; there were things we thought we could do without the church structure that we have not been able to do really."

Monica Appleby emphasized the consequences of losing the church's institutional support, as well: "[When we] left Glenmary and formed . . . the Federation of Communities in Service, [we] lost institutional support. I didn't realize that even though we were at loggerheads with the institution, we had some pillars there or a language there, words that were understood there that we didn't have in other places.

The years have also provided them with the longer lens of history for reflection.

Evelyn Eaton Whitehead argued that the group would never have fractured if it had limited itself to its work in the South:

I think if we had stayed south we could have lived out the internal renewal of Glenmary, and continued our work for at least another ten years. . . . Then I think . . . we would have been older as individuals, the congregation would have been stronger as a structural entity. And by then, ten years later . . . lots of strong congregations of women were facing the same issues that we faced in 1966; we would have been part of a larger fight. And . . . a lot of us [might] have stayed as Glenmary Sisters instead of the fractures in 1967. We would have found companionship in . . . the Leadership Conference of Women Religious [all the major superiors and women religious]; I think they have been certainly since the mid 1970s . . . one of the most prophetic structural organizations left in the institutional Catholic Church.

Yet the Glenmary women were not the only congregation struggling against the church hierarchy over the issues of renewal and self-governance at the time, and their leaders were aware of this. In a letter to friends accompanying a copy of her final press release, Mother Catherine noted: "Similar developments are being experienced in other religious communities: therefore, ours is not a unique situation."[10] And of course the similar developments ultimately prevailed. Kay Kaercher Barnett observed: "It wasn't that our ideas were so far out, but only that we were about ten years ahead of our time. The changes we wanted and felt necessary for our mission work are commonplace in religious communities today."[11]

In reflecting on the history of the Glenmary Sisters and that of the other orders who came into conflict with the hierarchy at this time, theologian Elizabeth Bounds commented:

All the orders wrote this letter to Rome saying, "This is what we're about"; and clearly Rome was so upset with what the Glenmary Sisters were about that they had to get the archbishop to send in a priest till the order settled down. And that exactly expresses what Vatican II has meant to the Catholic Church. These Sisters understood probably far greater than the hierarchy the spirit of change that was present, and they acted on that spirit of change. The hierarchy was not, and is still not now, ready for the implications of that change. Even though Vatican II is obviously part of the Catholic institution, the spirit that underlay it was so much more radical than the Church is still prepared to understand, that when Sisters like the Glenmary Sisters acted on it, the Church wasn't ready for that. I think that if they were an older order they might not have left.[12]

Joan Weingartner, too, felt that the Sisters may have stayed if their members had not been so young: "You know, if you think about it, our mother general was only forty. How young forty is! Part of the problem was we didn't have any sage women, any crones. We didn't have any clout. The most vocal people were in their late twenties, or thirty-year-olds. I think the community would have broken up eventually anyhow, but there wasn't anybody there to say, "If you want this to continue you can't just say, 'I gotta be me.'" Collectively, everybody was a teenager.

Yet even though they may have reacted without the resilience of an older order, Elizabeth Bounds recognized their exodus as a genuine response to a bitter and abiding truth: "You can be as radical as you want about the poor, but you can't question the power of the Church and the way the Church does things and the hierarchy of the Church. The Glenmary Sisters understood intuitively the enormous lack of scope which is still true for women in the Catholic Church."[13]

For her part, Lenore Mullarney felt the youthfulness of the Sisters was merely one factor among many that combined to dismantle the young group:

I think there were a lot of reasons why we could not weather the storm at the time. One, we were small and young as a religious society. Two, there was a preponderance of youth in Glenmary, and youth is not inclined to see the whole picture but must rush impetuously to whatever end it sees. Three, financially it was difficult to break even under the system—rather token remuneration from the parishes who had Sisters working in them; and we were not permitted to take a regular professional position at regular pay even when a Sister was qualified, and in fact was really doing the same type of work on mission. Four, society was changing with more outlets for people wishing to dedicate their lives, e.g., Peace Corps. Five, some theologians would say that probably very few are called to a life with a vow of virginity.

It was not only the issue of virginity the women leaving the order would soon confront in a non-theoretical way. These women who had been not just governed but also sheltered and supported by the Catholic Church since their teens were destined to lose a kind of structural innocence as well.

Touching upon the material and financial matters with which they were now gaining closer acquaintance, Catherine Rumschlag summarized:

There were forty-four of approximately one hundred who wanted to form this new organization, which we called Federation of Communities in Service, and there was about an equal number that just left as individuals and didn't want to deal with any of it anymore. And there were about sixteen who . . . [wanted] to stay within the canonical community . . . [and] continue to be Glenmary Sisters. So that's the way it worked out. We lost a lot of what we had built up through the years. The material things. We had three houses. We had this one place in Fayetteville that could house up to a hundred people. We put a hundred thousand dollars and lots of labor into making that a beautiful place. Each person who left got a thousand dollars. The people who joined FOCIS each got two thousand dollars, one for them and one for the group. But when you join a religious community you are not getting a salary, you are not getting compensation, you are not promised anything when you leave except your dowry—that's kind of a joke from the Middle Ages.

PART 2

Forming FOCIS

Chapter 6

FOCIS:
THE FIRST YEARS

I was really excited about being able to enter in lay clothes . . . and just be a "people."

In 1967 at their commitment ceremony to FOCIS, the former Glenmary Sisters promised "to live, love, work for the building up of the Kingdom of God in those areas where Christian influence is minimal."[1] They planned to continue a life of mutual sharing, celibacy, and communal service. They envisioned a continuation of Sisterhood, free of the patriarchal, authoritarian control of the church. What they did not fully realize was that in breaking away from the church's control, they would also lose its support and protection. They would be just "people," living in an economically depressed region, seeking to become part of a community in the "poverty pockets" of Appalachia. Searching for places of service, they settled in the poorest rural communities. There, they had to find jobs to support themselves, despite high unemployment, and places to live, despite the scarcity of adequate housing and—in some areas—suspicion and prejudice toward Catholics.

After their experiences with the Catholic Church, the women were anxious to avoid an authoritarian structure. They envisioned that each FOCIS group would be self-governing, autonomous, and democratic, yet linked so they could continue the same kind of work they had been doing in Appalachia. This proved to be impossible.

As Glenmary Sisters, commitment was complete: the community was safe and secure, and the community and their work came first. In FOCIS , their separate and secular jobs and the communities where they lived began to take precedence over the community of FOCIS.

They all went through incredible personal changes. Some reverted back to their family names. They developed new identities and had to rediscover or reinvent who they were. They had to learn how to shop for and wear secular clothes again, budget, and handle their finances. They had to make decisions about where they would live and work and apply for jobs in secular organizations. They had to learn how to be just "people" and develop working and

*platonic relationships with male colleagues. They were no longer sacred or
special; they had lost the protection of the habit. It was difficult to maintain
the same daily and spiritual lives as before. They had to make new rules and
routines to fit with their new communities, communities that were also going
through rapid social and economic changes.*

*These first years were busy, exciting, and creative, but also frustrating.
There was dissonance as they realized the type of organization they had envisioned was not working. Like the small towns in which they were living, they
had to rethink what type of community they wished to be. FOCIS women no
longer had the patriarchal church to look over them, provide for them, and
control them. Similarly, the coal mining communities no longer had the pater-
nalistic coal operators to provide them with secure jobs, housing, and the protection of a closed, "company town." The changing world came in on both of them,
and together they would need to develop new ways of defining themselves.*

In August 1967 at the Glenmary Center in Fayetteville, Ohio, the group
solemnized their transition to the new organization. André Abecassis,
freelance writer and photographer, photographed and wrote the following description of the commitment ceremony for *Ave Maria* magazine:

Slowly the women rise and silently leave [the building] to gather again in the
dusk outside. Softly they sing,

Some people run, some people crawl,
Some people don't even move at all;
Some roads lead forward, some roads lead back,
Some roads are bathed in white,
Some wrapped in fearful black

and it comes out a hymn, filling the night with their voices and the strumming of
an accompanying guitar. Then as a group, they walk away from the building. Now
a great, old maple tree spreads its dark leaves against the sky as they pause to hear
a reading by flashlight from Paul's letter to the Hebrews, describing how the
Israelites lived a nomadic life, but organized it into a federation of tribes. The ex-
Sisters walk the lovely land and sing of past and future. "Shout joyfully to God,"
came the voices as they walk around the small lake carrying torches against the
darkness. Finally they settle near the water where they build a big bonfire. Out
under the open sky they meditate. Some share their thoughts: "After leaving things
behind, standing on all that has been, thanks to our Father as we say 'yes' to all
that we'll be." And "I feel we are women who can make the Church live and
express in today's world the strength that was Mary's." And "Fire can't exist

without burning, the Church can't exist without mission, and we can't exist without each other."

On Sunday morning in nearby St. Patrick's church [sic. Fayetteville Chapel][2] where Fr. Jack Trese, brother of a Federation member, celebrated Mass, the forty-four make their commitment. Monica Kelly [Appleby] slowly makes her commitment:

"Lord Jesus Christ, I rejoice that I am able to continue my commitment to live, to love, to work for the building up of your Kingdom in those areas where Christian influence is minimal. For the sake of this service I commit myself to our Federation of Communities.

"Sisters, with you and through you I accept my invitation from Christ. I promise to give and receive in mutual sharing, remaining unmarried so that I will be more available for our communal service."

"Amen" say her Sisters. These words are repeated forty-four times, often in a choked voice, as each ex-Sister comes forward individually. Several times Father Jack must offer a steadying hand.

Through the cool, white chapel there are muffled sobs, handkerchiefs dabbing at eyes, tears streaming—the strain of relinquishing vows and greeting a new commitment. The 20-year-old ex-novice is joyful, for the new Federation allows fulfillment of her original goal—to do social work in a Christian context. Without the new group "I would have simply been a convent dropout." The 27-year-old nun who made her final vows only last year feels today's pledge is a deepening of those vows. Enthusiastically she starts her commitment, "Oh, God, I'm so excited!"

But for another woman who has been a Sister for nearly twenty years, the feelings are sometimes painful: "Christ teaches you something to imitate. You have to lose something to gain something greater." Tears now help relieve the joy and the grief: "Sisters always meant a lot to me. So I had to lose an association, an image I'd had from childhood. I'm cutting myself off; it may have been a false image, but it still hurts to admit it."

Communion, and the Mass is ended.

Fifteen minutes later, at a champagne party toasting the new Federation, the "uniforms" are gone. The women are stylish in colorful suits and dresses, slingback shoes.

At the last Sunday supper in Fayetteville, the Federation surprises Mary Catherine Rumschlag (who had sent thirty-five of her Glenmary Sisters to college) with a scholarship so she can finish her bachelor of arts degree, and Marie Cirillo receives a large wooden cross which had been put together with the odds and ends of a successful Glenmary building project which she had coordinated. The cross [is] a tangible memory not of what is lost, but of what has already been accomplished.

Before the women start loading cars for the long drive away, an ex-Sister lifts her glass and captures the spirit of this Sunday: "My friends, God is alive and well!"[3]

Many meetings were held throughout 1967 to finalize the form of the new organization and work out practical details. In addition to the allocation of money to the departing Sisters, Glenmary held financial workshops before the final leaving. The FOCIS women developed policies and plans to handle insurance, pensions, and costs of living. Cars would be owned by the Federation. A yearly budget of $2,700 for an individual was proposed, including such items as clothing ($200), housing ($400), travel ($480), and food ($360). Members of the group had to make many other arrangements quickly, particularly concerning location of regional centers, employment, and housing.

In December 1967 FOCIS became a non-profit 501(c)(3) corporation in the state of Illinois, with a president and board of directors. The constitution specified that FOCIS members would be organized in regional communities comprising at least five people. Each region would be responsible for planning and developing specific services related in some way to community development and would select a coordinator and a representative to the FOCIS board. A central organization would facilitate the services of the regional communities and coordinate activities among the regions.[4]

The purpose of FOCIS was initially formulated as "build[ing] a community of members who will give themselves for charitable, religious, educational, and scientific purposes." Later, when incorporation and tax-exemption papers were finalized, the statement was stripped of legalese; their goals were then defined as "build[ing] a community of members who have the capacity to give themselves to a life of dedication, service, and integration."[5] FOCIS members would "participate in the life and culture of Appalachia" by "involvement with the . . . people in the process of making their lives more meaningful"; "working within institutions affecting . . . Appalachian life"; and joining their work to that of others with similar goals. Through their interactions, members would "[grow together] toward an integral life of prayer and service."[6]

The new group outlined its administrative structure and membership criteria. The Executive Committee included the president and coordinators from each region. The Communication Committee provided public relations for the organization, while the Financial Committee handled expenses and taxed members through their regional communities. The Mission Development and Liturgical-Theological Committees created events, proposals, and study materials. Although FOCIS's charter members were former Glenmary Sisters, they did not limit membership to former religious or even Catholic women. Rather, those who qualified were "members of a regional community who subscribe to the Constitution and policies of FOCIS in regard to corporate service, common life and worship, group authority, and the sharing of goods and funds." The region recommended individuals for membership, to be ratified by a two-thirds vote of the Executive Committee.[7]

Responding to the years of conflict with the church hierarchy, FOCIS empowered each regional group to "administer its own affairs to the extent of its capability." The Executive Committee gave each regional group the responsibility "to determine, according to its own goals and values, the specific norms for the delegation, exercise, and limitations of authority among its members."[8]

Monica (Kelly) Appleby, the first president of the Federation of Communities in Service, had been the superior at the Holy Cross Center in Big Stone Gap, Virginia. Reporter André Abecassis described her: "Monica is young, pretty and energetic, a good choice to head the new group since she has plenty of experience working and living in Appalachia; she can be

Former Mother General Catherine congratulates Monica Kelly on being elected president of FOCIS, 1967. Photo by André Abecassis.

firm but diplomatic, [and] has administered poverty money all over the area in ecumenically sponsored programs."[9]

The FOCIS women sorted themselves out among the centers, going with friends, moving where they could find jobs, or returning to places where they had been on mission. Some entered school and others moved around looking for places where they could best fulfill their commitment.

Although most accounts say there were forty-four Glenmary Sisters who joined FOCIS and became members of a region, actually by the time they enrolled there were forty-seven, including two novices. Five left during the first year: Therese Elliot, Carolyn Kraemer, Helen Burgoin, Carol Corbin, and Nancy Griffin. By 1968 forty-two FOCIS members were associated with four regional centers:

Chicago: Evelyn Eaton, Kathleen Harkins, Dolores Meyer, Elizabeth Roth, Catherine Rumschlag, Rosemary Smith, Gail Addy

Cincinnati: Susan Bland, Lorraine Doll, Carol Duesing, Mary Catherine McCann, Karen Nagel, Alice Trese, Mary Catherine Wine, Virginia Carnes, Linda McDwyer

Tennessee: Bernice Bathauer, Marie Cirillo, Rae Anne Gasiorowski, Margaret Gregg, Mary Agnes Kempenich, Barbara Kuess, Mary Jo Leygraaf, Jean Luce, Mary Kay Rougier, Sue Romain

Virginia/West Virginia: Margaret Antes, Beth (Elizabeth) Busam, Patricia Eagen, Donna Haig, Kay (Kathleen) Kaercher, Monica Kelly, Anne Leibig, Maureen Linneman, Kathleen McCrady, Lenore A. Mullarney, Deborah Prenger, Joan Weingartner, Karen Linzmaier, Ginny Remedi, Mary Lee Dwyer, Rochelle Stroub

Each of the four regional centers developed separately and differently. Each region had its own particular issues, although they shared some of the same problems. Following are stories of how FOCIS settled the four regions: Tennessee, Virginia/West Virginia, Cincinnati, and Chicago.

Tennessee. Bishop Durick of Nashville[10] knew the Glenmary Sisters through their work with the Commission on Religion in Appalachia (CORA) and had wanted them to work in the state.[11] He had funded a study while they were still Sisters, and several of the women had traveled to Tennessee to formulate recommendations of the type of ministry they could provide. As an outgrowth of this preparation, in 1967 Bishop Durick invited FOCIS member Marie Cirillo to come and work for him as a community developer.

Marie made contact with the director of the Office of Economic Op-

Liturgy at Sullivan Road house in Knoxville, 1968: Monica Kelly (Appleby), Linda Ocker (Mashburn), Mary Jo Leygraaf, Jean Luce, and Margaret Gregg.

portunity (OEO) Poverty Program in Claiborne County, who was looking for someone to run a community center in the town of Clairfield, a mining area in the far northwest corner of the county. The director particularly wanted someone from outside the area because the residents were strongly divided between political factions. Since Jean Luce and Mary Jo Leygraaf needed places to go, Marie had invited them to accompany her to Tennessee, and she recommended Jean for the community center job.

Jean, Marie, and Mary Jo settled in Clairfield and another FOCIS member, Bernice Bathuaer, found a job as a nurse in nearby Lafollette. Lenore Mullarney got a job as office manager for the newly organized CORA and moved from the Virginia region to Knoxville in October 1967. Other FOCIS members settled in the vicinity. Barbara Kuess taught special education in the Sneedville public schools and Mary Kay Rougier did parish work in Crossville. Mary Agnes Kempenich started a health clinic in Sneedville with another former Sister, Shirley Martin (who still lives and works there). In Knoxville they had access to a large house on Sullivan

Road owned by the diocese. The house became an important gathering place and residence for FOCIS members enrolled at the University of Tennessee or working in the area. Lenore lived in the house and acted as an informal center manager. Margaret Gregg moved her art supplies there and set up a studio.

Marie remembered how excited they were about entering a community in their new secular status, but they still encountered suspicions and prejudice from local residents.

I was really excited about being able to come even though it was as an outsider, but to be able to enter in lay clothes . . . and just be a "people." Then when I found out that some people thought I was a nun that had come in incognito, trying to be subversive, I thought, "Oh shoot!"

When we came together everybody had their eyes on Jean [Luce] because she had the job. As far as I knew I was a little less talked about . . . so I was able to sort of move around and watch and talk and build a different kind of a base for how to move.

Since the FOCIS women were unknown entities in rural Clairfield, residents had to find labels for them. Marie recounted: "In the early days the first bad word they called us was 'Communist,' the second was 'VISTA,' and the third was 'Catholic.' The Catholic thing was the only one that could stick because I hadn't been a Communist or a VISTA, but they tried them all. Every once in a while people around here would start to tell the stories they used to hear about Catholics. They had stories about Catholic nuns carrying off babies. I mean there was as much prejudice towards Catholics as there was towards Blacks."

Shelby York, a native of the valley and retired coal miner who came to work very closely with Marie and Mary Jo Leygraaf, described his reaction to their coming:

I was just like the rest of them, I had been taught against Catholics and Communists . . . all my life. But I had learned a lot and my eyes had been opened when I was in the [military]. Some of my closest buddies and friends were of the Catholic faith. So I said, "Well, I'll just watch to see what you do." They were very dedicated to their beliefs and for me, your religion is the least concern I have. When Marie and the other people came in they were actually practicing their religion. Mary Jo is Catholic, I go to Church of God, but when I'm in need of religious consultation, I'd ask Mary Jo to intercede for me. To me, all religion is sacred.

The residents' perceptions of the ex-Sisters gradually changed. Mary

Jo Leygraaf felt an increasing acceptance of their work over time: "People were really suspicious of Catholics and so we didn't talk about it much. Some people probably didn't associate with Jean and the center because she was a Catholic. I don't feel it at all now. I don't know if it's because of television and stuff where people have had more exposure. I mean now people will say 'Well, I don't know what you believe but this is what I believe.' . . . They're willing to talk about it, where before they weren't even willing to talk about it."

Marie and Mary Jo felt that their experience in Chicago informed their work in Clairfield and helped them fit into the community. Marie said: "The experience in Chicago was good because I felt like I learned more about Appalachians and I think they accepted us because we were up there living with them and saying that we had been part of this experience."

Mary Jo used Chicago techniques to get acquainted with their new neighbors: "I had just come from Chicago, and we did interviews up in the inner cities with people that were from the mountains. So I still had that sort of way of thinking in my mind, so when I'd meet people at the center when Jean had meetings, I would always be sort of interviewing them, asking them questions about their family. I got to know a lot of people that way."

Postmaster Louise Adams was one of the first to welcome the women to Clairfield. Louise proved to be a very important contact, acting as a bridge between the ex-Sisters and other residents. A community leader and World War II veteran, she was very civic minded and always willing to help others with their problems. Marie recalled the importance of her early assistance: "When Jean Luce and I came in together and the post-master invited us and welcomed us, that was very helpful. She found us some space to live, and a few people that were part of her clan accepted us because she did. And that's something that I got to understand very early, other people take you on if one that they trust passes you on to them."

Virginia. In Virginia Monica Appleby had already created the Appalachian Development Office funded by Bishop Hodges of West Virginia, who continued to support the work of the ex-Sisters as FOCIS members. With Monica working full-time as FOCIS president, Anne Leibig became the Office of Appalachian Ministry field coordinator. FOCIS's Virginia region purchased the former Holy Cross Center in Big Stone Gap. It became the physical hub for the region, providing housing for members and space for Monica's office and community activities.

In its new incarnation, the FOCIS Center continued to offer social services, meeting space, and resources for local craft groups and other organizations working in the Appalachian movement for social change.

A Kingsport, Tennessee, *Times-News* article at the time of the leaving featured Monica, Anne, Maureen Linneman, and Deborah Prenger (all Glenmary Sisters in Big Stone Gap at the time of the transition) and local residents' reactions to their changing habits. One man said that although he had "heard something about" their withdrawing from Glenmary, he'd been in Big Stone Gap a long time and had always known them as "the ladies who don't ask any questions like the Welfare does when you need help." Another said, "I been a Methodist ever since I been on this earth, and I'm a-telling you them ladies are good Christians. Ain't nobody beginning to know how much good they do up in the hollers 'round here."

In the article Anne expressed the group's new focus: "We're stepping toward something rather than running away from something. What we are doing and what we want to do is our understanding of what it means to be a Christian. We see it as a deeper religious involvement." Maureen observed, "Now, as lay persons, we're not bound by canon laws, we are free to do what we feel needs to be done for people in this area."

On the subject of dress Monica said, "As a lay group, we'll be able to wear clothes like everyone else. I'm a great one for bargains. I'll probably have fun shopping for clothes to express my personality." Anne commented, "I've never really noticed what women wear. Guess I'll have to pay more attention now. There has been this apartness. Like maybe people are putting us on a pedestal as though we didn't have the same feelings as all women. Clothes will probably make a difference. Maybe they'll no longer look on us as different."[12]

The Big Stone Gap group had a big party in the fall of 1968. Ginny Remedi, who taught art in the public school, designed the invitation. It posed the tongue-in-cheek question: "What in the Hell Are We Doing Here?" The house was crowded with FOCIS members, Glenmary priests, local friends, colleagues from schools, and VISTA volunteers. Helen Lewis, who was then teaching at East Tennessee State University, remembers it as a "great party": "I especially remember Anne Leibig. I had only met Anne . . . as a Sister, and with the uniform, her veil, and her serious discussion of religion, I thought she was a middle-aged woman—at least fifty years old. Here I met a young woman in a miniskirt with fishnet stockings who was sitting on top of the refrigerator, giving one of her speeches which she delivered to young people about "Potentiality" and punctuating her remarks by tossing herbs: oregano, thyme, parsley to the rapt audience in the kitchen."

West Virginia. Margaret Antes, Kay Kaercher (Barnett), Kathy McCrady, and Rochelle Stroub continued the work they had been doing as Glenmary Sisters in Welch, West Virginia. One was teaching in the schools, one was doing parish work, and two were working with the religious survey of the Office of Appalachian Ministry. Others were sent to join them. Joan Weingartner remembered the move:

I was part of the group committed to go to West Virginia. We drove down from Fayetteville, Mary Lee Dwyer and Carolyn Kraemer and myself . . . to Berwind, West Virginia, where Mary Lee and Carolyn were already living. We lived in what used to be the clubhouse of the owners of the mine there. The former tennis court was the parking lot, and then this big mansion was divided up into real depressing apartments with faded floral wallpaper. We were in one of the apartments, the three of us. . . . We worked at one of the first OEO centers, which was called the Council of the Southern Mountains. Mary Lee and Carolyn were hired as "indigenous leaders"; that's how I learned the meaning of "indigenous."

Living in the region, the women were exposed to racism for the first time. Joan recalled the dramatic fallout from a casual social evening:

I was in a non-paying position to do arts and crafts at the community center across the road from the clubhouse where we lived. . . . in the White coal camp of Berwind. There was a Black coal camp nearby, and the community center allowed Black and White youth to come; it wasn't an issue. I had never talked to a Black person before, and I was curious. . . . so I invited some Black teenagers over to our apartment for lemonade and popcorn one night. . . . And the next day we were evicted. Mary Lee came to me and said, "We're out." Maybe I shouldn't have done it . . . I don't know. . . . But . . . it was a nice evening. It was just pleasant, and we talked, and I guess I found out Black teenagers are like White teenagers mostly. It was a non-event in a lot of ways. But we had to move over to Welch and commute.

In Welch we lived on the fourth floor above the Giant Dollar store, on Main Street, all eight of us, jammed up in this apartment. Some months later we got a phone call from one of our friends in Berwind, Gracie Rowe. She liked us. You know, there's always in the community somebody who likes you. She said, "I just want you girls to know that the FBI was here investigating you." It was the summer of '67. "Well, what in the world about?" "Well, Junior, who owns the company store, called the FBI on you girls and said you were trying to start a riot with the niggers. But when they came and talked to me I said, 'They weren't trying to start a riot with those niggers; they're Catholic, and it's part of their religion to like niggers.'" So that was how we left Berwind!

Cincinnati. Karen Nagel was working in Cincinnati the summer when the break with the institutional church occurred. She decided to stay on there, continuing her service work with FOCIS:

It was just a matter of I was here and there was a group forming, so I stayed. We found a place in Mohawk to live, which was an inner-city neighborhood. . . . There were six of us who wanted to live in that particular area. . . . As I look back on it now it was a collection of people that each had something they wanted to do in the area of service, so it was a networking of what each person was doing and bringing it together. Many of us were new to the whole area of service. Some of us had only worked very limited missions before we went into FOCIS.

Susan Bland (Murphy) remembered their life in Cincinnati as a time of successful service and community-building, despite limited resources:

[T]here were enough of us that we had two houses, Vine Street and the Mohawk house. And we shared expenses and some of us needed to work to support the others. . . . Mary [Wine] was working at the Neighborhood House, and she was bringing in the most income. And I wanted to go to school but I also needed to work. So, I worked at Kenner Toy factory. . . . and went to school in the evening. I was able to experience a job and the life that I thought a lot of Appalachian people would have. I had enough to contribute to the community and to go to school. You know, money went a long way then. I got connected to a group of young boys in the neighborhood and sort of formed a Boys' Club. We would do little activities. I remember taking them fishing and they figured out how to make fishing rods out of sticks and line and bought hooks and bought a rubber ball and cut that up and made little corks, on meager, meager money. I took them to the river several times to fish. They were eleven or twelve years old.

Living in Mohawk was crowded but it was fun. We helped each other transition out from the convent into the real world, so to speak. We [were] . . . doing different things during the day but at night we would sit around the table. . . . We all contributed. We had a fund for the food and we'd put in twenty dollars a week or something like that and manage to live off of that.

I remember sitting around the table long hours just laughing and really enjoying each other, and being very connected with the people, . . . people in the neighborhood, kids always at the door. We would sometimes have some kids in to eat. It was pretty much a community center and had we been older, we probably wouldn't have been able to tolerate it, but we were young, enthusiastic, energetic, and we were on a mission.

Their tolerance extended to an acceptance of less-than-ideal living quarters, as well. Karen remembered: "Our apartment for the six of us didn't even have a shower or a bathtub. It just had a sink and toilet. So on Saturday we would all get our towels and go visit Carol Duesing's family and take showers for the week and have a good meal. . . . It was stressful living."

Chicago. In Chicago FOCIS members settled into several houses where some had lived as Sisters. FOCIS continued to conduct the Appalachian training program in cooperation with Marquette University as well as Loyola faculty member Martin Corcoran. Members lived and worked in Uptown with Appalachian migrants. During the changeover, Evelyn Eaton White-head remained at the Appalachian Field Study Center, which continued for at least two additional years. FOCIS sent members from Cincinnati and Virginia for training. Donna Haig went to Chicago from Big Stone Gap in 1967:

I had seen people in the mountains and visited people in their homes. And then to see the same people, families from the same area up in Chicago with the cement sidewalks and the crowded apartments and no trees, and the poverty. The poverty somehow seemed even more stark in the city. . . . The experience in interviewing families was focused on really appreciating their culture and the ways in which their beliefs helped us understand their life. That was a real grounding experience for me. . . . And I've carried that way of thinking about the way of being with people in the work that I do.

Yet only one training was held in Chicago for FOCIS members. With members employed and regions having less money for travel, each group instead organized their own training, or members learned by doing. Evelyn Eaton Whitehead, who had entered graduate school at the University of Chicago, described a more radical change: "What happened is the people living there each got married." When the Chicago regional center was terminated in June 1969, Chicago members continued their affiliation through Virginia or Tennessee. Although she also married, Elizabeth Roth Turner continued her work in Uptown:

[After] I became a member. . . . initially FOCIS financially supported me to work full time in the neighborhood. . . . When we became FOCIS, it was not necessary to explain anything to the community as we did not change in their eyes. . . . People still called me Sister Joan for a couple of years. We continued doing what we had always done in the neighborhood. We were their friends—

sharing in their good times and agonizing over the bad times, comforting those who were homesick for the South, helping to problem-solve conflicts with their kinfolk, bringing understanding to parents about the schools, helping newcomers overcome their fears of the city, and listening to husbands' conflicts on the job.[13]

The central staff was set up to coordinate the work in each region. As president, Monica (Kelly) Appleby's job in helping to facilitate the work in the regions was both grueling and rewarding. In December 1967, when FOCIS had been in existence five months, she summarized her activity for the first board meeting: "I have been a traveler, communicator, reflector, representative, meeting goer, decision maker."[14] She met with members of the Executive Committee ten times in the following year. There were countless other committee meetings and much travel over difficult mountain roads ("driving mostly in second gear")[15] to see members in their districts. In West Virginia, Joan Weingartner remembered, "Monica would either come up or we would go down once a month, so she would spend four days a month on the project."

By 1969, FOCIS had members and ongoing projects in Chicago, Cincinnati, West Virginia, Virginia, and Tennessee. Yet its situation was hardly static. Like its members, the young organization was in a state of flux. At the time of the 1967 commitment service a reporter observed: "The women of FOCIS lead about the same daily and spiritual lives as before, but they are freer now to make their own decisions and to adapt to the situations and the problems around them."[16] This increased freedom, initially focused on achieving corporate goals, perhaps inevitably led to the exploration of personal choices as well. The rapid reality of dating and marriage caught the group unprepared. Economic pressure and evolving values would cause members to request changes in financial arrangements, central staff, and even the basic purpose of the Federation.

Maureen Linneman was the singer-songwriter-minstrel for FOCIS. She wrote songs expressing the feelings many were experiencing. Many of her songs became "theme songs" for the group. Maureen's song "Don't Go 'Way" commented on the process of entering communities and gaining acceptance. She explained and elaborated on the meaning of the Appalachian expression "Don't go 'way":

The expression "Don't go 'way" is something I often heard while living and working in Appalachia. Upon leaving a home, folks would say, "Don't go 'way, stay with us, sit a spell." Invitations were not only to stay now but to return, "Come back and see us." "Time is something I got plenty of." Underneath these sayings is a cultural expression much different from the often expressed phrases of "Got to run," or "I'll get back with you." Mountain folks knew of time when folks felt special just being together.

The song "Don't Go 'Way" relates these experiences and feelings:

> They asked me where I came from
> They wondered why I'd stay.
> Had I no home to go to?
> Was home too far away?
> Is family made of blood ties?
> Are friends gained just in strife?
> Does it happen when you're living
> That you're thankful for your life?

The song was also an expression of wanting to "stay with" relationships, love, community, and the bonds of family. Again as I reflect, many of my songs are voices from inside me that are asking me, "Why do I stay?"

At this time, I also knew that I was going to be physically leaving the FOCIS community to get married, and I wanted to stay in touch and continue being a part of FOCIS. The question of going and staying was felt by many of us as we all struggled with our choices. I really wanted to stay in the presence of community. I also wanted to convey the belief that a similar intensity exists when we are truly in connection with another individual or community.

The next verse expresses these feelings:

> Is it only when you're leaving
> That we say "Don't go 'way?"
> . . . But lately I've been saying
> When you're far or when you're near
> That it's not just when you're leaving
> That I'm wanting you to stay
> But it's even when you're with me
> That I'm meaning "Don't go 'way."

Chapter 7

MAJOR CHANGES

Obedience went first, then chastity, and then poverty.

By 1969 the new organization and its members had gone through major changes. Without the support and resources of the institutional church, it was difficult, and in some places impossible, to continue the type of organization and life they had envisioned. For many, FOCIS served as a halfway house, a means of transition to secular society. Some left the region to find jobs. Some married, and FOCIS opened their door to men and their families. The convent model of Sisterhood no longer fit, so in order to survive they developed a model that fit their evolving status. For some it seemed to be a disintegration of the faith community. For others it represented the loss of a dream of a strong activist women's community. For still others the rise of individualism and loss of mutual sharing and collective work was traumatic. Some, on the other hand, welcomed the change and freedom to move and work more closely with local communities.

Through a series of workshops and serious discussions in 1968, FOCIS members changed the structure and direction of their organization. Members became even more autonomous: they could remain members of the communities where they had settled or were free to find new groups with which to work. Yet they maintained FOCIS as a web of friendship, a network of support. They produced a model for their mobile, rapidly changing society, which allowed members to adjust to their many transitions yet maintain a sense of identity—through support, spiritual nurturing, protection and care—from the group itself.

The first two years after the break with the Glenmary Sisters were busy, exciting, frustrating, and creative. Above all they were crowded with changes. One of the women observed, "Obedience went first, then chastity, and then poverty."[1] Within a two-year period, many of the women were dating and some were married. In response, the group opened their ranks to men and non-Catholics. Its members also saw increased independence. Employed members were keeping the bulk of their wages, and some were living alone. Many were working for secular organizations or working ecumenically. Some members were attending secular schools and non-Catholic church services.[2] In an important sense, FOCIS functioned for the former Sisters as a halfway house to the modern world.

Maureen Linneman wrote a song about the many changes they were experiencing and the feelings of being in a time of transition. She called the song "Times in Between," and it was sung at many gatherings. She remembered its creation:

I wrote this song while living in the Knoxville apartment. I was in a time in between. I had left Big Stone Gap still with the vision of working in the mountains. I wondered where I was going. Wondered if I was on track for my life and asked where I would go from here. Many FOCIS people were in flux—coming and going with new jobs and new challenges daily. The past was gone and we were feeling the essence of change, looking for a new paradigm and having to create it as we went along. In this song more than any other, I know I was saying things so true and universal that I didn't totally understand at the time.

> Now it seems that the times in between's getting shorter in between
> All the coming and the going the laughing and the crying. . . .
> And when you really go,
> I hope you really know where you're going. . . .
> Life can be playing some kind of game with you.
> I've played that game too.
> Run from it, hide from it, play with it, toy with it,
> Learn how to stay with it, knock the shell off it.

As the song said, they were learning how to "stay with it," like adolescents leaving home. They were parentless and struggling to make it on their own. They were broke. FOCIS began operation with meager funds and no financial backing by the church or any other source of financial support. They planned to share their income, and the women working for wages would support others doing volunteer work or maintaining the organization. But the realities of their new situation soon displaced their structural intentions. In the original agreement with Glenmary, each FOCIS member was to receive $2,000, half for the member and half for the group. This was limited to professed Sisters[3]; those who left as novices received only $250. The Glenmary Sisters transferred $12,000 to FOCIS as a first payment. The balance of $60,000 was discounted over the years for any

Maureen Linneman recording her songs with J.P. Fraley at Appalshop Media Center in Whitesburg, Kentucky, 1973.

member who subsequently left FOCIS, so the full amount was never remitted. In 1971 FOCIS accepted $20,000 as a final settlement of Glenmary's obligation. Two-thirds of the money for the Federation went to the regions and one-third remained with the central office.

In the beginning, in keeping with the organization's plan of "sharing of goods and funds," each wage-earning member presented a budget for her living expenses and then contributed the excess money to a common pool. In this way the group supported members enrolled in school or doing unpaid community work and met other special needs.

The women modified this approach to income after less than two years. The Tennessee Region represented the views of the majority when it stated, "After living out the policy on personal budgets, we feel that everything related to it is on shaky ground. On the whole we were faithful to our dues and stipends to the region but are leaning toward the idea of a pledge system or higher regional dues."[4] In June 1969 the Board of Directors decided that members would simply pay dues to the regions, which would in turn contribute to the support of FOCIS. This change had a significant impact, especially on the lives of those who had been supported by the community.[5] The time available to Elizabeth (Roth) Turner for mission work in Uptown was diminished:

When I no longer received a FOCIS stipend, I first took a job at Senn High School to support myself. Then I began to work as a Kelly Girl [temporary job agency], doing temporary office work in the Chicago Loop. . . . I divided my time between office work, neighborhood activities and community meetings.[6]

When FOCIS was conceived, the idea of marriage was not included. Monica promised celibacy in her commitment statement. FOCIS would also be a women's religious community. Their lives would continue to be much the same as when they were Glenmary Sisters, they planned. However, differing lifestyle options became a major shift that came fast and without guidelines. Gail Addy was the first FOCIS person from Chicago to marry, in May 1968. FOCIS members were totally unprepared to embrace Gail in this new relationship, nor did she ask them to do so. She and her husband, James, left for Detroit the day after their city hall wedding. Gail was required to turn in her FOCIS ring.[7]

Sue Bland Murphy was the first from the Cincinnati group to marry. She commented: "At that time . . . I didn't see staying in FOCIS as an option. I just saw my getting married as choosing a different path than FOCIS. . . . I just didn't see that as fitting in." Donna Haig (Friedman) sensed an atmosphere of disapproval about dating while living in the FOCIS Sullivan Road house in Knoxville, so she and Maureen Linneman moved out to an apartment.

But the collective climate shifted quickly and the Board of Directors hastened to sanction the changes. In August 1968 it recognized that "members have a variety of attitudes toward the possibility of marriage for themselves and accordingly members have the right to make personal decisions in regard to their association with men." It therefore offered "the possibility of . . . complete membership for men and married couples."[8] FOCIS eventually returned Gail Addy's ring, which she loved. Afterward, Elizabeth Turner recalled that Gail wore it coupled with her wedding band from Goldblatt's department store.[9]

FOCIS women were quickly sought after as romantic partners by men who had maintained secret crushes on them while they were Sisters. For many of the young women this was both exciting and frightening. They had to learn new ways of relating to men with whom they had formerly worked as colleagues. Dating and becoming sexually active was a big challenge. One member commented on the difficulty of being a "thirty-year-old virgin." She recalled telephoning a FOCIS friend in the middle of the night to confess that she had just experienced her first orgasm.

The FOCIS women soon discovered that FOCIS membership did not provide the shield of protection that being a Catholic Sister provided. They no longer had the protection of the habit and the church. The women had to learn how to flirt, date, and deal with sexual overtures. They could no longer be as open with people. As Anne Leibig discovered, "It changed things when you weren't a nun anymore." Anne talked about changing how she related to people and learning to play the "dating game":

There was a protection about being a Sister: it was like we had had a kind of open, present way of being with people, which didn't have any sexual meaning. But when . . . I wasn't a Sister anymore I got responses that I thought, "Oh, I didn't mean it that way!" It took me a long time to learn how to flirt. If you're flirting then you know that it's flirting and it's part of playfulness, but it's not that you're going to go to bed with everybody.

Catherine Rumschlag was taken aback by the rapidity and extent of the shift:

Lifestyle changed more than I anticipated and it changed a lot more than most of us were saying. In this way it strikes me as a kind of dishonesty which bothers me. Like, we were saying the reason we were stepping out of the structure was to continue the life and work, and there was really nothing about wanting to get married. You know nobody said that, and yet half of them are married now. I think it would have been better if people had said that they wanted to get married or at least . . . to consider it, . . . but maybe it wasn't on their mind then; maybe it did happen later. . . . I think I have much more of the ways I had when I was a religious, and I think [the younger members] are much more in touch with young people. They understand them. Sort of a generation gap.[10]

Even so, marriage was not necessarily an easy decision. Kay Kaercher Barnett recalled her trepidation at contemplating matrimony:

Two years [after returning to Minnesota] I received a phone call from Jack Barnett, my childhood friend, classmate, sometimes date, and long-time neighbor. He saw my name and number in our high school reunion book. "Can I come a-courting?" he asked. His wife had died seven years before, leaving him with four daughters. My feelings about marriage were very ambivalent at this time. He came. We visited back and forth and prayed a lot. Finally I decided to make a retreat with Father Hugo, a retreat master so appreciated by Dorothy Day. It was a good retreat. He helped me to "accept the human condition" and come to a decision. Jack and I laugh about that a lot: him being the "human condition."

Lesbian relationships lived in the closet both in Glenmary and in FOCIS. Only recently have a few couples revealed their relationships or brought a partner into the network. Ginny Remedi and her partner invited FOCIS members to their ceremony of commitment. Ginny discussed her coming out and her current relationship with FOCIS:

My first sexually intimate experience, when I defined myself as a lesbian, was when I was twenty-eight. I was out of the convent then. At first I didn't want to call myself a lesbian; I didn't like the word. But I did like being physically close, being loved and appreciated, the giving and receiving. I came to a point where I had to accept the fact that I was a lesbian. Since that time my fear has lessened and my resistance to defining myself as a lesbian has changed. FOCIS is significant in my life; they accept me as a lesbian, they value my relationship with God, foster and encourage my relationship with Christ. . . .The FOCIS group is a family: I feel like I'm part of a healing community. The healing has something to do with growing with many people who have a long history together and a particular view of the world.[11]

The first males and non-Catholic joined FOCIS in 1969. The men were Phil (later Patrick) Ronan, then a Glenmary Brother employed by Monica in the Office of Appalachian Ministry, and Glenmary seminarian Peter Cook, who had come to Virginia the year before as a volunteer. Patrick would marry FOCIS member Beth Busam in 1970; Peter later trained as a psychologist at the University of Tennessee and married a former FOCIS volunteer, Pat Bensman. Presbyterian member Linda Mashburn had earlier crossed paths and been deeply impressed with the FOCIS women through her pioneering work as an organizer of health fairs and clinics in the region.

By August 1968, FOCIS members, paid and unpaid, were wearing many hats in Appalachia. They were educators in school systems and trainers of community action employees and volunteers. They were involved in recreation, drama, music, and art programs, both as participants and consultants. They served as social workers and Office of Economic Opportunity (OEO) and Community Action Program (CAP) board members and employees. FOCIS people took part in Catholic diocesan and parish programs as well as ecumenical efforts with other religious groups.[12]

As the women became more rooted in their communities, beginning projects, grappling with local politics, and helping to build new organizations, they began to question their organization and suggest changes in its structure. Some conceptualized FOCIS as a support system and a fellowship of friends rather than as an instigator and administrator of large projects. Others wanted FOCIS to be a more stable organization capable of developing and carrying out regional programs (just as they were then beginning to do with an ambitious community arts initiative). All seemed to want clearer structural definitions and a rethinking of purpose, along with their own duties and responsibilities as members.

At its June 1969 meeting in Berea, Kentucky, the board decided to undertake the definition of FOCIS membership, organization, and ideology. In August they sent a questionnaire to all FOCIS members, and these were compiled and used to plan a series of workshops in October.

Participants at the workshops concluded that the centralized organizational model adopted by FOCIS in the beginning was not fitting the needs of Appalachian communities. They wanted FOCIS to be a support group for members working at the local level. The workshops favored a structure more like that of a family or communication network. It was also thought the term "FOCIS project" was misleading since many projects were developed by FOCIS members in concert with other people or agencies and were not directly supported by FOCIS funds.

Later that year Evelyn Eaton Whitehead presented a report to the board based on the workshops' conclusions recommending a major change in the structure and direction of FOCIS:

FOCIS would be reorganized so that local regional communities would assume full responsibility for whatever operations and norms are locally useful. Interregional communication and cooperation would exist through committees or task forces formed around common interests such as a particular project (FOCIS ARTS) or theology or fund raising. The task force groups would be basically autonomous in their operations. There would no longer be a central staff.[13]

Monica (Kelly) Appleby reflected on these dramatic changes to the group's organization:

[W]e decided we didn't want to maintain a large organization. In the Glenmary days a core of us had to go to churches and . . . basically beg for money. We . . . didn't want to do that anymore. So . . . we decided we didn't want to maintain an organization where we had to spend so much time fundraising and also contributing to the maintenance of the organization. So we decided not to have full-time staff as an organization. That meant my job as president was not needed, because we neither wanted to raise money for it nor wanted to contribute toward it. That was hard. People were earning their own money and we were asking them to do things like they were in a convent, like have a budget for their personal needs and then give the rest to the community; and people didn't want to do that anymore either after the first couple of years. . . . It was taking the model we had for ourselves as Sisters and using it in this new organization. So that didn't go.

Also we tried to make ourselves democratic and participatory but it just wore people out. So many committee meetings. I would go to one almost every weekend, and for people who had [regular] jobs . . . to go to so many meetings . . . was just too much to ask.

The organizational shifts affected Monica both professionally and personally. As her role in FOCIS diminished, she began to seek other ways to serve individually:

And then personally I said to myself, "This is a time to take a break." Anne [Leibig] had taken over the Office of Appalachian Ministry. Others were involved in Big Stone [Gap] groups and projects. All I had was FOCIS, and it was disintegrating in my view. So I applied to go to Harvard. I had met Michael [Appleby] the previous summer at Goddard; we spent two weeks together in Boston in early January and we got married in March.

Though not the first to marry, Monica's status as FOCIS's leader made her 1970 wedding a major turning point in the group's history. Kathy Hutson picked daffodils from the roadside for the altar. She remembered the ceremony as a festive occasion: "The black youth choir, Richard Lomax's group, sang. Their voices filled the small basement worship area. . . . Michael and Monica wrote their own vows, [pledging to work for social change and live in community], and Michael said he was marrying a woman with forty sisters." They spent their wedding night in a little house up the street from the FOCIS Center that Catherine was using as an office for a to-mato-growing cooperative. The next morning Michael entertained some of his forty sisters-in-law "with an embellished story about the bed falling down in the middle of the night."[14]

In spite of the festive nature of the wedding, Anne Leibig recalled feeling some mixed emotions at Monica's decision to marry:

They were married three times—had three weddings. One in Massachusetts; one in California; and the one in Big Stone Gap was the first one and Monica's family came in. It was a real celebration. Granny Cox from Artesian Well Holler made her a double wedding ring patchwork quilt top and Monica made it into her wedding skirt. There was a gospel choir from the church in Derby. . . . Monica asked me . . . to be the main witness and to have the rings. And when the ceremony actually happened and we were up there and it came time for the rings, I had forgotten the rings. So . . . I had to run out, and I remembered that I'd left them out in the hallway. I realized later it was probably a blocked thing for me, that I didn't want her to get married. . . .

When we left the Glenmary Sisters we all thought we were going to keep the same promises—. . . the poverty, chastity, and obedience which is money, sex, and authority—that these three areas we could keep on doing, but without the institu-tional church. . . . But we were maturing young women and trying to shape our lives. The median age of the group was twenty-eight. So, when Monica decided to marry . . . she was setting a pattern for FOCIS that you could be married and be a member of FOCIS. It was an opening time that we all were learning and celebrating in, and her wedding was like the coming together of her family and the local community and FOCIS people in a celebration that really did feel joyful and accepting.

Though some members accepted the union right away, Marie Cirillo felt such pain at Monica's choice that she did not attend the wedding. She recalled sadly that "at the time I couldn't go to the wedding because it didn't seem appropriate. And I always felt bad. But it just seemed like a real violation to me at the time."[15]

Once married, Monica brought Michael into FOCIS, and he became an active member. Linda Mashburn remembered that after the triple wedding, the inclusion of families "became a natural phenomenon. About that time Maureen [Linneman] and Bob [Eaton] got married and Peter [Cook] and Pat [Bensman] and Beth [Busam] and Patrick [Ronan]. All of these stayed connected in the FOCIS community."

In October 1998 at the Highlander Center workshop, members came to reflect on their shared history. When Joan Weingartner asked Monica why she had left the group in Big Stone Gap, her reply surprised the gathering: "Because the group left me. The group decided not to pay for a staff person and so I gave up my job as the director of FOCIS. The group did not want projects, they didn't want FOCIS ARTS, so I gave up that too. And I had already given my [Office of Appalachian Ministry] job to Anne. So . . . I met Michael during that period, and I've always been good at falling in love, and I had fallen in love with him at that particular point. And I got married."[16]

Monica's leaving the region and subsequent marriage were in part related to the loss of a dream. Along with a new source of happiness, the change brought her a great sadness and sense of personal inadequacy:

I always had this dream that I believed in of this community of women. But it turned out when I met Michael the dream was fading, and I believe the timing was the right time for Michael and me. We also seemed to have similar kinds of desires and dreams; he was doing theater and we were big into the arts project; the whole thing of doing change through art fit. So the timing was really good . . . . And I thought I would get married and continue to do the same kind of things, but that I learned wasn't possible.

In a 1992 letter to Marie Cirillo, Monica reflected on the loss of their initial dream for their community:

I know we didn't do what we thought/hoped in the beginning. . . . I remember back to the fall of 1969 when I organized [the] series of three workshops. . . . At least for me, this was the turning point in FOCIS. People in the group decided at that time that they did not want to be an organization with goals and programs but rather a community of support to each other to do the work they personally found meaningful and right. And that, I think, is basically what happened.

Those of us who stayed in the region or close by can give informal support to each other, we get together once a year for a big live-in/pray-in and then most of us go on to a life somewhere else. We have no common place. . . .

I think we may have lost something irretrievable in those [fall] '69 meetings. When I think back, I sometimes think I could have been a stronger leader and pushed harder for a common work. But I went along with what I thought were the group's wishes.[17]

In a 1979 interview in the *Blacksburg Sun*, Monica discussed the structural dissonance inherent in the organization the women created to replace the Glenmary Sisters. Ironically their changed, more independent status gave rise to a new set of impediments in the pursuit of their great hope in common:

Without the supporting environment of the larger institutions like the church, it's very difficult for individuals to live a community life. Economically, we were having to go out and find individual jobs while still trying to live in a community group. Different schedules made it difficult to coordinate activities that had previously been part of the community's normal routine. It was often impossible in the new group to pray together. Before, in Glenmary, . . . it was usually one person out of the group who had a job in the community and others worked for the parish. But the parish workers were not able to keep their jobs after we left the order. Group members became more aware of their personal needs, jobs, cars, clothing, and were not able to concentrate so deeply on their mission as they had previously. There is also an identification problem. With many of the people where we lived not knowing who we were, we were neither fish nor fowl. We didn't feel the local support we had felt before. FOCIS decided to become a support group for each other rather than an organization with common goals and financial base. Members were more interested in following the goals of their individual professions and had less time to devote to local and regional Appalachian issues.[18]

Chapter 8

THE DISPERSED COMMUNITY

I came to realize that our FOCIS community was not to be the lay religious community I envisioned.

FOCIS became a dispersed community of members, with some "settlements" in Virginia and Tennessee. There were many spin-offs, and a network of resources developed as members worked on projects in communities throughout the region. As Glenmary Sisters, they had gone into communities as missionaries, to help the poor as servants of the church. As FOCIS they were still committed to service, but they were now members of the community and their commitment was to participate—using their skills and resources with the community, not for the community. This shift changed the style and method of their work and their identity. FOCIS became a network that provided resources for each community and personal support to each member. It became a communication system that helped build connections between many community groups in the region and supported a regional movement that was developing in the late 1960s and 1970s in Appalachia. Later as Catholic Sisters from different orders began to enter the region to find places of service, FOCIS became a support to them and a model for their way of working in the region.

After the reorganization in 1969, FOCIS members had to learn how to be a dispersed and mobile community of colleagues, friends, and sisters who would continue to give each other support.

From the beginning, FOCIS members moved around trying to decide where they wanted to settle and often relocated where they could find work. Some who couldn't find jobs in the economically depressed region had to leave. Personal choices like marriage and schooling drew others away, and some left because the communities where they lived and worked were too isolated to provide adequate support. For a significant number, FOCIS essentially served as means of transition from Glenmary to secular society. Yet FOCIS also attracted new members—colleagues from shared work and activist newcomers to the region—along with volunteers who joined the clusters for short periods of service. Beth Ronan accredited the dynamic nature of the group to its leadership: "FOCIS quickly evolved from women and religious roots. I attribute this to Anne and Monica because they were so eclectic, so widely involved. They kept in touch with lots of mountain activities and groups. Other people were coming in to be part of that action."

The 1970 FOCIS directory contained sixty-three names and listed "Friends" (non-member volunteers and valued colleagues) in each one of the three surviving regions: Cincinnati, Virginia–West Virginia, and Tennessee. Of the forty-seven original FOCIS members, thirty-one remained. The group lost about sixteen additional original FOCIS members in the 1970s. Many married, others moved out of the region to work or go to school, others became so involved with their residential communities that they left the FOCIS membership. Since 1980 there has been a stable group of twelve to sixteen original members, who have remained in the network or come back to the region and rejoined the group. Today's membership is thirty-seven, with sixteen being original Glenmary Sisters and fourteen, founding FOCIS members.

In this process of moving into and working with different communities and organizations evolved an incredible network of people along with an informal, "grapevine" communication system. Some kept in contact with former Sisters who did not join FOCIS, who provided other links in the complicated web of relationships. The sense of community among members became something different, less physically tangible but equally real. FOCIS not only continued to provide a strong circle of friendship but also an emerging old girls' network, which offered support and access to resources for community development.

Evelyn Whitehead described her many moves and the role that FOCIS played in providing a constant support network:

I got married in January of 1970 with the sense of continuing the relationship with FOCIS; Jim and I spent the summer of 1970 in Big Stone [Gap where] I was involved with the Appalachian Arts project.[1] We moved to Boston the next year. Monica was in Boston soon after that, so we had that informal network. Sometime after that we were at [the University of] Notre Dame. In the new network of FOCIS, you didn't have to be doing a job paid by FOCIS; you didn't have to be doing a job in one of the traditional settings, where Glenmary/FOCIS had worked, but you did have to have a relationship with something. FOCIS was working out

Networking and Organizational Development
Building Capacity and Accessing Resources Through Institutional Involvement of FOCIS Members

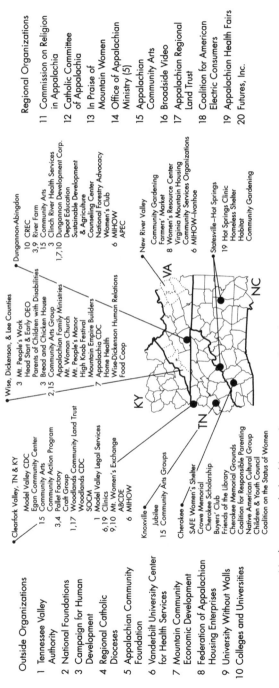

Outside Organizations

1 Tennessee Valley Authority
2 National Foundations
3 Campaign for Human Development
4 Regional Catholic Dioceses
5 Appalachian Community Foundation
6 Vanderbilt University Center for Health Services
7 Mountain Community Economic Development
8 Federation of Appalachian Housing Enterprises
9 University Without Walls
10 Colleges and Universities

Regional Organizations

11 Commission on Religion in Appalachia
12 Catholic Committee of Appalachia
13 In Praise of Mountain Women
14 Office of Appalachian Ministry [5]
15 Appalachian Community Arts
16 Broadside Video
17 Appalachian Regional Land Trust
18 Coalition for American Electric Consumers
19 Appalachian Health Fairs
20 Futures, Inc.

• Clearfork Valley, TN & KY
  Model Valley CDC
  Egan Community Center
15 Community Arts
  Community Action Program
3,4 Pallet Factory
  Craft Group
1,17 Woodlands Community Land Trust
  Woodlands CDC
  SOCM
1 Model Valley Legal Services
6,19 Clinics
9,10 Mt. Women's Exchange
  ABCDE
6 MIHOW

Knoxville
  Jubilee
15 Community Arts Groups

Cherokee
  SAFE Women's Shelter
  Crowe Memorial
  Cherokee Scholarship
  Buyers' Club
  Friends of the Library
  Cherokee Memorial Grounds
  Coalition for Responsible Parenting
  Native American Cultural Group
  Children & Youth Council
  Coalition on the Status of Women

• Wise, Dickenson, & Lee Counties
3 Mt. People's Work
  Head Start & Early OEO
  Parents of Children with Disabilities
3 Bread and Chicken House
2,15 Community Arts Group
  Appalachian Family Ministries
  Mt. Woman Church
  Mt. People's Manor
  High Knob Festival
  Mountain Empire Builders
1 Model Valley Legal Services
7 Appalachia CDC
  Home Health
  Wise-Dickenson Human Relations
  Food Coop

• Dungannon-Abingdon
10 CREC
3,9 River Farm
15 Community Arts
3 Clinch River Health Services
1,7,10 Dungannon Development Corp.
  Depot Education
  Sustainable Development & Agriculture
  Counseling Center
  National Forestry Advocacy
6 MIHOW
  APEC

• New River Valley
  Community Gardening
  Farmers' Market
8 Women's Resource Center
  Virginia Mountain Housing
  Community Services Organizations
6 MIHOW–Ivanhoe

• Statesville–Hot Springs
19 Hot Springs Clinic
  Homeless Shelter
  Habitat
  Community Gardening

KY TN VA NC

Numbers next to the local/regional organizations indicate their connection to outside and/or regional organizations.

Abbreviations: ABCDE—Appalachian Based Communities Development Education; APEC—Appalachian Peace Education Center; CDC—Community Development Corporation; CREC—Clinch River Education Center; MIHOW—Maternal and Infant Health Outreach Worker; OEO—Office of Economic Opportunity; SOCM—Save Our Cumberland Mountains.

Cartography by Matt Servaites.

new levels and new ways of networking, which involved a core of people who had been Glenmary Sisters, . . . but more and more, [incorporated] people of like vision who wanted support, . . . who dealt with one another on a social and value level rather than a day-in, day-out work level.

Some, like Beth Ronan, left FOCIS and later returned:

After I was in Big Stone Gap for a while, I didn't like the control I felt from FOCIS. . . . It wasn't too long after moving to Wise that I didn't want to continue going to Big Stone Gap. That was sort of my leaving Glenmary. . . . I felt smothered by too much organization. . . . [After the reorganization of FOCIS] we could deal more with each other as individuals, but some people never did connect if they lost the group or they left the area. People came and went.

The group is great now. We come as friends to be a group. Our loyalty is to each other, not an entity outside us. Now we are a congregation of trust, continuity, that happens because of sharing. It is not constraining. We come and go, expand and change.

As FOCIS became a dispersed network it included individuals who (like Evelyn Whitehead) moved out of Appalachia or chose professional careers outside of community development. Anthropologist Mary Schweitzer taught college in South Carolina and has done field research in locations as far away as China, but she values her membership in FOCIS for the connections it provides her:

I really do like [being a part of FOCIS] very much because it brings out the community dimension of people with similar values even though the outward appearance of life can be very different. So I sense a much deeper unity and caring about one another, what it really means to be a Christian in this particular part of the world. And even though many of the FOCIS people['s] . . . main work is obviously an option for the poor and mine isn't because I teach, . . . I still feel very much a part of FOCIS, because of the underlying values and the sense of commitment.

As the organization changed and grew, husbands and children were integrated into FOCIS. Richard (Dick) Austin had a long history of activism as a Presbyterian minister and leader in the battle against strip mining in West Virginia. When he joined FOCIS and wed Anne Leibig in 1975 he embraced a new family: "When Anne and I got married she gave me her FOCIS ring; she had it stretched and expanded to fit. I was marrying the whole group. I make that joke all the time, but there was a truth in it. . . . FOCIS for me was a family experience. I had been raised as an only child in a rather dysfunctional family, and the nurturing I needed wasn't there."

Without a central staff, FOCIS became a network of both individuals and the communities where they lived and worked. These communities became hubs in the web, centers from which activity began and spread. Most such centers were impermanent, dissolving or relocating as members moved or were newly recruited. Some, built around a committed individual or core group who found their place and settled in, lasted for a long time.

Chicago. The FOCIS community and the Appalachian Field Study Center in Chicago formally ended in 1970, although Elizabeth Roth Turner continued both her membership and her work in Uptown until 1975:

There came a time in 1970, when I was the only FOCIS person and the only one . . . in the . . . apartment. Evelyn Eaton married Jim Whitehead in January 1970, and moved out. Margaret Antes Bell lived [there] while she was in transition. But now I was by myself with a lot of space. . . . Tony and Barbara [Sister Marie Bernadette Kuess] Locricchio came from Detroit and stayed several weeks. Tony represented two defendants in the Chicago Eleven Draft Resisters trial. I sponsored a VISTA volunteer with room and board while she was in service at the Hull House on Beacon Street. Through her I met two conscientious objectors, each named "Jim," who were doing alternative service as architects at Rodney Wright's design center in Uptown. The two Jims came for the evening meal as they had no cooking facilities where they were staying. People from the neighborhood would drop in as usual and took a lot of interest in my visitors. So even though I was living alone, I was continuing to create community.

I kept in touch with FOCIS in Knoxville and tried to be a part of the FOCIS organization as much as possible. It began to feel less of a community for me. It was impractical to link in any real way with direct service projects or with members. However, . . . FOCIS continued to be my link to mission for as long as I served the Uptown Appalachian community.[2]

Elizabeth mused about the difficulty of breaking ties with the organization: "I am still wondering how one quits FOCIS? I've asked the question of several persons with no clear answer as to whether there was a procedure or not. I thought I wrote a letter of resignation. . . . My best answer . . . is that one did not "quit" FOCIS. FOCIS meant sharing a common history, having a dedication to a personal ministry of serving others, and sharing friendships that had developed in the arena of service and the struggle to remain true to oneself."[3]

Cincinnati. In 1969, the Cincinnati group reported nine members, some of whom also had paying jobs, involved in serving both low-income, Black and White Appalachian neighborhoods. They worked with a goal of bringing the two ethnic groups together. The report noted: "One of the conditions of an urban inner-city neighborhood is that most of the people have been subjected to a variety of projects that they feel have exploited them rather than helped them. Consequently, one of our approaches to the problem has been to identify with the neighborhood and to de-emphasize our role as a FOCIS organization. Our approach is not to bring in projects and programs but to develop what the neighborhood people are developing as their projects at the time." Like members in Virginia and Tennessee, the Cincinnati women were shifting their focus away from the idea of a centralized organization in favor of the specific needs of the communities where they had settled.[4]

Along with other involvements, they sponsored summer arts programs (part of FOCIS ARTS) in the Mohawk and Lower Price Hill communities. Mohawk was largely Black and Lower Price Hill, White Appalachians.

Joan Weingartner had worked as a FOCIS member in West Virginia for a year and a half before she "ran away" to Cincinnati, where she taught art in grade school and joined the Cincinnati women. She felt out of place in her first FOCIS assignment among the urban Blacks of Mohawk: "I felt like I didn't fit in the FOCIS group there. I moved. It just wasn't a good experience for me. So I got the job in the FOCIS ART project in Lower Price Hill, which was really the Appalachian community. And it was a wonderful experience."

In Cincinnati, Joan remembered feeling outside of the FOCIS core: "The Cincinnati people didn't feel they were part of FOCIS. . . . They thought a small group controlled the rest." Having to drive four hundred miles to meetings in Virginia and Tennessee was an added disincentive to continuing their affiliation. The Cincinnati "participating community," as regions were called after May 1970, finally opted out of the Federation in September 1973. Some of their work continued through local community organizations like the Lower Price Hill Community Development Association, which is still in operation.

Mary McCann Thamann recalled how FOCIS "petered out" in Cincinnati and the sad circumstances of her own leaving: "There were two houses in Mohawk, and when I left they went down to one house. . . . There were few meetings of FOCIS. . . . Seems to me it petered out at that point. We were still a group in name for a year or two. We continued party-type stuff. I don't think many were going to church then. [Three of the women married and left.] I left to take care of a niece who was in a coma for two years. I lost touch with everyone. My niece died. It was hard. I didn't have Glenmary, I didn't have FOCIS."

West Virginia. Like Joan Weingartner, all but one of the West Virginia contingent left the region within the first three years. Kay Kaercher Barnett, the last to depart, stayed until 1976, when she relocated to live with her aging mother in Minnesota:

At the beginning, the transition [from Glenmary to FOCIS] did not seem difficult. We were still a community. I intended to continue living the same life of prayer and service though we were officially dispensed from our vows. We were accepted in our various dioceses to work for the church and whatever other organizations we chose. Many began working now in various types of community development and in public institutions so much in need of qualified personnel. During my first year in West Virginia I worked as a religious education coordinator for several parishes. . . . It was during this year I came to realize that our FOCIS community was not to be the lay religious community I envisioned. Some were going through a crisis of faith and did not even attend Sunday Mass regularly. This disintegration of our faith community was a traumatic experience for me, but gradually I was able to accept the situation and to find faith support from others in the parishes and with the Virginia community that I visited occasionally. . . .

At this time the schools were just beginning special education. Licensed teachers were in short supply in those areas. The government offered federal grants to teachers who would study for an M.A. degree in special education. I did this and for eight years taught retarded children and those labeled retarded because of their extreme poverty. The hills and hollers of West Virginia hold much beauty and much misery, but they certainly captured my heart.

Our original West Virginia FOCIS community . . . dispersed; others had come and gone, and I lived alone for a couple of years. Quite often I traveled to Big Stone Gap, Virginia, to spend time and be refreshed by our group there. They were still a vibrant and faith-filled community, as they are to this day.

When FOCIS members gathered at the workshop at Highlander Center in 1998 to reflect on their past, a discussion of why some groups survived and others did not took place. For example, even though the Cincinnati and West Virginia regions were important early sites, they did not last as long as the communities in Tennessee and Virginia. Joan Weingartner, who had been part of the FOCIS groups in both West Virginia and Cincinnati, led the discussion of the West Virginia situation as participants sought to identify reasons for the group's demise:

JOAN WEINGARTNER: Why did ten of us leave West Virginia? We all got along and it wasn't like a bitter thing, but we all left. We lived in West Virginia two years. . . . And all of us left for different reasons. It wasn't like there was a fight or we didn't like FOCIS any more. . . . I was trying to think on the way down here why we left, why we didn't form a [stable] core group, 'cause all of us liked being part of the Virginia region, and all of us liked the work. . . . Kay Kaercher Barnett was the last one to go. I think [she felt the group] in West Virginia . . . had let her down.

HELEN LEWIS: You didn't have resources.

MONICA APPLEBY: Or support.

JOAN: I think it was just so lonely. We didn't have a connection to the community. It was just ourselves. I remember when . . . *Bonnie and Clyde* came out, and that was such a controversial movie . . . 'cause the heroes were violent. So we decided, well, let's get a whole bunch of people to go see the movie and then bring them back to our house and we'll discuss it. . . . And then we realized we didn't have any friends in the community. You know, we didn't have people [with whom] we could discuss honestly our feelings. . . . You know, a lot of times when you're in a community of a different culture, in respect to that culture, you don't always say what you think. And so we realized that we edited a lot. And there was no one that we could be with that we didn't need to edit, except ourselves. . . .

MONICA: Well, Joanie [Weingartner] and Margaret [Antes Bell] . . . and I visited McDowell County a few years ago. . . . We went to Welch [and] we went to Avondale; and we went to the church where you had the Christmas party with the VISTAs; and we went across the road and they told stories. But I remember my experience of that [trip] was, how in the world did we ever ask people, young women, . . . to go there in the first place! . . .

ANNE LEIBIG: It's that Appalachian cultural emphasis we had, and McDowell County is [the heart of what we defined as Appalachia]. You know, we had a mythology about it. . . .

MONICA: And it was really rough on people that lived there, although they loved it. It captured you in some way. . . .

HELEN: There was more support for Big Stone Gap. You had a house. They didn't have a house. They didn't have a place to live! . . . Those centers were very important.

ANNE: We didn't understand the importance of space.

JOAN: Also the lighting wasn't that good! . . . The mountains were on either side of Welch. If you go through there, it's just a creek, a railroad track and a road. And the sun wouldn't rise until noon; and it would set at two o'clock. And it was gray, it was gray all the time. . . .

ANNE: But I think the instinct of FOCIS was to go to McDowell County and [we had] seven women who were willing to be there. How did it happen that we went there, Monica?

MONICA: . . . . It was through the Office of Appalachian Ministry. There's a lot of Catholics in McDowell because of the mines: Hungarians, Polish, and Italians. And so that was the place in West Virginia that OAM [and] the bishop . . . said would be a good place for us to go. . . .

HELEN: I think you didn't realize what the church and what the Glenmary Sisters as an order, as an institution, provided. . . . You were going to do the same kind of great mission work, but you didn't have the connection [and resources you had before].

MONICA: The connection with the institution . . . was a love-hate relationship, but there was a lot of support.[5]

Tennessee. In the early days of FOCIS members lived and worked in Clairfield, Crossville, Sneedville, and Knoxville. In 1969 the region reported that the members from Crossville had resigned but work was continuing in Sneedville with the formation of a Health Council. Marie Cirillo and Mary Jo Leygraaf were active in Clairfield. Knoxville was an important hub for the Tennessee FOCIS group for several years. Members came to Knoxville to attend the University of Tennessee, seek funds and resources from the Tennessee Valley Authority (TVA), or just to take a break from rural life for shopping, a concert, or a visit with friends. The house on Sullivan Road loaned to FOCIS by the diocese was more than just a residence; it was also a site for inter-regional committee meetings and workshops and a gathering place for activists, musicians, and people from other parts of the region. However, by 1974 no FOCIS members remained who wanted to maintain the house except Lenore Mullarney. In that year Margaret Gregg, who had left Sullivan Road early on to live and work with ecumenical Epworth Ministries in downtown Knoxville, relocated eighty miles away to Johnson City. At the same time, the members attending UT had also graduated and departed to take jobs in other places. The Tennessee group felt that there was no longer a need for a physical center, so they returned control of the house to the diocese in 1974, and it was sold to a church group.

The closing of the house and Margaret Gregg's leaving Epworth changed Knoxville from a center of FOCIS activity to a place where several members continued to live and work in different agencies and schools. The Knoxville group now organizes the FOCIS annual meeting in January. Members stay in motels or with friends and gather in a downtown Catholic church.

Virginia. The Virginia community also underwent many changes. The FOCIS Center in Big Stone Gap ceased to be the organization's headquarters; there was no central staff and Monica Appleby had married and moved to Somerville, Massachusetts. Still a gathering place, the Center provided housing for volunteers and other short-termers who came to the area.

A Glenmary volunteer when FOCIS was formed, Kathy Hutson joined FOCIS and worked in the public schools as a speech therapist. After completing graduate work at Vanderbilt she returned to Big Stone Gap and lived at the FOCIS house. She described the changes in the Center during this period:

I moved back into the FOCIS house when I came back. It had really changed. Ginny [Remedi] and I lived there one winter, and Catherine [Rumschlag] lived with us part time, and we had a lot of college kids living with us. . . . Well, it was just musical beds for a long time. . . .

[W]e needed to keep the house filled to keep it going financially and we had a lot of space. The agency I worked for [Dilenowisco—an educational cooperative] always had people coming in from out of the area, I bet we put up at least four or five people for several months. . . . But people [in town] didn't really like us. One lawyer told us the first job he was offered was to get us out of town any way he could. He said we had beer cans in the alley and people with long hair and beards on our front porch. . . . These were local people, local kids. . . . Russ Cravens, a conscientious objector to the Vietnam War, was living there. There was the University Without Walls group that Anne was involved with. . . . I am sure some of them did smoke pot or whatever else young kids do, and people didn't like that happening in their neighborhood, but mostly people just guessed that they did.

I had the house for two years and people kept moving in and out and Ginny left. It was too much for me to take care of that big house. . . . The neighborhood didn't really fit our style so the big house was sold[6] and the monies were split. . . . I bought this little house in the southern section of town and Catherine and I fixed it up and we lived there about three years.

Big Stone Gap, the headquarters of Westmoreland Coal Company, was largely an upper-middle-class town that housed the company managers and other professionals. The FOCIS house was located in a middle-class neighborhood, while most of the families and communities the members worked with were on the fringes of town or in the coal camps up a series of hollers around the working class town of Appalachia, five miles distant. First Anne Leibig moved the Office of Appalachian Ministry from Big Stone Gap to Appalachia to be closer to the people they were serving. Then, with the help of local community leader Jeanette Getsi and a loan from FOCIS, Anne bought an old hotel for sale in the middle of Appalachia that housed elderly residents the two feared might otherwise end up being evicted. The renamed Mountain People's Manor with Jeanette as its new manager became a center for various groups and activities such as the art fairs and puppet shows that were part of the summer arts program.

In the early 1970s the town of Appalachia was a vibrant hub for many FOCIS-connected activities. Anne Leibig explained the group's push for arts education in a 1974 article in *People's Appalachia*: "We began to work on an arts approach to community development. This was from the conviction of starting where people are, individually and communally. The people we know had talents and a love for music, storytelling, crafts, painting. In the existing institutions there was no reinforcement for these gifts. We felt people could come together to do these things in an individual way at first and as they were appreciated by others they may begin to act more in community."[7]

In 1968 Anne and other FOCIS members had helped area women start the Mountain People's Work Craft Cooperative, which then established a regional marketing consortium with craft groups in Tennessee, where Marie Cirillo, Mary Jo Leygraaf, and others were active. In turn, the existence of the Appalachia women's co-op had inspired a group of men to form a building co-op to rehab houses and install needed plumbing and bathrooms. Some of the craft co-op women also went on to work in a restaurant and bakery co-op in Big Stone Gap founded by Catherine Rumschlag.[8] Appalachian Community Arts (the umbrella organization which had evolved from FOCIS ARTS) had seeded two local groups, which used Appalachia's old train station for their programs. Other offshoots were a community-based newspaper, photo shop/darkroom, and Ginny Remedi's Redeemed Earth pottery shop. In 1973 Anne helped all these groups and others come together to form the Appalachia Community

Quilters in the Crazy Quilt Craft Co-Op in Newcomb, Tennessee, in 1970.

Development Corporation (ACDC) to augment "planning, . . . fundraising [and] mutual support."[9] Jeanette Getsi was its first president.

Anne noted that in addition to supporting twenty-five jobs in the community, ACDC facilitated the interrelation of its three hundred members "in a new way" and empowered "a growth of consciousness that could lead to common actions for larger freedoms. Paulo Freire has spoken of this process of persons creating their own tools and institutions and then beginning to see that their situation can be changed and that they can be the agents of that change."[10]

Virginia FOCIS members were also involved with Concerned Citizens for Social and Economic Justice, the legal assistance and counseling service in Wise; the Dickenson County Food Cooperative, a community-owned co-op, which Patrick Ronan helped develop; and Appalshop, Inc., an OEO-funded media center across the mountain in Whitesburg, Kentucky, where young people were starting to document the problems and culture of the region.

FOCIS members helped found the Wise County Welfare Rights Organization in 1971. *Mountain Life and Work* reported: "The WRO worked with hundreds of people in the county trying to get fair welfare hearings and getting the Welfare Department to abide by regulations and give people what they are entitled to."[11] In addition to its advocacy role, the WRO set up a transportation co-op to take poor people to food stores, doctors, and social agencies.

A 1973 *Mountain Life and Work* article quoted Jeanette Getsi in discussing the importance of the Appalachia CDC and community development groups' work in Wise County:

Mrs. Getsi says, "People who aren't in the mines or on the railroad don't have any way of living. And most of those companies are owned by people who live heaven knows where and don't really care about the area and what happens." CDC members believe that outside help may be appreciated, but that the important thing is for local people themselves to figure out ways to handle the problems they face in their county and communities.[12]

Catherine Rumschlag, who had regularly visited southwest Virginia since the 1950s as her community's superior general, moved to Big Stone Gap for good in 1970. She worked part time at the Catholic church and quickly began to explore other ways to be useful in the community. In that first summer she and FOCIS member Karen Linzmaier started a to-mato-growing venture with a group of teenagers. Catherine remembered:

> I had noticed the summer before that high school boys came to the house to ask for work so they could earn some money. We had little work for them, so most of the time we had to turn them down. I thought we could employ them in a tomato patch, and share with them the profits. We arranged for a piece of land . . . with a tomato-growing cooperative that was operating in the area. We borrowed money from the charity fund at the Catholic church to buy the plants and pay the workers. We worked for fifty cents an hour and a promise that at the end of the project, the profits would be divided according to the hours worked. I learned a lot about grow-ing tomatoes as we received technical assistance from the cooperative. Later in the season our plants were struck with the blight, so many of the tomatoes could not be sold to the cooperative. We sold some locally, we canned some, and many went to waste. When it became evident that there would be no profits to distribute, the workers' enthusiasm waned. A few workers carried on, but we ended the season with a debt to the charity fund, which was kindly forgiven.

Catherine's enthusiasm for cooperatives, planted decades earlier by Father William Howard Bishop, was not quashed by the tomato bust. In the mid-1970s she would initiate two long-term projects in Big Stone Gap: the regionally renowned Bread and Chicken House and Christ Hill, an intentional community and homeless shelter.[13]

The small agricultural community of Dungannon, Virginia, became a center of FOCIS activity in 1972 with the purchase of The River Farm by Monica and Michael Appleby and Helen Lewis of Clinch Valley College. Anne Leibig and Helen had cooperated for several years in hosting college students who came to Appalachia to volunteer or learn about the region. With the sale of the FOCIS Center in Big Stone Gap, their Field Study program now needed a place to house students and hold workshops. Monica, living in Massachusetts, longed to return to the area; she and Michael envisioned a future in which they might combine educational work with farming. Anne and Helen began a search for a piece of land that would meet all of their needs. They found and purchased a place near Dungannon in rural Scott County—an isolated but beautifully located 150–acre farm with a mile of frontage on the Clinch River.

Dungannon was already a familiar spot to ex-Sisters Monica and Anne. Its small Catholic church had been built in 1947, and the Sisters had often come to a nearby valley to picnic in the summers and to hold Bible schools in the town.

In 1972 Michael and Monica moved south to their new home. During the first two summers about twenty people—musicians, actors, FOCIS members, and college students—camped in the barn and orchard and helped with the disused property's reclamation. Their labors were punctuated with frequent music and spontaneous theatrical eruptions. One night Bread and Puppet Theater group members from Glover, Vermont, capered on twelve-foot stilts in the parking area, their performance illuminated by the headlights of cars.[14] Members of the group came to help Michael and Monica because Michael had worked with them in New England.

Monica, Michael, and Helen soon decided to open the Farm to other members. Several young people from Clinch Valley College and Wise decided to join. They had worked with Helen and FOCIS in the arts program and various social movements, especially on the issue of strip mining. Frankie Taylor and Becky Bingman joined first, followed by Rich Kirby and Becky's sister, Beth. Anne Leibig was an early member. Together they spent many hours in planning how the Farm could become a community with the combined functions of home, working farm, and study center. The members had wanted a land trust but the legal problems proved too great, and they settled for business incorporation, specifying that the land would be used for farming and education.

In 1974 Anne returned from West Virginia with a future husband and a master's degree in social work. Environmentalist Dick Austin initially helped her build a house on The River Farm. Then he bought the farm next door. The couple married in 1975, and Anne moved upstream to help Dick begin organic farming practices on Chestnut Ridge Farm, where both still live. During the 1970s other artist and activist friends settled in Scott County, drawn to the like-minded circle whose hub was The River Farm. The influx of outsiders, a demographic first, caused quite a stir in the small agricultural community. Rumors circulated of the presence of hippies, Communists, and nudists and their shocking activities, such as skinny-dipping in the river.[15] Although many of the group were native Appalachians, most were not born and bred inside the county, and they brought with them a lifestyle quite different from the conservative local norms.[16] However The River Farm circle's immediate neighbors, amused by the newcomers, were cordial and very helpful to them. They protected them from those in the county who wanted to run them out, especially in later years during a heated environmental controversy. After the first couple of years, The River Farm lost its charm as a "hippie commune" and the stream of youthful volunteers slowed to a trickle, but it became and continued to be a major center for international visitors and other groups interested in community development, Appalachian issues, and rural culture and living. Spearheaded by Anne, the Farm members soon became heavily involved in community development projects in Dungannon. Chapters 11 and 12 describe these and other innovative educational and economic projects initiated by Monica, Helen, and other FOCIS and River Farm members.

Chapter 9

ARTS AND DEVELOPMENT

The arts program was putting theology and action together.

The first FOCIS project was an ambitious, creative, region-wide Arts and Development initiative. The project brought together two expressive cultures: Appalachia and FOCIS/Glenmary. The arts had played a major part in Glenmary life and work from the beginning. For women repressed in many significant ways by the congregation's training, doing art in liturgy, celebration, and mission activities provided an opportunity for personal and community expression. Members carried their vital habit of art into FOCIS. They expressed themselves and created community through graphic and fiber art, poetry, music, film and video, and the organization of arts events. They developed a rationale and methodology from their mission work, creating Bible schools to involve whole families and communities, which they brought into the Arts and Development project. It was also through this ambitious project, which began in the summer of 1969, that they learned how to work with communities in a different way and developed a new organizational structure for FOCIS.

The late 1960s and 1970s were the beginnings of the Appalachian cultural revival movement, and the FOCIS ARTS project became a source of support and a participant in this. As Glenmary missioners and later as FOCIS workers, the women became appreciative of the many skills and talents of the Appalachian people, whose creativity was shown in their quilts, crafts, music, and storytelling. The FOCIS members saw the possibility of using this creativity for community development, personal growth, and a means of improving Appalachian residents' self image. This self-esteem boost was particularly important, given that this was a time when the images in the national media of Appalachian people and communities were that of depressed and fatalistic people.

The government and most development programs had used the "culture of poverty" model to explain the economic and social problems.[1] This explanation of causes blamed victims for their oppression, explaining their poverty as a result of their culture: their values, attitudes, and way of life. Although as missionaries the women came to the region with some of those preconceptions, as active members of the communities they began to redefine the situation and see the creativity and potential for development in the people. From their own experiences with oppressive structures, they could identify with the dependency and powerlessness caused by the social, political, and economic system in counties where much of the land and minerals were owned by outside land companies, where surface mining was destroying the environment, and where mechanization was forcing migration of families to urban industrial centers.

They joined the Appalachian movement, which began to define the area as a "colony" and mobilized opposition to the exploitation of the land and people. The FOCIS ARTS project became part of this Appalachian revitalization movement. They did not seek to merely preserve traditional arts but rather cultivate and innovate them. They brought in new techniques with video, film, and photography; new designs for quilts; new methods of marketing crafts for income generation; and new ways of using music and storytelling to mobilize communities, to dialogue about the region's problems, to make constructive changes, and to begin a social and economic development process to improve the quality of life there. In the region, this was the beginning of local music festivals, craft fairs, community heritage days, arts councils, and many efforts by communities to show and tell their stories.

Through the arts initiative, FOCIS women developed a different role, a different way of working in community—not as missionary but as participant. As catalysts who encouraged creativity, expression, and discovery, they were animators of social change. In this process, they learned how to disassemble, decentralize, and give up control. Afterward, FOCIS members no longer brought in a project; instead, they helped the community organize and develop its own.

In FOCIS's second year, even as it was gravitating towards a new structure that would leave it without central staff, the organization initiated an ambitious and multi-faceted two-year program linking art to community development. Centrally planned but locally focused, FOCIS ARTS activities took place in Chicago, Cincinnati, and a number of locations in Appalachia during 1969. Members' experiences from those projects accelerated their move to decentralize the organization and taught them new ways of working in communities. In various incarnations the arts program would continue into the 1980s as one of the most important strands of their work.

FOCIS ARTS's Discovery, Expression, Communication, funded chiefly by the Irwin-Sweeney-Miller Foundation, involved collaboration with many other organizations and individuals.[2] It underscored the importance of helping communities develop projects from within while it strengthened the paradigm—first developed on mission in Glenmary—of art as an essential aspect of community development, creating a model which would continue to inform members' work for decades.

The program's planners believed that involvement in local arts projects would lead participants to greater self-confidence and a stronger sense of community. As a by-product, they hoped the activities would "enhance the opportunities and abilities of the individual Appalachian to become self-sustaining economically."[3]

Each community site developed projects and special events in liaison with the other sites, and all came together in August 1969 for an Arts Fair in Knoxville, Tennessee. FOCIS encouraged locations to develop permanent community groups that could support ongoing activities.

Maureen Linneman remembered working with a talented group of women doing crafts in Saint Paul, Virginia:

The women did a lot of the patchwork quilting, music, pottery, and crafts. That was important, the whole craft work and arts. I think we saw the women creating quilts and then looking for a way they could earn money through this natural talent they had. Margaret [Gregg] helped them develop different designs.

Ginny Remedi and Barbara Locricchio with pottery class in Dickenson County, Virginia, 1969.

The first thing they did was produce banners and handbags, and then the women started making a little money to spend and it was a sort of pre-economic work. Once the women got into knowing they could make a little money, they began to see how they were employable. Before that they didn't see it. They had no self-image—[thinking,] "Nobody would ever pay me for what I do." I think we were helpful in changing that mentality. The crafts became the way to do that.

Maureen felt they were breaking new ground with the arts initiative: "I think the summer arts program embodied new concepts; the proposal was beautifully expressed, like theology. It was putting theology and action together. I think the arts program validated [our whole approach to service], but it was work- and thought-provoking to make it happen."

A gathering in Buffalo, Tennessee, illustrates the way film and slides were used to encourage community participation. The Osborne family viewed and discussed a multimedia presentation that community members had created over the summer. "Appalachian Environment" featured film and slides from the rural and city project locations; voices of mountain people and summer staff; and local folk music and music from the film *Midnight Cowboy*. Viewers' remarks progressed from a critique of the images to a discussion of economic problems in the mountains:

ESTER OSBORNE: It [the slide show] showed the farming, the man planting, then the corn and the cattle. Then they showed the mountain with the timber. One part showed a shack that was vacant for a long time—that is raggedy country. The showing brought back memories.

NERVIE OSBORNE: There are so many who don't know anything about these mountains back here. They'd enjoy seeing it.

ESTER: In some places they would think it was an outcast place, with rundown houses and places like that . . . and then again they could enjoy it and think it was wonderful. . . . I think it's a wonderful place in the summer, but in the winter I think anywheres else would beat it. . . . but there's nowheres else to live. Our little bit of income wouldn't pay the rent anywhere else. . . .

NERVIE: I was born and raised in the mountains, and understand the mountains and the work, the wood gitting [sic] and farming and everything. If they moved me to the city, I wouldn't know no more than a kid how to start to make a living.

ESTER: When my grandfather came to this part of the country, he came from North Carolina, and you know how he got here? He hooked his milk cows up to the wagon, and he rode in the wagon, and the cows pulled their household stuff, whatever they had. You know, I fell out with my grandfather from the time I heard that he'd leave North Carolina and come back to a country like this.

Facilitator Margaret Gregg suggested that the group think of another name for the presentation:

ESTER: Maybe something like "The place that's forgotten." "The forgot place."

JIMMIE OSBORNE: "The forsaken place."

ESTER: Yes, I do think at times it's forgot. I think the government should be able to do something. Any place can be improved, no matter how far out it is. . . . It should be built up. There's plenty of ground. You could put up some kind of workshop, plant, or anything. Roads could be built; the creeks could be worked on. Used to be people raised cattle, hogs, sheep, and always had something to sell. There ain't nobody around here now that's buying things.

The group decided another movie was needed to give an accurate picture of rural Appalachia, one that "would show more of the hardships of winter and work and life."[4]

During the second year of the ARTS program FOCIS expanded the roles of local project staff and communities. Monica Appleby explained the reasoning behind the shift toward increased community authority:

We raised money to develop those projects but we learned that by having money resources from the outside and entering into a community, there is still that insider/outsider relationship with resources coming from the outside and somebody outside controlling them. It was like it always has been in the coal mining camps. We would raise the money as FOCIS and we were controlling how it was spent, so after we did that for one year, we then decided rather than the money coming to FOCIS and us sending out these teams, that communities could decide what they wanted to do within the parameters of the art expression of building the community. And they could apply for the money and it would be sent to them. So they were in control. After that we raised money directly for the communities and that went on for about five years.

FOCIS sponsored ARTS projects in Price Hill and Mohawk in Cincinnati; Clairfield and Knoxville in Tennessee; and in Big Stone Gap and Appalachia, Virginia.

The Mohawk program, designed largely for an interracial group of young people, began to work with the Mohawk Improvement Association, which was involved in problems of housing, recreation, and services. Local people took over the decision making and expanded the group by forming a board based on membership from different streets in the neighborhood. Strong leaders emerged from the community-directed Price Hill project, and several local groups worked together to form an arts organization in affiliation with the community council. A community celebration attracted three hundred people, and the formation of the Lower Price Hill Arts and Crafts Committee was a spin-off. The Lower Price Hill groups became a major force in the community. They took over an old school building to develop an adult education program and helped support an Appalachian cultural festival that is held annually in Cincinnati. They work closely with the Urban Appalachia Council.

Epworth Ministry, an ecumenical parish in the Fort Sanders area with which Margaret Gregg was already involved, sponsored the arts project in Knoxville. The Epworth community comprised activists, artists, musicians, university students, and faculty, and used FOCIS ARTS to integrate many of their activities and interests.

Two church buildings and several houses provided studio, performance, and gathering space. There, summer events included rallies, craft projects, music, covered-dish suppers, dances, Bread and Puppet Theater performances, and political demonstrations. From the confines of her studio, Margaret produced posters and flyers for many events and social movements in the region. One famous product was a sweatshirt bearing a portrait of the indomitable miners organizer Mother Jones, captioned with her pithy slogan, "Pray for the Dead—Fight Like Hell for the Living!"

The music and theater events became incredibly popular, attracting performers from throughout the region and visitors from as far away as Chicago and Washington. Epworth's first event was the Youtopian Folk Music Fair, with its theme of "Make Love—Make Revolution—Make Jubilee." (Its spin-off, the annual Jubilee Music Festival, continues today at Knoxville's Laurel Theater.) There West Virginia activist-musician Hazel Dickens made her first public appearance singing songs she had written about coal-mining issues. Doug Yarrow and Mike Kline premiered their slide and music program on strip mining, entitled "They Can't Put It Back." Rick Diehl from the People's Appalachian Research Center presented his mixed-media program about Appalachian social movements, music, fairs, and generations.

In 1970 FOCIS sponsored the wildly successful "Appalachian People's Old Timey Folk Rock Camp Meeting Music Fair!" in Wise County, Virginia. Margaret Gregg produced a poster and flyers for the festival and made quilt backdrops for the stage from old Glenmary Center wall hangings. She remembered the excitement surrounding the seminal event: "All the activists of the mountains were involved. It was something like an

Kathy McCrady with music class in 1969.

Appalachian Woodstock and was the beginning of a series of music festivals and the revitalization of traditional music in the mountains."

One of the organizers, Jack Wright, wrote the following account of the many obstacles they surmounted in producing the festival:

I had been involved in the Appalachian Studies Program at Clinch Valley College and had helped organize several programs of traditional music at the college for the seminar. One of these became the annual Dock Boggs Memorial Music Festival.[5] We had also had programs featuring Jean Ritchie, Ralph Stanley, Mike Seeger, and other local musicians.[6] Soon I began thinking about putting on an outdoor festival that would include traditional music, gospel, and rock and roll. Several of my friends and fellow students, including Frankie Taylor and Beth Bingman, worked tirelessly in the planning and execution of this first outdoor festival. The effort took on a communal tone. Our first challenge came when we tried to find a suitable location for this small outdoor dream.

In those days, just the mention of rock and roll in the aftermath of Woodstock gave local leaders cold feet, to say the least. National friction between the generations seemed at a new high. To oppose the war in Vietnam, or to be for equality and a clean environment at home, was considered un-American by many. Student strikes and takeovers at colleges across the nation often erupted into violence. Idealistically, we hoped that the local music might bring different people closer together. Dock quieted some of my fears when he told me that I could count on him to play at the festival.

We approached local leaders about using the county fairgrounds. After several weeks of waiting for an answer they turned us down cold with no explanation. I went back to Clinch Valley College to ask about using the picnic area on a wooded section of campus. The chancellor dismissed me with a quick retort, "We are not gonna have any rock festival around here on this campus." The National Forest Service offered help, but they had no open space large enough to accommodate us.

Finally, a cousin of Frankie Taylor's agreed to let us use a piece of property he owned at Chestnut Flats bordering the Jefferson National Forest on High Knob near Norton. This rolling, open meadow surrounded by lush forest had no water or electricity. It had last been used as a skeet-shooting range in the early '60s. The water and mud-filled ruts in the one-lane access road left it almost impassable. But this spot pleased us immensely. Its quiet beauty and remoteness made our dream intimate and real.

After securing the space we had less than a month to prepare the site. With no budget, our task was formidable. A couple of hundred dollars left over from the spring festival would have to get us through. We built the stage from found and "borrowed" lumber. The Old Dominion Power Company seemed delighted to bring "juice" to an isolated area. Maybe it would be developed. Service amounted to an eighteen dollar hookup fee. Ma Bell put in a pay phone out on the entrance to the site at the main road.

We hauled "red dog"[7] from the most visible and largest slag heap in the county, located on the outskirts of Norton. Each trip, the loaded dump truck strained five miles up the narrow blacktop road, passing hemlock and rhododendron, around sharp curves and switchbacks to the top of High Knob, the county's highest summit. Though we unloaded twelve truckloads and it put our road in good shape, we hardly made a dent in the smoking gob pile it came from.

Portajohns failed to [materialize], with the nearest vendor sixty miles away. Our budget allowed us to dig two latrines, his'n and her'n. We fitted our newly constructed wooden thrones over the holes and surrounded our privies with olive drab canvas strung up on poles. Both johns were open-air affairs with a late summer night's view of the star-lit heavens. The latrine design came from one of the Vietnam vets on our volunteer crew.

We mowed and raked our grassy eight-acre meadow with a borrowed tractor rig so that we could have festival seating and plenty of parking. During the last two weeks we pitched our tents, hung a flag, and set up a campsite, where we worked night and day to get ready. Often we bathed in the chilly waters of nearby High Knob Lake. At more than four thousand feet above sea level we labored, cooked, laughed, and breathed pure mountain air, readying our grounds for the county's first alternative music festival.

We drove Dock Boggs up the mountain that warm Saturday afternoon to the festival site. He was dressed in his trademark dark suit, necktie, and polished dress shoes. There was a mix of ages in the audience, mostly young folks with longer hair, several were shirtless, some barefooted and wearing shorts. Other folks brought lawn chairs but most sat on the ground. About one hundred and twenty people out in the sunshine for the afternoon's performances saw Dock's arrival.

Three handmade crazy quilts hung down from the back of the primitive wooden stage. Their asymmetrical patterns slowly rippled and folded into one another as the bottom edges blew about in the early fall breeze. In back of the audience, across the meadow, a frisbee sailed between two friends. Dock gave his big smile and a small wave to the crowd. He took his banjo out of the case and tuned a little. Then he shuffled over and sat down on a folding chair in the middle of the stage and picked into the microphone. He was alone, doing a twenty-five minute set. He worked the two mikes easily. He addressed the crowd. Looking out across different faces. Talking between songs, telling the story behind a song or about himself. The late afternoon sunshine gleamed off of his eyeglasses. He finished with "Oh Death." The local film crew was only aware of the young White female blues singer from Knoxville and a Vietnam veteran turned protest singer from West Virginia. Little did we know that this was to be Dock's last public performance. It was September 12, 1970.[8]

Frankie Taylor, of The River Farm in Dungannon, was one of the local organizers of the festival. He recently commented on the event and its lasting effect on him and other local participants:

Over a three day stretch there were over two thousand people who drove to the meadow on High Knob in the Jefferson National Forest. They came from all the surrounding states, but mostly from the small communities in southwest Virginia. We were generally young, hippified people in love with music, but there was also a scattering of hunters and other woodsfolk who were just curious. Many of us were politically active but probably wouldn't have used the term, and there was no shortage of folks who saw the event as a prototype for social awakening and necessary for the coming revolution. It was hugely successful except for maybe the revolution part. There was wonderful music, great food, and only a couple of fights, not serious, and we considered ourselves lucky in that respect. The hippie love thing really did work.

That was thirty years ago, and I still live close by. I occasionally run into the rest of us who put it all together, moms and pops now. Without fail everyone feels like it was a special thing, a positive experience in their life. A kind of lore has developed around the event and (as one who secretly hoped it would further the revolution) I see that lore as a kind of affirmation. I think we're all more likely to trust group activity. And then it helped create our identities, really cool identities, something that tied us to where we lived and more importantly to where all our kinfolks had lived. It was organic to say the least, but again, we probably wouldn't have used that term.

Margaret Gregg recalled the next stage of FOCIS ARTS as the organization grew through grants and external funding: "After the two-year project, we got funding through the National Endowment for the Arts's program for community arts. Actually, the NEA was pretty new and we were one of their first projects. Then each time we'd develop a grant we'd say to a group, 'Well what do you want to do?' and pull that together for a bigger package. And then just gradually people just kept going more on their own."

Seven community groups grew out of the FOCIS ARTS initiative and continued programs around crafts, film, video, theater, music, visual arts, and festivals. After FOCIS decided not to be a major developer of projects, it joined local groups in organizing the Appalachian Community Arts Project to support existing activities and encourage further community-based efforts through help with developing proposals and financial and management skills. The groups wrote up projects for inclusion in the "FOCIS ARTS portfolio." FOCIS continued to act as the sponsor and received fifteen percent of the grant total for administration.

One of the FOCIS ARTS spin-offs, Appalachian Community Arts (ACA) was the brainchild of Marie Cirillo. Through this structure the NEA Initiative in Expansion Arts Program supported a number of local efforts, in part because the fast-track bureaucrats found it difficult to deal directly with small groups who typically were not incorporated or fiscally sophisticated. The setup represented something of a compromise that was not without difficulties. Marie, who had become a strong voice for the region, served on the awards panel for the Expansion Arts Program for several years and became ACA's liaison with the National Endowment of the Arts. Many national funders looked to her as interpreter and to FOCIS as a source to recommend programs in the region—roles sometimes resented by community groups who felt that they should be able to access funding directly without FOCIS or Marie as guardian angels.

Expansion Arts funded a regional cultural festival in 1973 at Lincoln Memorial University in Harrogate, Tennessee, to showcase community arts programs. Margaret Gregg's festival brochure offered the rationale of strengthening community among both artists and audience members: "The Jubilee environment will lend mutual support to groups and individuals by furthering the growth of communication and the understanding of the cultural, political and social issues associated with the life, labor and land of the Appalachian people."

Organizers Michael Appleby, Rich Kirby, John McCutcheon, and Jack Wright brought together more than fifty individuals and groups who played from three stages.[9] Performers represented both traditional and contemporary music with regional roots: bluegrass, old-time fiddle and banjo, dulcimer, ballad singing, gospel, and country. Displays included banners, quilts, craft demonstrations, photographs, and continuous showings of films and videos. There were giant puppets and Punch and Judy shows as well as theater groups from throughout the region. Rich Kirby remembers:

About a week before the festival, Lincoln Memorial University tried to cancel the whole thing. There was this huge uproar having to do with lifestyle and morality. The college was insisting that there be no men and women in the same dorms at night. It didn't matter if they were artists who had been married for years. We finally realized that if we broke that rule nothing was going to happen. . . . The college president was most upset about the "drunken barbarity" on his campus. As the president was raving about that Helen Lewis said to him: "Do you realize that the best fiddler in the southern mountains is on your stage right now?," meaning J.P. Fraley. It was the first time he had ever stopped to think that maybe there might be some artistic merit in some of this stuff.

When Monica moved to Dungannon in 1972, she helped organize the Scott County Arts group to participate in the FOCIS ARTS program and later developed the county Arts in the School program utilizing the influx of newcomers along with local artists and musicians.

In Clairfield, Tennessee, a group of local women organized a craft co-op in the valley. Teacher and community leader Tilda Kemplen recounted its beginning: "Most of the women had learned to sew. They had quilted and made clothes all their lives. They helped the family make a living by making things that the family used. One of the first groups we organized was a crafts operation, Model Valley Folk Arts, in support of the community women who wanted to craft items such as quilts, pillows, and handbags."[10]

Mary Jo Leygraaf majored in arts and crafts at the University of Tennessee. When she returned to Clairfield she began teaching pottery.

I built an outdoor gas kiln, and taught classes at various locations, some at [Marie Cirillo's] house, some at churches, some in other people's homes. I would just travel around and bring all my supplies with me and then bring all their work back to the shop to fire. Then I'd bring it all back to the people and they'd glaze it and bring it back again. . . .

Somebody would hear about it and be interested and they'd get enough to have a group of people, and we'd have classes. Some people just made it for their own interest and things they wanted. There was a woman from Mud Creek that had a family with a bunch of kids and it was an outlet for her. She just loved to come and play in the clay and make things. She did some nice things.

We would go to craft fairs not just with our pottery but there was a craft group in the valley too that . . . did all kinds of quilts and clothing and things like that. We'd usually go with them, and set up. We'd go to Cincinnati and we'd go to Knoxville, just wherever.

Ginny Remedi and Mary Jo Leygraaf, potters at kiln, 1968.

The Model Valley craft group existed for some fourteen years. Their products were marketed by Vanderbilt students and an Appalachian store in Cambridge, Massachusetts, run by Monica in 1971. The experience local women gained in this group helped them go on to other ventures.

Margaret Gregg, July 2000. Photo by Bob Hurley.

The art director for the original FOCIS ARTS program, Margaret Gregg has continued to serve as the FOCIS "Artist in Residence." Margaret has been central to FOCIS work and helped all the communities with workshops, publications, and celebrations. A display of the posters, flyers, and program designs that Margaret developed for grassroots community groups provides a social documentary of the progressive social movements in the region since the 1960s. She makes art central to all FOCIS work, and she encourages creativity in work, play, and everyday living. She always brings a spontaneity and lightheartedness to meetings. She can make chaos out of order, which breaks conventional thought patterns and brings a critical outlook to social issues.

Margaret's personal story shows how both Glenmary and FOCIS

helped her develop her talents and how her art has enriched the life and work of the group:

In Big Stone Gap, in the parish, I found women, young and middle-aged, who had a lot of sewing skills, so they could do a lot of embroidery. I worked with them and we made some big wall hangings. The theme was the seasons, and these were based on how you see the seasons in southwest Virginia.

I would do silk-screen projects with people and sometimes leave equipment and they could do their own thing. I would try to do things so that people could have some income. They'd silk-screen cards, I'd pay them for them and then I'd get paid for selling them.

I learned about Happenings, a free-form, participatory-type of involvement, a little bit of theater, heavy on visuals. And I just loved it, just loved it. I remember doing a Happening project at Fayetteville, the training center. We used a huge roll of paper, five or six feet high, a gift from a paper mill up in the north. We'd unroll big pieces, eight feet long, everybody painted big figures on them and we covered the tennis court with the figures for a fall festival, in about 1960.

You could summarize my artistic work as a Glenmary Sister as doing publication layout and design, liturgical graphics and decorations, instructive as well as participatory art education, as well as the *Community* statue . . . I was a very young member of the community and I remember, the day of the big Council in Fayetteville, it was in the summer which was an unusual time for such a meeting. . . . I was working on trying to reproduce this particular piece of sculpture, a ceramic group that became known as *The Community*. We planned to use it to create income for the community. In order to fire the piece in the kiln, I had to cut off the head of the biggest figure in the community group, and I remember thinking this was like what was happening in our community.

The Glenmary Sisters continue to offer [the statue] for sale. My niece is a good customer. [She buys them for friends and new members of the family.] Once she called them to get background information on the piece. When she asked who the artist was they responded: "Oh, somebody that was with us a long time ago and we think she's dead now." More recently I saw the *Community* statue which she gave to new family members. I noticed a new level of distortion in the work which made me think that they must be using a new mold or that the old one is totally worn out. It looked beat up. I felt shock, anger, and sadness. I resorted to the comfort of metaphor: the old molds, even if they are supposed to be copies, just don't work—no integrity.

I served FOCIS as graphic designer, arts program originator and developer, fundraiser, and project director of the Community Arts program. In 1968 the Tennessee Arts Commission purchased one of my paintings, *New Generation*, for its permanent collection. The Dayton, Ohio, school system purchased one of my first designer quilts in 1972.

Working with the FOCIS summer arts program was exciting; we were young, restless, sweaty, lots of motivation. Sometimes we'd give people cameras or sometimes set up scenes or make stories to film with super-8 film, and then silkscreening, painting, photography, music. Some people would really be skillful with getting people to tell stories or to perform or to create plays. You know it just depended on the person's inclinations or experience. In some ways it was probably on the model of Bible school—you know, what do kids do in the summertime? And then you bring in the adults and try to find some local leadership, and start to talk about things, and get together and see that lots of people are thinking about the same thing. We had people assemble in Knoxville bringing all these things they created and showing them together. And then there were staff people that were not part of Glenmary or FOCIS. They brought a lot of talent and motivation. And usually there'd be people, who might have been church-related or community center related, that would just be so thrilled to have this project and these resources come in and they'd really work hard with you and have great ideas.

I have a tendency to be maybe a little open-ended and ambiguous and sometimes it was difficult to explain to staff what it was we were supposed to do. What is art? I never quite got through those definitions to many people's satisfaction. People wanted to perform well and needed to do what they thought they were supposed to do. Sometimes that could create *real* problems, because you can't just say "Oh its supposed to look like this and this is how you do it." That doesn't come off. . . .

I don't know how to assess . . . what impact [the summer arts project] had. It was FOCIS's first community project, which was rural and urban, which gave jobs to a lot of people. There were staffing positions to be filled, some were coordinating, some were directive in the community, so this created new areas to resolve. Like, if you are working for FOCIS, how do you work for the community which is something else, and how do you work from a theory about community arts? It was very exciting, very relevant as far as turning on to new work ideas and things, also very frustrating, because I felt myself . . . involved in something that I didn't know how it all related to the parts. And sometimes found that I was a person who was a source of disruption and confusion for people. Because they thought I had some notion of art or work . . . that they wanted to be able to understand and I wasn't able to communicate well what it was all about.

With the FOCIS ARTS project, I was working just as the organizer, the coordinator, and I was doing things for projects, doing PR or if they needed a hanging to put somewhere I'd do that. And then things for newsletters, drawings and all that. I was starting to sell things and I needed to do more of that. I was very drained [from] being totally available. And I remember I thought I would do something for myself. And I did it.

I did research and film production with the James Agee Film Project [for] Ross Speers. One project was collecting photographs that would show the history of

Washington County, [Tennessee], so that meant going around to people and [saying]: "Hey, let's see what you've got stashed away!" . . .

And then working on the film *Electric Valley*, the fifty-year history of [the Tennessee Valley Authority]. I'd find the people and we'd talk, and then set up film interview times when there was a crew. And I organized a reunion of all the Fontana Dam workers, which was really, really exciting. . . . TVA liked it too; it was sort of like we performed a service for TVA. It helped me appreciate the impact of such a huge organization, and everywhere you go somebody remembers something about TVA.

It was exciting to meet people and they would be excited because somebody was listening to them, and there was this sense of it being in a larger context that had historical significance; it was very affirming. I had that community development skill to go find people and get things going. And it taught me, gave me a much deeper appreciation of what you go through to come up with a good product—something that has a lot of substance. And it was the most in-depth and comprehensive film, and I learned more about research than I had ever done before. . . .

And then, I made an animated autobiographical film. I was at that age where personal issues were becoming something I needed to look at and try to sort out what's personal and what's political. I looked at photos of my parents, I made it chronological and I incorporated the political projects I was in. I could throw in some cuss words. I had an abortion and I made an image of that. I had an egg broken on a rosary bead, . . . and it was a way to make a statement about that, make it public. It wasn't that I hadn't talked to people about that, but I put it in a context. And then I could be playful about some things in the media. It was a way to integrate something. Autobiography is a good way to come to terms with yourself, it's like a powerful healing process. And the animation was a lot of lively discovery, because I could only learn by doing.

REFLECTIONS ON 25 YEARS: SEPT. 4, 1959–1984

I dressed up to marry Jesus.
I changed my name to Ruth—
    became Ruthless.
Daddy didn't come.
I ran away from home.
I decorated and discovered dreams and disasters.
Sisters are women—rejecting women,
    loving women, searching women.
Women loved me, women opened me.
I clung and cried and created.
I left home again.
I changed my name to Margie to Marge to Margaret.

I decorated and discovered Appalachia.
Women are workers and flirters and flowers—
    decorators and doers, drinkers and dancers.
Men loved me and opened me.
I clung and cried and created.
I left home again.
    Decorated and damned.
    Digging, dying, dreaming.
Love's layers ripping and waiting.
And now we talk from our hearts.
    Welcome home.

            Margaret Gregg

PART 3

Working in Communities

Chapter 10

SOCIAL SERVICES

Hot Springs Health Services shows what a community can do when it sets its mind to it.

The 1960s and 1970s were a period of great change and considerable unrest and organizing in the Appalachian Region. The War on Poverty, which had mandated community participation and control, fostered the poor and marginalized people's realization that they could participate in decisions which affected them and make changes in the social and economic situations in which they lived. FOCIS women encouraged and joined with citizen groups who were working to make these changes. They listened to what people were "fussing about," and two of their first major efforts focused on primary health care and legal services. Nationally, there was interest in developing primary health care centers for rural and depressed areas. As a result, FOCIS was able to tap into foundation and government funding programs that emphasized health education and prevention programs. Members collaborated with college student activists and church programs to develop health fairs. The group added the model of the Bible schools and the arts programs, which they found worked to mobilize the community. OEO programs had legitimized community control and the United Mine Workers reform agenda included providing primary health care for coal mining communities, which would be controlled by miners and their families. The coalfield clinics would also provide occupational health programs such as respiratory therapy for black lung victims and health education programs for families. The building and developing of the clinics in rural communities became the impetus for developing other community projects. The clinics became community centers dealing with broad community health problems rather than medical treatment centers. Owned and operated by the community, the clinics gave the region both a sense of pride and belief that they could rebuild their communities.

However, all the services—welfare, education, health, and transportation—for people living in these isolated and poor communities on the "back side" of the counties were controlled by the elite in the courthouse towns. Glenmary/FOCIS family visitors soon recognized that many people in the counties were not receiving the services they were legally entitled to. FOCIS members began developing legal aid clinics and training local people to be legal advocates for those who received welfare, disability and medical care compensation, and pensions.

This chapter details FOCIS's early social service work to promote health care and legal services in the region and their later project to provide transitional housing for the homeless in southwest Virginia. In all of these programs, FOCIS's way of working is clear—they do not tackle the medical institution or the legal institution or the housing programs directly. Rather they work with the community to develop alternatives to the existent, or in most cases nonexistent, programs in their communities. They set up alternative structures under community control, and then they confront the institutional structures with a community-wide base of support and knowledge of the problem. Some of these clinics influenced the development of statewide programs. Other clinics and the bulk of the legal aid programs did not survive, however, as governmental regulations changed from support of community-oriented programs to more "cost-effective," and "efficient" models. Yet while these programs were operating they provided care for many, functioning as a model of community-based services. Through their social service work, FOCIS members gained an education in management and the workings of government and helped to build a socially conscious constituency able to use their education to tackle future problems in the community.

With the reorganization of FOCIS, the members developed a different way of working in community. They became a presence, a resource, a partner. They did not bring in projects; rather they brought skills, energy, ideas, commitment, and a network of friends and resources. They encouraged, taught, shared power and expertise, and helped develop local leadership. In this way they stimulated (and occasionally spearheaded) the creation of some of the region's first community-based projects in the areas of health, arts and recreation, legal services, education, economic development, housing, and rural infrastructure. A number used their professional skills in schools, clinics, and hospitals. The FOCIS committee structure made it possible for them to cooperate in larger projects even without a central staff. "FOCIS projects" were supplanted by projects in communities. The women's successful involvement in developing social services in the region testifies in part to the potency of their network structure. Members first helped create these services in the Clairfield–Clear Fork Valley[1] area of east Tennessee.

Much of the Clairfield group's early work centered around the Office of Economic Opportunity (OEO) community center where Jean Luce was director. Initially Jean, Marie Cirillo, and Mary Jo Leygraaf listened to residents to find out what problems were most important and which issues people wanted to work on. Citizen organizing work from the previous year made it clear that health was a primary concern. Marie and Jean got the assistance of Linda Ocker (Mashburn), who was organizing health fairs in the region through the Presbyterian Church and the Council of Southern Mountains. Working with Jean, the Youth Corps, and a volunteer medical team from the Palisades in New York, Linda organized the valley's first health fair. Vanderbilt University medical student Bill Dow, who had founded the Student Health Coalition (SHC), continued the health fairs in Tennessee and developed a close relationship with Marie and the Clairfield community. The SHC sponsored a series of health fairs in the valley, but their beginning effort drew a mixed reaction. Community activist Shelby York remembered:

Well, the first that I heard of the students was in 1969. . . . They had a two-week health fair over at the old county school building, which was a mile or so over in the other holler. I saw all this activity up there in that old school yard. . . . I asked about it, and the reply I got was, "That's a bunch of hippies down there. It's supposed to be some kind of a health thing." They didn't know what it was. They didn't bother to investigate."[2]

With the help of Louise Adams, the postmaster whose son had died of hepatitis, Marie got other local people involved, and they repaired the old school building and developed a community clinic. Volunteer doctors were recruited to come in several days a week until a physician, Dr. Carl Rountree, offered to come full-time when the clinic was ready.

The spin-off effect of their efforts quickly became apparent. Marie Cirillo recalled how other groups sprung from the original clinic: "I encouraged the group to form their own non-profit. . . . This was the first self-help non-profit . . . [and] a spark which led to other development. Groups that followed included a development corporation, craft group, a folk school, child care, legal services, and three other health clinics in the valley: White Oak, Frakes, and Stinking Creek."

Before coming to Appalachia, nurse Linda (Ocker) Mashburn had worked in Presbyterian missions in India and had studied at Union Theological Seminary. Working with the FOCIS network, first as a colleague and then as a member, she made health fairs happen throughout the mountains. She recalled her pitch to health fair organizers to establish her role as a year-round position:

> In 1967 the Presbyterian Board of National Missions was looking for someone to coordinate a summer program they were calling Health Fairs . . . [with] volunteer teams they had recruited from affluent churches. The teams had a doctor, nurse, dentist, and some professional medical people along with some teenagers in a sort of work camp group, to put on a health education program with some diagnostic screening. It could be done in the rural areas and used as a tool for community organization. I got very excited about the community organizing potential of the program. . . .
>
> I said to the church, if you really want the community organization aspects of the program to be developed, you need to have somebody in the region year-round to work with the communities on long-range programs. The one-time summer committee could plan a health fair and talk about local needs, but . . . you need to have a lot of follow-up to make longer-range things come to fruition. They bought that idea.

Because Linda believed it was unwise for the project to be coordinated in New York, Presbyterian minister Phil Young, then president of the Council of Southern Mountains, put her on the Council staff (headquartered in Berea, Kentucky). She felt this approach was necessary to obtain maximum local involvement and "ownership" of the process. Linda recalled the meeting as her first opportunity to meet FOCIS members working in the region:

> The Commission on Volunteers sponsored a meeting [in February 1968 in Berea] about how outside volunteers could be best used in Appalachia in the service of the community rather than with other agendas being superimposed on this region. It was a really good conference. . . . Monica Kelly [Appleby] and Margaret Gregg were there, and so these were the first FOCIS members I met. I learned a little about FOCIS through them and about Glenmary. I was very impressed with their contributions to the meeting. It wasn't a very large gathering, but some of the most strategic people working in the region were there. Myles Horton from the Highlander Center was there, Appalachian Volunteer folks were there.[3] It was an opportunity for me to make contacts with folks already working in the region. . . .
>
> As it worked out, we did health fairs in a number of areas that summer, including Sneedville and Clairfield. Eventually I did one in Wise and Dickenson counties in Virginia, and in Welch, West Virginia, where FOCIS member Kathy McCrady lived. Later that fall I participated in a meeting FOCIS held in Cincinnati in which they got together the health-trained people in FOCIS to see if there was a specific project or effort that the medical people were interested in pursuing, parallel to the

arts program. . . . [There] I met Rae Ann Gasiorowski, a nurse and FOCIS member who later worked with me to develop the Hot Springs, North Carolina, clinic. She later went to become the first nurse at the Stinking Creek Clinic in Tennessee.

I had worked in the Appalachia Region for a total of three years. . . . I was feeling burn-out from the work I was doing for the Presbyterian Church. I averaged forty thousand miles a year traveling for them on those mountain roads, going thirty miles an hour. I worked eighty hours a week at this job or more, because I worked days, evenings, and weekends; . . . and during the summer when I had responsibility for the volunteers, there were no days off. . . . I couldn't keep it up. And I began looking for something different.

Hot Springs, North Carolina. Linda had first visited Hot Springs, a small community on the French Broad River, to do a health fair in 1969. She immediately sensed its need for a more permanent heath clinic:

It was apparent to me that Hot Springs, and that whole end of Madison County, was in desperate need of a primary care center. They had a simple concrete building, built for health care and used by a succession of physicians in the 1950s. During the years it had stood vacant, . . . but the community action agency had renovated it. The community was hoping that a solo physician was going to move a practice into it, but I knew that wasn't going to happen.

I told the people in the community that if they were willing to work, I and another nurse would come to Hot Springs and try to develop a primary care program for them.[4]

A local working group quickly coalesced to cooperate with the two FOCIS women on the clinic project, helping to raise money and facilitate community input into the new organization's bylaws and articles of incorporation (Elizabeth Hunter, "Hot Springs Health Care Pioneers," *Appalachia* [May–Aug. 1997]: 20).

Under Linda's leadership, the Hot Springs clinic opened in the spring of 1971:

In 1971 when Rae Ann and I moved to Hot Springs, I had a model in my head of a rural clinic staffed primarily by a nurse practitioner with physician back-up. During the four years I had spent in the region, I had watched nurses moving into expanded roles because of the great need for medical care in remote communities. I spent time with nurses working for the Frontier Nursing Service in eastern Kentucky who diagnosed and treated common health problems using standing M.D. orders. . . . Martha Stucker, [then] a Dominican Sister of the Sick Poor, . . . evolved a similar expanded role in the Clairfield, Tennessee, clinic after I helped find foundation money for the community to hire her.

Rae Ann and I opened the doors on the Hot Springs Clinic May 1, 1971. Dr. Michael Kelleher, a surgeon from Asheville, was our first physician and he came weekly to hold clinics on Saturdays. After a few months, we found another physician at the V.A. [Veterans Administration] hospital who was willing to come out on his day off.

Until the Hot Springs Health Program received a five-year grant from the Appalachian Regional Commission (ARC) in 1972, it stayed afloat on a very limited budget. Linda recalled how they "'operated on fees, volunteer labor, and a little foundation money. We paid the physicians who came out to help us a little something, but the nurses, nurses' aides, and the bookkeeper basically worked for nothing. I lived on my savings'" (20).

Linda helped finance their lean first year by paying Rae Anne's salary via contributions through the tax-deductible FOCIS books. To eke out their resources further, Linda also taught sociology part time at Mars Hill College. Patient fees covered some of their expenses. Despite the tight finances, the working group planned a cluster of three clinics for the community: medical, dental, and home health services. With the arrival of the ARC grant in May, Linda then in double-quick time "had to hire a staff of twenty-six, open three clinics, furnish a dental clinic, and license a home health agency":

[FOCIS] did a wonderful job of referring people when I was hiring staff. One of the nurses I hired was Kathy Johnson. . . . She visited in Big Stone, and FOCIS members called and said, "We have a nurse here you might be interested in recruiting." She had been working at the *Catholic Worker* in New York.

The first several years were very stressful, and being the only medical people in Hot Springs during the first year meant being on call all the time. FOCIS was essential to my "re-creation." When I needed a break, I escaped to Knoxville and enjoyed the hospitality of the house there and the company of those members living or visiting there.

Hot Springs was one of the first rural health programs in North Carolina, along with another started by Jim Bernstein in Orange County, with the encouragement of the University of North Carolina. The governor then proposed funding for rural health programs all over the state, based on the models of the first two programs. When it was funded, Bernstein was hired to direct the Raleigh office and is still running the state program after all these years.

Today the sole primary care provider in the county, the Hot Springs Health Program runs four medical centers. In a 1997 feature article on the Hot Springs Clinic, the Appalachian Regional Commission declared Linda Mashburn a "pioneer" in their magazine, *Appalachia*. They quoted Jim Bernstein, director of the Office of Rural Health and Resource Development of North Carolina, and North Carolina governor Jim Hunt, who alluded to the innovativeness of Linda's work:

> Building a rural health-care practice using a community corporation rather than a private physician as a base was [a] groundbreaking idea back in the early 1970s when Mashburn and the Hot Springs community decided to try it. [Their model] was a great concept "because doctors . . . and nurse practitioners come and go. When they do, you're not back at square one. You still have your base to build on." . . .
>
> Linda's pioneering work and the highly praised program have influenced health-care policy in the region. Hot Springs is "a spectacularly successful example of what rural health services can be, not only in the state, but in the country. It represents the cream of the crop, shows what a community can do when it sets its mind to it," says Jim Bernstein. "We helped establish seventy-one rural health clinics in North Carolina based on what we saw in Hot Springs." Former North Carolina governor Jim Hunt agrees: "I have watched over the years as local determination and . . . leadership developed this first-class homegrown enterprise that is a shining model for rural communities throughout our state." (20–21)

Because Linda had married and wanted to start a family, she left the Hot Springs program after four years. Yet she returned after nine months to run the home health agency for almost a year during a nursing shortage and later helped the program weather a major transition when a lot of the original staff left. She then continued to serve on the board of directors until her family moved to Statesville in 1979. After her marriage to Bill Mashburn, both she and he studied public health administration. Her subsequent career could have been different had she not put her family's needs first.

Satisfied that the program remains alive and healthy, Linda is not altogether above more personal emotions: "When I started it, there were four full-time doctors providing services in Mars Hill to the community and the college, and they gave me a lot of opposition even though I cultivated their cooperation. They saw what we were doing in Hot Springs as 'socialized medicine' and attacked it. [W]e had a few ugly meetings there. Eventually, when they retired a few years ago the Hot Springs Health Program bought out their practice and buildings. It was a sweet victory."

Southwest Virginia. After earning her nursing degree, Beth Busam (Ronan) returned to southwest Virginia as a FOCIS member. She started the first home health service program in the area during her time at the Appalachian Regional Hospital (ARH) in Wise. "I always wanted to go back to the mountains. I wasn't interested in Chicago. The swinging bridge over the Powell River made more sense to me. . . . I was a new graduate and the day I passed State Board Exams I became Head Nurse in O.B. [at the ARH]. I was an instant expert, the only R.N. in the department. . . . Yeah, head nurse in a day!! It happened all so quickly. That was real good and I did learn a lot."

Linda Mashburn then recruited Beth, who left her job to do health fairs over the summer and returned in the fall. Beth recalled her motivations—both professional and personal—for choosing to work in Wise and with the health fairs:

Wise was one of the few hospitals in the Appalachian chain that didn't have home health . . . I wanted to do a home health program and they wanted to have one, so they let me start one. . . .

Before that in 1968, Patrick Ronan [was the first guy to officially join] FOCIS, [as] a Glenmary Brother in Dickenson County. [When] I came down after graduating from nursing school, he was there at a FOCIS meeting in June of 1969 in Big Stone Gap. . . . Glenmary men didn't like Patrick joining FOCIS since it was a dissident group of women. We were not to be trusted.

We all went out to dinner at the local fish house, and then at Christmas he asked me out. He was still a Brother, but he had to sing at this local Baptist church and wanted me to go with him. That was my first date: at a Baptist church at a potluck supper singing "And They'll Know We Are Christians by Our Love." . . . This "date" was Christmas of '69. . . . Through that spring he left Glenmary, and . . . he would come visit me at each of the health fairs. . . . It was really nice, and the last health fair we got engaged. It was the end of August; we got married in December of '70.

When Monica Appleby moved to Scott County in 1972, one of her first efforts was working with Anne Leibig and Dungannon area residents to develop a health clinic. Monica and a local Methodist minister recruited the Vanderbilt students to do a health fair in Dungannon. In its wake a lively community group came together and raised the funds to build a clinic. Anne helped with fundraising and became the first administrator of Clinch River Health Services in 1977.

The FOCIS-connected health centers introduced a new concept in rural primary care to the region: locally owned services controlled by communities rather than physicians in private practice—a market-driven model which had produced a chronic shortage of health-care facilities in Appalachia. Members further served as skilled professionals, which were also in short supply.

FOCIS members were able to bring resources from state medical schools, health departments, and the Appalachian Regional Commission to the rural communities to help build and staff the community clinics. The health clinics that grew from the health fairs represented the power of the FOCIS network. These clinics did not simply dispense treatment but inspired further development in the communities. For example, creation of the Dungannon clinic led to the development of a town water system and a community center and education program.

During the 1970s regulations and government resources encouraged development of community health programs. Later federal regulations began to emphasize cost-effective management, forcing a number of clinics to close or consolidate. Preventive health programs and community-building activities were no longer funded. It took very strong boards and local support to survive. The Hot Springs program even made the risky decision to forego federal funding and become self-supporting so they could continue their community mission unhampered by Reagan-era strictures.

Through the leadership of another new FOCIS member, Mary Herr, the FOCIS network was also tapped to support the development of legal aid clinics in the region. Mary entered FOCIS via the Sullivan Road group in Knoxville, after serving as a VISTA in Charleston, West Virginia. Mary lived in the house on Sullivan Road and helped to develop the recreation and arts program and coordinate the festival and craft fair at Epworth. Later she coordinated the newsletter and served as president of FOCIS in 1975. Mary recalled how Marie Cirillo got her involved in Clairfield early on:

I started going up to Clairfield because I had experience in bookkeeping and they were trying to get some groups like the pallet factory and Model Valley Mountain Crafts started. . . .

You know Marie, if she finds someone [with] a skill she recruits them. . . . So I just started going up there one day a week, then two days a week, and then eventually I moved up there. . . . in '70 or '71. All I got was a stipend from Marie but no job. Things in my life seem to evolve and I thought it was the thing to do and did it. It didn't cost a lot to live in Clairfield.

Mary spent her first two years in Clairfield doing on-the-job training in management, bookkeeping, and secretarial work. She succeeded in getting the State Area Vocational School to pay her to teach a typing and bookkeeping class there. This was a welcome first, as students had formerly been required to attend classes in Jacksboro—impossible for those without transportation. During this time Mary, who had a natural interest in "legal stuff," became increasingly aware of a lack of legal resources:

That was when all those people were trying to get their black lung benefits and miner's pensions, so we got Greg O'Connor, a lawyer, to come to Clairfield one day a week. So we got together and eventually I applied for a Ford Leadership Development Grant to help get training as a paralegal and open the legal services in that area. . . . Greg O'Connor would come up one day a week and I would be there the other times.

Eventually we got a grant from the Campaign for Human Development to hire a full-time attorney. So then I started training local people to work as paralegals, and then I started paralegal training in the region . . . with community groups. They wanted to do the same thing we had done in Clairfield . . . I taught people about dealing with black lung, Social Security disability, and miners' rights.

Because so many people in the valley received black lung or other benefits, legal services was a vital resource. Community activist Shelby York recalled the challenges in getting the program running:

We had a lot of disability people, trying to get disability services, trying to get black lung, trying to get the different benefits. We had people that should have been drawing Social Security ten years prior to coming to talk to us, but somebody in this valley had told them, "You can't draw Social Security, you can't draw that." It was people telling them that were just trying to keep power over people is what I call it. Just plain keep them under your thumb. But it took us about three years to overcome that and to get people to realize that you aren't obligated to nobody but yourself. So it worked.[5]

The Ford Foundation grant allowed Mary Herr to travel to Connecticut and California to study legal service provision at various institutions. Mary came back from her training convinced that the answer to the legal service needs in the region was to train more paralegals. She believed that legal assistants could advise people of their rights and help them obtain their benefits:

Since only one percent of this country's lawyers devote full-time to civil problems of the poor, it would appear to me that the gap between legal needs and services provided is at least as readily remedied by decreasing the demand for lawyers as it is by increasing their supply. I feel the use of legal paraprofessionals is an important way to bring about structural changes to alleviate the legal problems which plague all but the very rich in society and which, in effect, cripple the poor. I am interested in developing a training program which would enable local residents to do this without extensive college experience.[6]

By 1975 other communities in the region began seeking paralegal training and asked Mary for her help. She moved back to Knoxville and got a grant from the Commission on Religion in Appalachia (CORA) to expand her work. "I would go to [the communities] to do training, one week a month. I didn't go to Clairfield anymore; they were pretty well trained and set up. I went to Morgan County and Wartburg in Tennessee, kind of west and north of Oak Ridge, then would go up to Hazard and Hindman, Kentucky, then to Clintwood, Virginia, and to Cherokee, North Carolina."

When the CORA grant ended Mary coordinated and taught most of the courses for a program through the University of Tennessee and Manpower to give unemployed persons paralegal training. As this program came to a close, Mary wondered what she would do next. "Then I got a call from Kay French, who was one of the people I had trained in Cherokee, asking me if I would consider coming to work for them as a paralegal and community educator. I had kept connected with her and Yogi Crowe, because Yogi was someone I trained too.[7] So I said yes and moved to Cherokee in November of 1978."

Cherokee, North Carolina. The community of Cherokee held special interest for Mary. Some of her ancestors were Cherokee, and although she was not brought up as a Native American, she was interested in learning more about her Cherokee ancestry. As such, she welcomed the opportunity to live and work in Cherokee.

Cherokee is the major town on the Qualla Indian Boundary, which is the home of the Eastern Band of the Cherokee, and it is the administrative, business, and communal center of the Eastern Band. A popular tourist attraction, Cherokee has a large casino and an abundance of souvenir shops, but outside the town, up the hollers, and along the Oconoluftee River are several communities with more traditional lifestyles—including Big Cove, where Mary Herr settled: "Big Cove is the most isolated of the Cherokee communities and has the most full-blood and traditional Cherokee speaking people. I learned about Cherokee legends, foods, medicinal plants and philosophy from my neighbors and friends by their daily lives as we spent time together."[8]

Mary worked for legal services in Cherokee until 1981, when the Reagan administration began cutting back social welfare programs. She recalled the effects of those budget cuts:

They told us they had to reduce the staff from twenty-five down to seven [and] would have to close offices, and told us to start looking for other jobs. In February of '81, Frank Gardner came here as pastor at the Catholic church. . . . We had just formed a parish council and I was the first . . . president/chairperson. He offered me a job with the church doing what I basically did with legal services as a paralegal and community educator with community groups. I took a six thousand dollar salary cut, and I worked for Our Lady of Guadalupe Church in Cherokee until 1995.

In 1993 alone Mary helped more than 300 people obtain over $98,000 in retroactive disability benefits.[9] Yet her service has not been limited to legal aid. Over the years, Mary has been a founder or active participant in many groups focused on community improvement both for the Qualla Boundary and the region, including a local food co-op; the Coalition for Responsible Parenting; Friends of the Library; an advocacy group for residents with substance abuse problems; several spiritual and cultural preservation groups; the Swain County Council on the Status of Women; the Mountain Dispute Settlement Center; and the Swain/Qualla SAFE House. The SAFE House offers a full range of crisis and advocacy services including shelter, referral, counseling, day care and support groups. This important project was the first joint effort between the Native American and Anglo populations in the area.

In 1988 Mary became the first *Guardian ad litem* on Qualla Boundary. Part of a child advocacy program established in North Carolina in 1986, the guardians are trained community volunteers who work with attorney advocates to protect the interests of children in courts.

In nominating Mary for a Nancy Susan Reynolds Award for Personal Service, a colleague from Swain/Qualla SAFE wrote: "She doesn't sign her work like an artist. Most of the time she does her work in such a way that she herself gradually withdraws and, eventually, all the work is being done by the people themselves. The results of her efforts are everywhere. . . . She is always stimulating the process and the end result is independence, self-sufficiency and self-respect for Indian people." The same colleague said about Mary's work habits, "She works from sun-up till the wee hours, and she once told me, when I had the temerity to ask, that meetings *were* her social life."[10]

Mary assessed her time on the Qualla Boundary and the scope of her work there:

Reflecting over the last twenty years that I have lived and worked in Cherokee, . . . I realize that I have learned much more than I have taught and received much more than I have given. From the time I first came to Cherokee before making the decision to move here, it felt like home to me. The Cherokee people opened their hearts and homes to me. They were willing to accept the talents, skills and knowledge I had to offer them, but they also shared their traditions, gifts and spirituality with me.

In all of the places that I have lived, I have never felt the sense of belonging and being a part of the community that I do in Cherokee. It truly has become home to me.[11]

Big Stone Gap, Virginia. Another social service project was developed in the mid-1970s in Big Stone Gap, Virginia, by Catherine Rumschlag and Kathy Hutson. The FOCIS Center had been sold in Big Stone Gap, and with cuts in federal money many of the OEO programs in the county were being phased out. Catherine became aware of the severe housing shortage in the area and the need for shelter for homeless, transients, and families needing emergency housing. Her prayer group decided to form an intentional community with a common ministry. They bought land and a cluster of buildings near Big Stone Gap, which they named "Christ Hill." Emergency housing became their ministry.

Catherine Rumschlag explained the group's move toward focusing on emergency housing: "In 1982 we set up a new corporation, Appalachian Family Ministries, to operate the housing service. I have been director of this project since its beginnings. Kathy and I are the only members of the original Christ Hill Community who have continued to live and work in this area. Other people have helped with the ministry as volunteers, especially two women whom we first knew as residents of the shelter. . . . Other volunteers help with transportation, computer mailing, and maintenance work."

Ginny Remedi moved her pottery shop to Christ Hill and joined the community. She recalled how her craft became a type of social service there: "[O]ur ministry was mostly reaching out to people who were in need. My ministry as a potter in that community was one . . . of sharing God's light through the work that I did and the scripture passages that I put on the pottery."

Catherine and Kathy lived next to the shelter facilities until 1999, when both retired. They enlarged the facilities in 1990 to accommodate ten people and they housed from 100 to 120 people annually.

Even though Kathy continued to teach full time in the public schools, she was always "on call" at the shelter when at home. Her newsletter account, "Diary of an Assistant," recorded a single, typical evening:

November 5, 1990. I came home after a busy day at school. One car was at the shop and Catherine had the other—taking a friend to the doctor in Kingsport, Tennessee—about 40 miles away. A storm was predicted so I decided against my usual walk and started a fire, preparing for relaxation with a novel. I hoped that the six people staying at the shelter would assume we were not at home and I could rest till Catherine returned. But the evening procession could not be delayed.

A young husband who had been doing community service through the courts came in to report that he probably had gotten a job and would move in the next week. Within minutes after I returned to my comfortable position, another young man who had stayed with us and had been recently hospitalized knocked and announced his return. He would be leaving for a group home within the week. As I began cooking supper, our only mother and her baby came in. She had started in a new program to help the homeless get jobs. . . . She talked a little about school, got a package delivered earlier in the day, and used the telephone. As supper was well on the way, the hospital called. A couple was stranded and needed a place. I wanted to be sure that Catherine hadn't also accepted a call and was getting information from the hospital when Catherine drove up. The older couple shared our meal and asked about staying until their Social Security check arrived. They had hoped to find an old friend, but had not. Supper worked out well in that I had started with larger amounts of garden corn and beans and used all the hamburger.

It was about 8:30 before all the knocking and phone calls ended for the night.[12]

People who sought shelter at Christ Hill came in all varieties. Some were abused. Most were young and local. Unemployment, which waxed and waned elsewhere during their twenty-nine-year ministry, remained ever high in the coalfields, due to steady job losses in the mines. Noting their purpose was emergency service, in a 1992 interview Catherine acknowledged the occasional development of longer-lasting relationships with residents and exposed the speciousness of welfare reforms enacted later:[13]

[We] don't expect to change attitudes. . . . This one family which came here in 1981 with three kids, she's been sort of a part of the Christ Hill community. She lived on ADC [Aid to Dependent Children] and housing subsidies. When she was doing workfare she was assigned here as a volunteer. Now she has a full time job at minimum wages: she actually likes her job, but it's really hard [to make ends meet]. I think we made a difference in her life, but it's not so much the shelter as the association.[14]

Beginning in 1992 Christ Hill began hosting a monthly meeting of Woman-Church.[15] Organized by two Catholic nuns of another order who held the initial meeting at their home in neighboring Lee County, it is a gathering for prayer, discussion, and encouragement. Themes of meetings include feminist issues dealing with the organized church and religion, justice and peace, and ecology. The core group have become an important support to each other.

When they retired in 1999 Catherine and Kathy moved to Abingdon, Virginia, to begin creating the innovative community of older adults that they and FOCIS member Dene Peterson had been designing and planning for some years. Catherine noted their transition in the Christmas newsletter: "On July 10 about 30 people came and packed and ritualized the big change in our lives. We had a pot luck dinner and a prayer and remembering service, led by Anne Leibig and John Rausch. The packing took all day and a few people worked in the evening and Sunday morning. On Monday the movers came."[16]

To honor her twenty-nine years of service, the Wise County Chamber of Commerce named Catherine Rumschlag "Woman of the Year" in April 2000. Making the presentation, Chamber President Rita McReynolds acknowledged the compassion and ministry Catherine had shown to the community for so long:

People didn't come to the back door and get a hand-out at Christ Hill, they were treated like family. Through Rumschlag's skills and compassion she made a significant difference to the lives of the children and families she has served. Their children were cared for and they were shuttled to meetings, doctor's appointments and agencies to help them find clothing, furnishings, permanent homes and a new beginning. They were often served food that had been harvested from the large garden maintained on the property. The assistance Rumschlag gave to others was not a once-in-awhile activity but rather an ongoing lifestyle that continued every day of the year. For many years the Chamber referred inquiries from the homeless to Christ Hill. We are now honoring the caring and trusting woman who opened her doors to those in need. She truly personifies Wise County's commitment of a caring community that honors a person's dignity in a time of need.[17]

Chapter 11

COMMUNITY-BASED EDUCATION

I was learning so much, linking intellectually and practically when we were doing this work.

The Glenmary Sisters' community educational work started with the Bible schools, which evolved into community meetings and discussion sessions. As both Glenmary and FOCIS they provided access to rural Appalachian communities for college students largely from Catholic colleges. At first they used the student volunteers to help with their mission work, but as FOCIS, they developed this activity into an educational field study program. Working with grassroots community groups dealing with major economic and social problems, they were able to provide students with rich educational experience which, for many, changed their lives. The students also had skills needed in the communities, and they found themselves doing important work, making a real difference. Their education was "relevant," quite different from the traditional classroom where learning is separated from doing, theory from practice, and education from work.

As FOCIS members became involved in the communities, they found educational needs and began to address them. They worked with citizen groups, many of which were led by low-income women, who were anxious to improve their own education. Together they developed community-based education programs, which they located in abandoned depots, company stores, or old school buildings, which became community learning centers. The local women organizers became the first students. The programs offered literacy, GED (General Education Diploma, the high school equivalency degree), and college courses through local community college outreach programs.

The communities had lost their economic base of mining, manufacturing, or farming, and these learning centers provided a place for community discussions, a space where residents could come together to analyze their region's problems and strategize ways of improving the quality of life in the community. Since many of the students were women, the centers provided a women's support service along with leadership development training.

The FOCIS women had been influenced by Paulo Freire's pedagogy and the philosophy of community-based education, which included experiential education, community control, and education for social change. All this found expression in the community education programs and the development of an Appalachian University Without Walls, which gave credit for life experiences.

Just as the Glenmary Sisters sought to reform the church, FOCIS women sought to bring reforms to the public educational system. In addition to providing field study experiences for college students and alternative community-based education programs in the rural communities, FOCIS women worked in the public schools to bring in new educational practices: teaching art, music, drama, speech therapy, and special education. They became part of the Appalachian Studies movement developing in the area, bringing together Appalachian scholars, activists, and community people. They developed Appalachian Studies curricula and helped finance these ventures by developing a non-profit organization, the Clinch River Education Center (CREC), which sought funding for teachers, artists, and community leaders to produce programs for schools and community.

Because FOCIS members lived in Appalachian communities, they were well situated to provide field study experiences for students from Catholic colleges who came to the region as volunteers. Earlier the Glenmary missions in Appalachia used college and high school students as volunteers in their summer work: helping with Bible schools, Headstart, and other projects which the Sisters organized first through the parishes and then through the OEO programs in which they were involved. As Appalachia made the news as the "poverty pocket" of the nation, student groups from other colleges and universities wanted to come to the mountains to help and learn about the problems of the region.

In 1969 FOCIS members Anne Leibig and Karen Linzmaier, based in Big Stone Gap, joined two instructors from Clinch Valley College, Tom Robinson and Betty Wham, to set up what they called an Institute for Cultural Exchange to provide college students with "an educational experience that is developed from the 'everyday life' of people in Wise County, Virginia. It is our belief that the life style of the people in this central area of Appalachia is unique. The mountaineer culture is a contribution to America and sharing in the life of this area is an educational event."[1] They planned a program, recruited host families, and hosted a group of students in January 1969 from the College of Saint Benedict, Saint John's University, Saint John Fisher College, and Colgate University. Participants' evaluations were strong and requests for educational experiences came from other colleges. In 1971 while she was in Massachusetts, Monica Appleby met weekly with a group from the Lincoln Filene Center at Tufts University who wanted to develop an Appalachian unit for their program in minority relations. Monica had completed her studies at the Harvard Graduate School of Education in the previous year, receiving a master's in community education. The director of the Tufts program accompanied Monica to the mountains and recorded interviews with people there and in Cincinnati, which were used to develop curriculum materials for the classroom. A group of high school students from Wellesley, Massachusetts, participated in the pilot project.[2] They visited the region and later hosted a return visit by students from Clinch Valley College. Clinch Valley students commented in a radio interview that students from Wellesley and Boston had come to the Appalachian Mountains to observe poverty, and they were returning the visit to Massachusetts to observe wealth and try to understand why some areas were poor and some were rich.[3] Jean Luce helped set up the arrangements in Massachusetts. Helen Lewis of Clinch Valley College traveled north with the students.

From 1969 to 1972 the FOCIS Center in Big Stone Gap, Virginia, served as an Appalachian field center for the Union for Experimenting Colleges and Universities.[4] The field center developed programs for students from Hofstra, Stephens, Antioch, and other colleges. Students spent from one month to a year working in community-based projects, learning and receiving credits.

In Virginia there was an extensive support base for student volunteers. In the Virginia FOCIS newsletters for 1970–1971, nineteen students were mentioned as staying with families and working in communities as part of their study program. After thirty years many are still in touch, grateful for their learning experience provided by FOCIS connections. Rich Henighan came to Big Stone Gap as a student volunteer and returned as a conscientious objector to do alternative service. He spent two years working with Anne Leibig on the Religious Research project. Afterwards he received a master's in community psychology from Vanderbilt University and wrote his thesis, "Coaldale's Religion," based on his experience in Big Stone Gap. He continues to live and work in Knoxville, Tennessee.

Clairfield, Tennessee, also has had a long history of providing educational placements for students and has hosted many volunteers. Marie Cirillo became an important mentor for numbers of students as she made use of their skills to improve the community. In 1971 she had Vanderbilt student volunteers do research to uncover many of the legal, land, and health issues in the

Clearfork Valley. Not only did their research produce change in the communities, but in the process the volunteers themselves learned things that impacted their lives. Sociologist John Gaventa[5] reflected on his experience:

> I had been on a very different path when I went to Clairfield. I had been taken by Chancellor Heard [of Vanderbilt University] to the White House when he did the mission on student unrest. I had been student body president at Vanderbilt, and I was on a more traditional upwardly mobile career path. I knew something wasn't right with it, and the whole summer in Washington I was disillusioned about what could be done. So I came back and got with friends at the Student Health Coalition and got involved—so that next summer and after that was so different and so much more rewarding and challenging. It was what I wanted to do. That period of time was so exciting. I was learning so much, linking intellectually and practically when we were doing this work. It has affected my work ever since. I would attribute Marie for being the support base, and several of the FOCIS women for being supportive. I think there is a long history of Marie encouraging, influencing, and supporting. She was always making contacts, bringing in resources, contacts to people outside.[6]

Caroline Kennedy worked with a video documentation project as a student volunteer in 1973. Her group produced a history on the effect of

Caroline Kennedy, summer intern at Clairfield, Tennessee, 1972, visiting with Pauline Huddleston.

coal on the land and people in three coal camps. She said, "Marie was really an inspiration to me. Her commitment to her work was so complete. Marie genuinely loves the area and the people. It is not like work to her."[7] Caroline has stayed in touch with Marie, who attended Caroline's wedding. Earlier, FOCIS shared another tie with the Kennedy family when a Robert Kennedy Memorial Fund intern came to Clairfield to assist with economic development projects.

Patricia Ronan, daughter of FOCIS parents Beth and Patrick Ronan, volunteered in Clairfield when she was seventeen. She came to appreciate the role members played in their communities: "I saw a lot how community organizing can work. None of the people in FOCIS were natives of Appalachia but their attitude was not, 'Here are these outside experts.' It was, 'Here are these people who want to live with you, and your problems are our problems.' I realized that when one moves, one is never going to be completely native. But you can take on things and you can become a part to some extent, but never completely."

In Clairfield Marie devised a way to combine the education and volunteer program with community development work through the Living Learning Center. Students from around the country spend working vacations in Clairfield and the entire community becomes their educational laboratory.

In 1990 the Living Learning Center hosted an international rural group and a national housing group. Global Exchange spent four days in the valley. The Center has contacts with other international programs: Heifer Project International, World Vision, and Save the Children Federation. They have hosted resident families from India.

Marie has worked with a regional coalition of private colleges to design Appalachian-Based Community Development Education (ABCDE), in which students and faculty from five Appalachian colleges work with communities in Virginia, Kentucky, and Tennessee. ABCDE is a partnership between communities and colleges to recruit volunteers and resources for the region and develop hands-on education for the volunteers. Some of the colleges have elaborated on this idea and recruited other community groups as partners in a new organization to create a model for participatory research related to sustainable community development.[8]

Marie's most recent project pulls together the ABCDE education and volunteer program with the Woodland Community Land Trust and the new land it has recently obtained in Eagan, Tennessee. (See chapter 13 for the story of the Land Trust.) Marie always works from the "big picture," attempting to link people, projects and movements, locally, regionally and globally.

In 1992 the Huber Land Company turned over an old school building and twelve acres of land for the use of Eagan's residents. Marie secured funding to establish a communication center in an unused building to provide computer, phone, fax, copier, and video services to the community. The communications center supported Eagan's efforts to initiate an oral history program, restore the old school, and begin a development project. Eagan native Mrs. Corella Bonner of the Bonner Foundation has provided a personal grant to begin renovation of the Eagan School as an education center and site for student interns. The Foundation's main program underwrites colleges' provision of student service to communities. Marie, Mrs. Bonner, and the ABCDE colleges' designs for a program involving these elements have become the basis for establishing the Clearfork Community Institute, the planning and development of which will be funded by a grant from the Appalachian Regional Commission. The Institute will include the Eagan School, the one remaining coal camp school building in the valley, and the 160–acre mountain, to be used for environmental education, which was purchased by the Woodland Land Trust in order to save it from being clear cut. Marie has brought all the groups in the valley together in the planning process. She shared her vision for the facility:

Clearfork Institute will be a physical center from which strategic development education can be achieved. The building itself will manage the training for a local sustainable economy, will be the repository of our history, the research center for environmental works, the cultural center for community enrichment. The center includes a mountain to be healed, a settlement to be built, a forest to be managed for sustainable development, sacred places from which to renew love as a culmination of life-giving power. . . . [T]his indoor and outdoor space will support our efforts to make the transition from a fossil fuel based economy to another. Together, with books in a library and spoil piles on the mountain, we will come to know where we have been and to consider where we want to go. We will give new life to our land and put new information on our shelves.[9]

Working with volunteers and students in the region, FOCIS members in southwest Virginia became interested in developing a program in which residents who hosted and taught these visitors could also receive college recognition for their skills and competencies. Since the students were getting credit for their activities, it seemed only fair that hosts should, too. In the early 1970s the Union for Experimenting Colleges and Universities was beginning to develop the University Without Walls (UWW) program. The nontraditional program was designed for adults who could not or would not attend a more conventional college. It would give some direction to these students and help them obtain a degree through a personalized process that was egalitarian and academically sound.[10]

Monica Appleby used a Ford Foundation fellowship to help start an Appalachian UWW program (AUWW) through the existing Appalachian Field Study Center in 1972. The founders aimed to create a "process of educative action for mountain people in their home communities," "build a network of people, organizations and institutions" to serve as a resource, and help residents "obtain a college education in a manner that fits their life condition and . . . aids Appalachian community development."[11] AUWW affiliated with Roger Williams College in Bristol, Rhode Island, as the degree-granting institution. When Monica and Helen Lewis moved to The River Farm near Dungannon earlier in 1972, they formed the Clinch River Education Center (CREC) to sponsor both the AUWW and field study programs.

AUWW's brochure lauded the program's scope and diversity:

[O]ur students combine their educational experiences into total educational programs that help them develop the skills, competencies and creative talents that they feel are the most important to them. . . . [W]e have students learning cooperative management skills, developing community arts programs, designing training programs for paralegals, putting craft skills to work in local elementary schools and developing creative early childhood education programs.[12]

A 1974 newspaper article described the institution in full swing:

For the past 18 months, completely without publicity, a branch of a major Eastern university has been operating in the mountains of Scott County.

The "new" college sports no glistening laboratories, no bustling campus, no corridors of classrooms and offices. It's the last place anyone would look for an ivory tower.

It's called the Clinch River Educational Cooperative, and it sits at the bottom of a narrow, winding trail, flanked by the Clinch River on one hand and mountains on the other. Not every car can cover the tortuous half-mile of rocky road leading to the school, which can't be seen from the road.

But the Farm, as it is sometimes called, is making itself increasingly visible throughout Scott, Wise, and Lee Counties.

Its 30 organizers, facilitators, advisor-teachers, and students have undertaken studies and sponsored programs ranging from Black Lung benefit seminars to mountain music revival sessions. The thread that holds the subjects and the Farm together is basic: the cultivation of an awareness among mountain people of their environment, their heritage, and their role in determining their own future. . . .

There are no "classes" or "teachers" at Clinch River. The entry requirements are just as informal. Depending on previous college experience and other factors, a student enrolled at the college can graduate with a Bachelor of Arts degree in Appalachian Studies in from nine to 48 months. Possible areas of study include community organization around environmental, health, welfare, legal, and economic issues; farm development and land reform; transportation, food service, home construction and repair, and crafts co-ops; and mountain arts.

The difference between studying at Clinch River and other institutions is action. In a conventional class, a student studies ways to implement recruitment drives for potential Black Lung recipients, for instance. At Clinch River, the student, aided by lawyers, health officials, and other facilitators, conducts the drive.

"We don't try and teach anything here. We simply hook the student up with the resources he needs to get things done," says Mrs. Appleby.[13]

The program began with thirteen students from five states. Nine were women.

Enrollees earned credit recognition for prior work with community and regional organizations, filmmaking, paralegal training, subsistence farming, house building, and other endeavors germane to the region's life and growth. The students used their experiences to make education work for social change in the mountains. During the five-year life of the program, nineteen students received bachelors' degrees, in the areas of community education, special education, music, art, human services, psychology, social work, filmmaking, women's studies, communications, and legal aid.[14] FOCIS members and faculty friends from Clinch Valley and other nearby colleges volunteered as mentors and teachers. However, insufficient financial support limited the number of students who could participate and eventually doomed the fledgling institution. Even with years of effort, Monica and the other founders could not find the backing AUWW needed to survive. In 1974 internal changes led Roger Williams College to transfer AUWW's affiliation to UWW/Providence; then because of logistical and financial problems UWW/Providence urged AUWW to find a regional college with which to affiliate. For a while it looked as though the AUWW had reached an agreement with West Virginia's Jesuit-run Wheeling College, but because of budgetary problems the deal did not materialize.[15]

Even though college representatives gathered at the Highlander Center in crisis mode to try to create a regional consortium and Monica developed a widely endorsed planning committee–advisory board structure to undertake a feasibility study for a "Rural College of Appalachia," no institution was willing to take on the responsibility of sponsoring or spearheading the effort. The demise of the AUWW in 1977 was a great frustration to FOCIS members. They had developed an alternative institution with exciting promise for the region, but lacked the clout and access to a financial base to assure its survival.

In 1997, twenty years after the end of AUWW, Beth Bingman of The River Farm was awarded a Kellogg International Leadership grant to study and potentially create educational opportunities for adults in the region who could have been served by a UWW structure. The community college systems in Virginia, Tennessee, and Kentucky provide some help for the first two years of post-secondary education, but many citizens are still left without credentials for better employment or simply compensation for skills they possess. Beth formed a committee of women seeking an external degree program. The committee surveyed existing college offerings and sought to work out arrangements for some of its members to further their education. The committee members also work as a support system for each other, sponsoring a study group to learn about new programs in distance education and explore other possible ways to meet their needs.

What began as a program to educate outside students about Appalachia built interest in developing Appalachian Studies for Appalachians. The local families and students who helped with the programs were empowered by teaching others their history, showing and explaining the problems of the region, and giving the visitors an appreciation of their culture. Monica Appleby crafted a proposal to provide Appalachian Studies for residents which was not fully funded but which spurred cultural work in the schools.

Monica and the Scott County group of musicians, folklorists, storytellers, local historians, and community educators who had been involved with the FOCIS ARTS program had formed the Clinch River Educational Center (CREC) in part to develop an Appalachian culture revitalization program for elementary and secondary schools. The program was designed to "create spaces for the contemporary carriers of mountain culture— musicians, outdoorsmen, storytellers, craftswomen—in the school system, thus . . . re-structuring the system itself to allow for community participation."[16] They sought funding to develop materials in print, video, and film for use by teachers and curriculum planners. They also supported a proposal for an Ethnic Heritage Studies project developed by Dilenowisco, southwest Virginia's five-county educational cooperative. Even though the entire plan was never funded, many of the group worked with the Dilenowisco program in a number of the region's schools. They also worked closely with the Appalachian Studies Program at Clinch Valley College developed by Helen Lewis in 1969.

Currently comprising about a dozen women as members, CREC has continued to serve the region as a flow-through non-profit to fund educational and training programs, including artists in the schools, performance artists, and rural peer-to-peer Maternal and Infant Health Care projects in four states. CREC provides fellowships and resources to groups and individual women who generate such programs. CREC established the Helen Lewis Leadership Development Award to support Helen while she worked with the community of Ivanhoe, Virginia, to write their history in the 1980s. Recently the organization provided computers to help two women community leaders in their work.

Anne Leibig has been the main FOCIS person in the Dungannon area, acting as organizer, catalyst, and even town manager. In 1977 she became manager of Clinch River Health Services, acting town manager for the town council, and chairperson of the Dungannon Women's Club Development Committee. In the latter role she inspired and oversaw the moving and refurbishment of the old train depot to a central spot in town where it became a community education center. The center became known as the "Depot," and Anne taught classes there along with other FOCIS members and River Farm residents: Helen Lewis, Rich Kirby, Beth Bingman, and Father John Rausch. With community involvement they created Project READ, an adult education/literacy program that was featured on a PBS program. Mountain Empire Community College in Big Stone Gap offered developmental programs, career studies, and certificate and associate degrees through the Depot. The building became a lively women's center, as about thirty women taking GED and college classes used it as a meeting place for mutual support. Quite a number were able to get their two-year degrees from Mountain Empire through the Depot. Carol Honeycutt, who earned her diploma through the Depot, recalled the big difference the program made in her life: "I got married when I was eighteen and moved in with my in-laws. . . . I had no house to run, no children to watch and a husband who was Mr. Independent. So for about

Helen Lewis and Lara Collis, Highlander intern, at Dungannon Depot Education Center, where Helen taught college classes, 1996.

five to six years I just sat around the house. And I gained about eighty pounds and I watched soap operas and I became a parasite; just living off the TV and the food and not doing much of anything . . . until I was so disgusted with myself that I even thought; 'Well I might as well just end my life because I'm not contributing to anything.'"

At this point, without giving it much thought, Carol signed up for some of the courses at the Depot she had vaguely heard about. Taking classes provided her with a new sense of self-esteem and opened her eyes to many previously unknown possibilities:

Education was a whole new life. New ideas such as: a woman does not have to have a home, children, or even a husband to be a worthwhile, completely whole, self-sufficient human. . . . I learned many things by going back to school and much of it was not in a text.

Taking classes at the Depot gave me a self-confidence that I had never had. I was at one time so shy and awkward. I wouldn't even order a hamburger for myself. It also helped me realize I wasn't quite as stupid as I thought. I finished my classes this year with a 3.56 GPA. That makes me feel very proud. One important thing my classes helped me do was get involved with my community.

Whatever I do with my life from here on out, I'll always be grateful for a second chance at education. Education had shaped me into a new complete person.

Here is a poem I wrote about the Depot education program:

"Classes at the Depot"

First Quarter:
I saw her walk into the classroom with her head and eyes down,
And she neither looked left or right.
She had her books clutched protectively to her chest.
And when the teacher asked her a question, she answered,
"I don't know," in a pleading voice.
She got a B in history.

Second Quarter:
I saw her walk into the classroom
And she glanced up and risked a shy, quick smile at me and turned a
    bright red.
And when the teacher asked her a question, she answered,
"I'm not sure, but I think it's this."
She got a B+ in math.

Third Quarter:
I saw her walk into the classroom with her head held high;
And everyone called her name and she yelled back, "Hello!" to
    everyone.
And when the teacher said, "Look, this is the way it is."
She said, "Excuse me, I think you're wrong."
And she got an A in English.[17]

The community-based education programs in both Virginia and Tennessee developed curricula to provide rural leadership competencies, skills, and knowledge needed for living and working in rural Appalachian communities. These were the communities in the more isolated parts of their counties that had been neglected and by-passed by more recent development. The community-based programs provided education for those who had been left out, pushed out, or dropped out of the education system.

In Tennessee, Marie Cirillo and others brought together the women's groups that had focused around crafts and thrift shops to talk about next steps. The new coalition called itself Mountain Women's Exchange (MWE) and decided to focus on a way of doing education in which they had a voice. MWE first contracted with Roan State Community College, in Harriman, Tennessee, to conduct courses at the storefront where they were based. Later, Carson Newman College in Jefferson City, Tennessee, agreed to offer classes, and MWE controlled the curriculum. The women developed an integrated community education program including literacy, GED and college courses, children's theater and education, and support groups on domestic violence. The education program, now housed in a former church building, has made it possible for many local students to complete college courses and degrees.

In 1985, through a class they taught at Mountain Women's Exchange, Helen Lewis and John Gaventa developed a participatory community-based economics education program to support development in grassroots communities. The syllabus was published as *The Jellico Handbook: A Teacher's Guide to Community-Based Economics.*[18] The handbook was designed to be used in the community college outreach classes in the rural communities. The members of the class not only studied community development but also researched their own community and strategized to make changes. The class was designed to provide skills that would enable and empower the students to analyze economic problems and to devise strategies to participate in, change, and/or develop their own local economy. The methods included oral histories to illustrate economic changes through peoples' own experiences; community surveys to develop research skills and help participants state and prioritize the problems to be addressed; and community mapping and drawings to help students analyze current problems and relationships in the community as well as to articulate visions for the future.

In addition to developing community-based educational programs, a number of FOCIS members taught and provided new services in the public schools. Appalachian schools were in need of trained teachers; in the 1960s and '70s there were essentially no teachers in special education, art, or other specialized areas. Kathy Hutson, the first non-Glenmary woman to join FOCIS, worked for thirty-three years in the public schools of southwest Virginia. For many of those years she was the only speech therapist in the region. When Kathy was not accepted as a Glenmary Sister, she was encouraged by Monica Appleby, superior at Holy Cross Center in Big Stone Gap, to come as a volunteer and apply for a teaching position in Wise County. She had degrees in speech and special education, and since the national Elementary and Secondary Education Act had just been passed, it was anticipated that there would be pressure on schools to develop programs for children with special needs.

Kathy recounted her legendary story of the challenges she faced as a groundbreaker in her field:

I talked first with some people in Wise who knew about the needs of special children. One of them said, "You are barking up the wrong tree; they will never start special education here in these schools."

Well that kind of made me angry. . . . so I went straight to the [school] superintendent's office. I was so naive, I just walked in and told him I was a speech therapist. He asked what a speech therapist does; he had never met one. I told him. And . . . he said it happened the school board was meeting the very next day. . . . he said, "I will put you on the agenda and if you can talk them into it you can have the job." . . .

Most of the questions they asked were, Had I ever been a Sister? Was I going to be a Sister? I said no. . . . I think I am the first Catholic they hired. It was 1965. They knew that money was coming and . . . they knew some new things were going to happen. . . .

There was a superintendent, assistant superintendent, two secretaries, and a book-keeper, and that was the school board personnel. They had never hired anybody except classroom teachers. They didn't have librarians, they didn't have special read-ing, they didn't have any special education . . . none. . . . they said I could come. I think my starting salary was $2,400 for the year; . . . it was really low; all salaries were low here. . . . my mother said, "What did I send you to school for?" . . .

As the first one who ever worked in special education in the county, I had no forms or supervision. I had four schools, and there were serious, serious problem kids, big tall kids in the back of the classroom. . . . I became the only person who would deal with these kids so I had lots and lots . . . with serious problems, as well as those with minor ordinary speech problems. After the first year we had a woman who became a social worker who had a retarded brother. So we started a retarded children's group with other local mothers. [T]hen she and I . . . and some others started working on a tutoring program in the one-room schools. We had a lot of tiny schools, . . . and so sometimes on Saturdays I would work with the tutors, showing them how to work with the kids with speech problems. Sometimes I would go to the kids' homes. . . .

Of course, I wasn't really sure at the time what to do. I had some ideas, but [the problems] were much more serious than most of the kids I had seen in my Saint Louis practice teaching. So it felt like a pretty big load. I didn't have the support; I mean there wasn't even anybody who asked what I did, because they didn't know what I did. So periodically I would go and visit the superintendent and tell him what I was doing. That got me in trouble, because by then parents had started demanding services for their children—kids had so many needs. And it put me in the middle. I was biting the hand that was funding me.

After three years Kathy decided to go to Vanderbilt University to graduate school. When she asked about pursuing a higher degree, the school authorities asked her to resign. She remembers being "totally burnt out by the work," and convinced that the schools were not going to start the programs they needed. "They really didn't want to make things better and it was frustrating."

She was at Vanderbilt for three years when a new educational resource center (called Dilenowisco) was established in Wise County, Virginia, funded by the Appalachian Regional Commission. A group of teachers went to Nashville and talked her into returning to Wise County and working with them in what they hoped would be big and exciting changes in the schools of southwest Virginia. They would be working with five school divisions. Kathy joined this enthusiastic and energetic group who, as she said, "wanted to get all this new stuff going":

One of the big grants was to start hiring the first psychologists, speech therapists, teachers for the deaf, and they couldn't find all these. They knew about me. My understanding is the superintendent told them, "She will work like the devil for you but I don't know if she is worth the trouble."

I worked with five superintendents when I came back. I was one speech therapist working in the sixty-five schools. I was trying to show other people what to do. And I had the idea that the way is to train other people. . . . I worked with one group a month in each school. Now each of these districts have speech therapists, so there are twenty-five people doing what I did.

FOCIS women like Kathy Hutson brought new ideas, new programs, and changes to the traditional education system. Because they also lived and worked in the communities with parents and concerned citizens, they developed public demand for services for students with special needs and organized support for better education throughout the region.

In retrospect, FOCIS made contributions in the fields of service learning, special needs, community-based education, and Appalachian Studies. They created a model for student volunteers in which local communities participated actively in hosting and educating the visitors. Valuable organizations created by FOCIS continue to function: the Clinch River Educational Center and the Clearfork Institute with the Appalachian-Based Community Development Education program. Graduates from the short-lived University Without Walls have become leaders in the region as filmmakers, teachers, community development workers, and artists. These include Mimi Pickering at Appalshop; Jack Wright at Ohio University; Mary Herr in Cherokee; Joyce Dukes at the Commission on Religion in Appalachia; and Marty Newell, co-director of the Rural Education Network at the Appalachian Center of the University of Kentucky.[19]

Chapter 12

COMMUNITY-BASED ECONOMIC DEVELOPMENT

Well, look, if you hadn't tried to start a factory you never would have gotten that forty acres, and if you hadn't gotten those forty acres you'd never have this village square, you'd never have twenty homes built.

As the economy was being restructured, many Appalachian communities where the FOCIS women lived lost their economic base. Unemployment was high, young people were leaving, and there was a great need to develop more job opportunities and stop the general economic decline. In response local citizen groups had sprung up to try to develop economic alternatives and improve the quality of life in the community. FOCIS women joined with them to work for community improvement. Since many of the community leaders lacked the educational background and skills that would be helpful for identifying and implementing economic development, FOCIS worked with them to first develop the educational programs described in chapter 11.

As community members developed skills and understanding, they gained confidence to try to rebuild and revitalize their communities. Many of the community development strategies were not only creative but also very different from the mainstream industrial development model, which sought to build industrial parks and recruit outside factories. They created new approaches to economic development, concentrating particularly on ways to develop human capital, services to meet the needs of families in the community, and home-grown industries. From their own economic experiences, women tended to define "development" in holistic terms, including not only jobs and income but also education and human development.

Beginning some of the first community development corporations (CDCs) in the region, FOCIS members worked to provide jobs and economic opportunities. Some of these developments, which included craft production, a restaurant, sewing factory, laundry, and housing projects, survived for seventeen years, and others are still operating. While in operation each of the programs helped provide income and a means of survival for a number of people. They all fostered development of community services and infrastructure, bringing to residents not only important technical and structural development such as roads or water but also intangible benefits like personal development and management experience, which they used in later development programs. They became educated about development policies and encountered the barriers rural communities face: They found that they could develop some community services and educational programs, but they still lacked access to capital and other resources needed to do substantial economic development. They began to challenge development policies, including the manner in which development money and resources were distributed to rural areas. Although they did not change the economic system, they made a difference in the quality of life in the community: houses were repaired and built, water systems were developed, health care and education were improved, recreation programs were started, some home-grown businesses provided jobs, and community spirit was revived.

The first major economic development project by a FOCIS member was the Bread and Chicken House, a bakery-restaurant cooperative started by Catherine Rumschlag and a group of women from the Big Stone Gap–Appalachia area in 1971.

While working with a local craft group, Catherine conceived the possibility of producing food products. Though talented at craft-making, the women were even more skilled at cooking and baking. With no bakery in town, Catherine envisioned putting the women's skills to work filling what she felt would be a strong local market for baked goods. She recalled the origins of the cooperative:

I had a long-standing interest in cooperatives, and we discussed starting a bakery as a workers' cooperative. I learned that a local restaurant had excellent bakery equipment that was little used. I went to Mr. Frank DeMoisey, the owner, and he suggested that I bake for him on a part-time basis. He would market the products and pay by the hour, and I would gain some experience with baking in this area.

I did this for several months and then Mr. DeMoisey decided to sell the restaurant. He also planned to sell a smaller business, "Mr. D's Chicken House," which operated out of a small building behind the restaurant. He suggested that we take over the chicken carryout and combine it with the bakery business. Four of the women in the sewing group made a commitment to the project, and we invited one more woman to join us. She was Oaklee Foster, who had been the chief cook at DeMoisey's restaurant and was living on unemployment compensation since the restaurant was closed. We agreed to pay Oaklee the amount she was getting from compensation, while the other members would work as volunteers to get the business started. Two members were working full time at a sewing factory, but donated time after work to the new business.

The Bread and Chicken House was legally incorporated as a workers' cooperative. Founding members besides myself and Oaklee were: Illinoise Mitchell, a Black woman who had been manager of the kitchen in the Black school before integration. She had also been cook and baker for private families at different times. She had jobs in the community action program, and when those funds were cut she worked in the sewing factory. Harriet Bush was also Black and the mother of eight children. Her husband had been injured in the mines and she worked in the sewing factory. Alberta Stanley lived in Derby, a mining camp. She was the wife of Jim Stanley, who played guitar and sang at many events sponsored by Glenmary Sisters and FOCIS. Jim Stanley and Willie Bush, Harriet's husband, did many errands and odd jobs around the Bread and Chicken House in the early days.

The business opened March 11, 1971. The FOCIS group loaned $2,500 to the business to pay our first bills. None of the members had any capital. We paid our bills out of the day's receipts. The chicken carryout business picked up quicker than the bakery, since it already had a clientele. But before many weeks had passed we felt the need of a full-time baker, so Illinoise quit her job at the sewing factory and took up her position in the bakery. I was the manager, and also filled in with baking, cooking, or selling as required. Oaklee was the main salesperson, and she also processed the "broasted" chicken and potatoes in the front of the shop. Alberta made slaw and potato salad, and helped with baking and selling as needed. We were quite excited about having our own business.

Two years later a progressive regional magazine gave the establishment a rave review: "The Bread and Chicken House deserves its reputation as one of the best places in southwest Virginia to eat. . . . Baked goods, chicken, sandwiches and specials are for sale. People who work in Big Stone Gap, where it is located, come there to buy carry out lunches."[1]

With such glowing recommendations, the cooperative grew quickly. Its success allowed it to hire additional people and offer an hourly salary to its workers:

We began paying all workers an hourly wage, beginning at somewhat less than minimum wage because we needed to economize to obtain things . . . to carry on the business. We also began to buy the building and equipment, making monthly payments. There was a good spirit of cooperation among the workers and when we had difficulty paying the bills, the members of the cooperative cut their own wages so that we could make it. We operated at a loss the first year but after that we made a small profit. We received a grant of ten thousand dollars from the Campaign for Human Development, which was a great help.

The business grew and we hired more people. Some became members of the cooperative and some did not. Most of the workers were women. We were crowded in the little shop and we dreamed of a larger, more efficient place. When a building which housed a restaurant and bakery became available, we sold our building, obtained a grant of ten thousand dollars and moved and renovated the new place. We moved in the spring of 1977.

I wanted to work only part time, so we hired a manager. I also received a scholarship for a program at Notre Dame University, and I arranged to go there in August of 1978. When I came home for Christmas break, I realized that the Bread and Chicken House was in serious financial trouble, so I felt I should help out by taking over the bakery and trying to make it more profitable. We also received another grant of ten thousand dollars [from CORA (Commission on Religion in Appalachia)] to help catch up on some bills and improve the cash flow. As things improved I again went to part-time work, but the manager had many family and personal problems and the local economy became more depressed and competition increased. After seventeen years of operation, the Bread and Chicken House closed and the building went back to the original owner.

The five women who started the project continued until the business closed, except Illinoise who retired (she was over seventy years old) and Oaklee who died of cancer before the change of location. Alberta took a job as cook for teenage boys in a resident program and Harriet worked part time for a program for older citizens.

At the height of the operation we had from fifteen to twenty workers. Salaries were not much more than minimum wage, but we did try to be considerate of workers' needs. . . . In starting this business, I thought it would be more simple than being head of a religious community, but I found that the administrative duties were surprisingly similar, especially the personnel responsibilities.

As the co-op closed some of the staff reflected on the experience. Harriet Bush remembered how shy she was when they began the business: "I was scared to death. I was a quiet person, off to myself a lot, and it was the hardest thing in the world for me to ask those customers what they wanted." Her seventeen years at the Bread and Chicken House helped her become active in community affairs and a confident public speaker.[2]

Economist and FOCIS member Father John Rausch evaluated the business after its closure for Mountain Management Institute, a provider of support services to community enterprises:

When the [Bread and Chicken House] began nearly a generation ago, there were no fast food outlets in town. Now Big Stone Gap supports a variety of hamburger, chicken and pizza places that competitively cut into the co-op's business. Its aging equipment and sometimes inefficient ways also robbed it of real business vitality.

While business analysts might criticize the cooperative for their lack of market savvy, many community people recognize their contribution. They created jobs with dignity. The jobs allowed workers to offer ideas and participate in decision making about the work place. They practiced flexibility about schedules because of family situations. The co-op stressed a commitment to community and frequently advertised school or community programs, helped with contributions of food. Coupled with work place democracy and respect for workers they contrasted sharply with outside corporations that prowl Appalachia extracting the mineral wealth at the least cost.

The co-op promoted personal development and workers learned practical business skills. The co-op also inspired other community groups. Bread and Chicken received visitors literally from all over the world. Scores of people from southern Africa to Nicaragua have seen the B & C during its seventeen-year history and have left excited and motivated. Their lessons will filter into future community efforts. Despite their business problems, their alternative vision remains their legacy.[3]

In addition to its economic contributions, Bread and Chicken House was also important in breaking social barriers. It was a woman-owned business and a racially integrated cooperative, both firsts for the community and region. It provided a livelihood for fifteen to twenty women for seventeen years.

As noted in chapter 8, Anne Leibig organized one of the first Community Development Corporations (CDCs) in the area. In addition to Bread and Chicken and other community groups, Appalachia Community Development Corporation included the Appalachia Builder's Co-op, created by unemployed coal miners and young men in the community. The co-op started from two years of evening carpentry work by Jim Stanley, who did odd jobs at the Bread and Chicken House where his wife worked, and Gene Coomer of Big Stone Gap. They had been remodeling and installing bathrooms and electric heat at reasonable rates—sometimes charging nothing to people in need. They decided to expand the operation to teach more people carpentry skills and provide much-needed rehabbing for houses in Wise County. Conscientious objector Russ Cravens worked as a volunteer with the group. They were able to obtain capital for a truck and tools through a loan and grant.

Together with Model Valley Community Development Corporation in Clairfield, Tennessee, and similar groups in four states, Appalachia CDC formed the Central Appalachian Economic Development Association. The Association encouraged a model of local, worker-controlled small business development.

Anne brought her experience from developing the Appalachia CDC to bear in forming the Dungannon Development Commission (DDC) in 1979. The DDC soon became the dominant planning and organizing force in the community and developed several innovative programs to meet community needs. These included maternal and infant health care; a crisis fund; SHARE, a food bank helping families stretch household dollars; and a parents' advocacy program to encourage closer involvement in their children's education. The Depot education program, described in chapter 11, became a way of training and recruiting women for these and other community-building projects.

In 1980 Anne recruited Nancy Robinson to help with DDC programs. Shortly after joining the DDC, Nancy was hired as its executive director. As town manager, Anne mentored and encouraged Nancy as she developed into a strong leader. Working together with a twelve-member board of directors and other community helpers, the two spearheaded a wide array of DDC projects.

Nancy had left home before finishing high school to work as a domestic with a family in Knoxville, Tennessee. After graduation from high school, marriage, and divorce, she moved to Ohio and worked for Caterpillar Tractor company until they downsized, closed, and moved abroad. At that time Nancy not only lost a good job but a house and ability to survive in the city. She moved back to Dungannon to live in a trailer near her mother. She began volunteering at the Depot:

I got bored and the first thing you know, I started volunteering—volunteering to help the women's club that had the Depot, volunteering work for the Development Commission . . . just to keep busy. Meantime, I did housework to give myself a little income. I went around cleaning people's houses. . . . And let me tell you, a Susie Homemaker I am not. I know how to cook and clean and wash and all that, but give me something else outside of the home. That's not my bag.

So that's how I became involved. The first thing you know, they made me president of the Development Commission and then a member of the board. Anne Leibig started training me. She says, "Nancy, you can do this. You are the type of person this community needs." And she just kept encouraging me and made me real confident about myself.[4]

In his economics class at the Depot, Father John Rausch taught about co-ops. A group of his women students who had worked at the local sewing factory decided to start a sewing co-op, and John agreed to help them. The resulting Dungannon Sewing Co-op employed thirty-four women for six years before the lack of capital and poor management forced them to close. In "The Legacy of Appalachian Cooperatives" John analyzed the reasons for the co-op's successes and final failure:

The Dungannon Sewing Co-op (DSC), which started in 1983, demonstrated that a small community suffering higher than 50% unemployment could organize its own alternative work place. After nine months of planning and preparation the co-op blouse factory opened with eighteen members, but throughout its existence it consistently supported as many as thirty to thirty-five workers. The decision to close stems from a variety of business reasons that reflect familiar marketing, financial and management problems. There was high worker turnover when demand for domestic sewing revived and new factories in the area lured away co-op workers.

The sewing co-op accepted contracts at first for inexpensive blouses in order to enter the market, but lost money in the process. Before it finally secured profitable contracts, the . . . co-op had incurred an enormous debt. In addition the DSC used old equipment that frequently broke down and caused production delays.[5]

Though it ultimately folded under economic pressures, while in operation DSC was in many ways a model co-op, providing training in sewing and management and allowing workers to participate in decision making and planning. Its employees became involved in the community and donated four hundred dollars towards a library facility. The co-op's concern and respect for workers contrasted sharply with the commercial sewing factory in town in which many had worked.

The DSC experience led to further development. When Dungannon's commercial factory burned, ninety women lost their jobs. A group asked the DDC to try to start another community-owned sewing factory. They named their new facility "Phoenix" for the mythical bird that rose from the ashes. The complex process of building Phoenix Industry involved helping the community construct a sewage system, buy and develop a site, erect a building, build a road, improve the water system and—above all— raise money. The DDC spent $120,000 on site preparation, construction, business planning, and training. An industrial psychology class at the Depot trained women to sew and develop personnel regulations. The government provided $300,000 to finish the building, buy equipment, and provide capital for a year's operation. The building and equipment cost more than expected, however, so the operational capital was less than planned. With that tight budget, they could not afford to make a mistake. Unfortunately, the manager made several mistakes, and the factory closed after one year, losing jobs for about sixty women.

Nancy Robinson and DDC board members Helen Lewis and Bill Kenny talked about what happened to Phoenix at a Highlander workshop. Bill, a Tennessee Valley Authority retiree, had come to Dungannon as a volunteer to help in the development projects. Even though Nancy felt that bad management caused the failure, she saw positive outcomes from the experience:

Some may think that Phoenix is a failure of business, but in essence, here is what happened because of the project that we started. We now have adequate water, we have a sewer system, we have a road that wasn't even there—paved and state maintained. All these positive things have come out of this. We have a building that's worth $150,000 or more, we have this equipment that's worth $80,000. We've got all these assets that we never had before. What bothers me about this whole thing is the business should never have failed. And had it not been an internal thing, a power play with the community factions, and had the board [hired according to] a résumé they sure wouldn't have picked the manager that they picked. It shouldn't have failed. This is where my bitterness comes in.[6]

Nancy resigned as director of DDC before the factory closed. She had tried to discuss Phoenix mismanagement issues with the DDC Board of Directors, but to no effect.

A board member at the time of the DDC downfall, Helen Lewis recalled the turmoil caused by the closing:

I was on the board after Nancy had left and didn't know anything about what was going on. Suddenly we had no money and were trying to figure out why. We were sewing dresses which we had under-costed and could not make costs. We were subsidizing these companies who knew we had some government money and had talked us into contracts which they couldn't handle because they were too complicated. . . . Bill and I were new and trying to figure out what was happening and didn't know where to turn for good information. Management training for managers of community-owned businesses is also important—knowing how to price, to cost, to market and deal with workers in a humane way. . . . The irony of it all is that the county received one million dollars for economic development that year and put it into buying some more land near Dungannon for a second industrial park, land from a politically important person, instead of helping a business which was providing jobs for sixty people to stay in business.[7]

Nancy noted that community-owned enterprises were considered "radical" or "socialist" by the established industrial development planning officials. Largely controlled by women and ordinary people, not the county seat politicians, the community initiatives are often ignored and shut out of the planning process.

Because the industry was new to them, Dungannon board members lacked the insight to push for early assistance. Board member Bill Kenny recalled some of their missteps :

We were subsidizing the big contractors who were sending most of their big contracts overseas to be shipped back. And the only thing we could get was the difficult or left-over contracts. That is where a cooperative of several small factories would be helpful who could share some marketing, costing expertise. [A]ll the small sewing operations [could] say, "Well, we're not going to take a contract if we're going to lose money . . . to . . . subsidize you."

We didn't know enough about sewing factories and the cut-and-sew business to ask the hard questions and those who knew didn't ask them soon enough. And now we have leased the factory to a man who runs it like a sweatshop, but he is providing 35 jobs.[8]

Nancy commented on the formidable challenges of making a community-based business successful, once it is off the ground. She felt that a community-based organization could construct a building and get it ready for lease, but she was in doubt as to whether a community-based organization could handle the operation. The lack of management skills and the need for education and training limited their ability. She also recognized the contradictory requirements of running a competitive market-oriented business and a community- and worker-oriented business. She said the board would tend to be community-minded, and the manager had to be "both hard-nosed and have a community perspective."[9]

When Nancy later returned to DDC as director of housing and economic development, she began to look for other ways of using resources. She conducted a housing survey to assess community needs and was amazed by the findings: "I can't believe the people that live in substandard houses still. . . . Even in this day and time, with all our modern technology, that we still got [sic] people who have to walk to outhouses. I mean some of these are elderly people. And yet the governmental system doesn't have a way to take care of these people, even for basic needs."[10]

Initially she established a volunteer program and began to bring in people from across the country to Dungannon to work on housing and other community projects every summer. They remodeled an old filling station to house a community laundry facility. When that venture proved unsuccessful, they remodeled it again to provide office space for the DDC. Under Nancy's leadership the DDC organized an annual Fourth of July celebration, the "Mountain Treasures Festival," which brings more than three thousand visitors to Dungannon and has become a major fundraiser for churches and community groups. At the urging of the DDC, the Nature Conservancy bought a former hunting lodge built by the railroads and then leased it to the DDC as a centerpiece for eco-tourism development. DDC operated it as a meeting and conference center.

Eventually Nancy began to put most of her energy into creating a housing project on the land they had purchased for the factory. Using volunteers and working with the regional Federation of Appalachian Housing Enterprises (FAHE), the DDC built fifteen rent-to-own, low-income single-family homes in a subdivision named Blueberry Hill. They also rehabilitated more than 150 homes. They developed the project—the state's first single-family rental subdivision—with the help of many partners and the Virginia Housing Development Authority–administered Federal Low Income Housing Tax Credit Program. Families pay around three hundred dollars a month for their two- and three-bedroom homes on beautiful mountain sites.

Nancy was diagnosed with inoperable cancer in 1997 and died in the spring of 1998. Before her death the road to Blueberry Hill was renamed Nancy Robinson Street, and she received commendations for her work from the governor and general assembly of Virginia.

In Virginia the co-ops and community-based economic development projects inspired and influenced many other communities to encourage and develop local businesses. In nearby Lee County in Saint Charles, they developed a health clinic, a community-based education program, and a community-owned sewing factory.

Even earlier than the Virginia CDCs, in Clairfield, Tennessee, Marie Cirillo and Mary Jo Leygraaf helped organize the Model Valley Community Development Corporation, which initiated a number of social and economic development projects. Mary Jo attributed the origins of the group to Marie's people-centered approach to development: "Marie got the Model Valley people together by getting the local men involved and having them . . . discuss what they thought the community needed. Then she also found people to work with them."

The development group met with state officials to ask for other federal monies to replace the defunded Office of Economic Opportunity (OEO) center. They were told that little could be done for rural development as most funds were going to urban areas through the Model Cities program. Shelby York, a community leader who became chairman of the Model Valley Development Corporation, explained what happened next:

Nancy Robinson, Director, Dungannon Development Commission, whose housing project, featuring lease-to-own housing, was a first in Virginia. Photo by Kenneth Murray.

"Louise Adams was really the one that caused the name Model Valley to stick to this organization. [On the way back] from . . . Nashville . . . Louise just spoke up, she said, 'Well, . . . we'll just go back and make us a Model Valley!' So that stuck, and it's been 'Model Valley' ever since."[11]

Model Valley Community Development Corporation (MVCDC) is now one of the oldest rural CDCs in the region. Shelby York, chairman of the Model Valley Board for over thirty years, recalled how he became involved with the group and its mission:

I got involved with the Model Valley project kind of by accident. When this whole thing started up here I didn't want any part of it. . . . I tried to resign in '73. I'd been with them that long, and I decided I didn't want to be tied down with it, and they refused to accept the resignation. So I told my wife, "Well, they're bent on me getting involved, I might as well . . . really get up there and do something."

Once I . . . set my mind to it, I saw opportunities, I saw doors that could be opened for this community. . . . I'd been around, I'd traveled pretty much the world over during the war years, and I'd seen downtrodden people in those different countries I'd be in. . . . This area up here was at a point that some of those countries over there were just about as well off as we were here. Well, I began to see if you just do this or do that, you're going to open up some ways and make some things happen.

There weren't many active members, not the ones that as the old saying goes, "As the going got rough, they got tough with it." You had people like Louise Adams that weren't afraid, they'd shot at her house and everything and she was born and raised in the holler. Threatened her and everything else. You had people like that that were willing to bump heads with the opposition.[12]

The opposition was varied. County officials who had always maintained control over the backwoods sections of the county resented outsiders and emerging local leaders pushing for services. Local families supported by county officials feared losing the special favors they received for their loyal votes. Outside economic controllers, land companies, and coal operators wanted no resistance, protest, or criticism of their exploitation. Local workers in the industry were fearful of losing jobs and protected the companies. As a result there was local opposition to the changes being made. Shots were fired into Marie's house, the office was burned, student volunteer's had brake lines cut in their cars, and many threats were made by phone, letter, and grapevine messages. The violence was directed not only toward the outsiders but toward their local supporters as well, even when they were developing needed services in the community.

Many of the Model Valley Community Development Corporation's efforts had to do with creating infrastructure in the valley. One of the most important issues was providing families with safe water. Mary Jo described the process of developing the water system that became a base for fire departments, housing, and many other changes:

It was important to get a water system because the water's so contaminated . . . . Here in the valley people could drill a well, but it's all been mined out under White Oak—you could drill and drill and drill in White Oak and not hit water. So people would have hundreds of milk jugs hanging on their porch and . . . they'd get a whole load of empty jugs [and] take them to a spring on [Highway] 25W and fill them up. . . . That's the only water they'd have. Or they'd have a cistern where they'd get the water off of their roof. So . . . people . . . were really desperate for water. . . .

Nobody had their water tested or anything. Years ago there was a hepatitis epidemic at the school and the lady[13] whose son died, she always thought it was connected to the water.

I was here through the whole process—all the meetings with the federal people. It was a phenomenal thing. . . . [I]n creating the water utility everybody was working together, people that didn't agree on other things.

The water system has increased the population because people come back now and it's easy to hook onto the water. You don't have to spend a thousand dollars to try to drill a well . . . that's contaminated. So it's helped in that way, and we hoped it would help bring industry, but so far we've not.

One of Model Valley's first economic development projects was an attempt to create another industry in the valley besides coal mining. They envisioned creating a pallet factory that could use local timber and be locally owned and operated. However, the American Association (the British land company which owned much of the land and minerals in the area) rejected their requests for land on which to build the factory. Access to land was critical to development in the valley, and its monopolization by the British multinational corporation severely impeded residents' advancement. Marie recalled the constant frustrations as a result of limited land rights:

I remember when we tried to start a health clinic, when we got to the point when we felt we could really build a factory, [or] . . . thought we could do a child care, or . . . thought we could really deal with housing, there was this major thing about, "Well, where's the land that we're going to put it on?" So there was a whole ten years of little groups having to deal with, "Where's the land? Where's the land?" . . .

Then I came to understand that because we live in these rural, unincorporated areas, that you have no kind of a planning mechanism, no kind of local government. You can't even say, well, . . . if we're trying to get a clinic and a child care, why can't we get enough land to have these things together? Instead of one thing four miles down the road because that was the only land you could find, and one piece five miles down the road because that's the only piece of land you could find.

When, after several attempts, the MVDC was finally able to buy forty acres of land for the pallet factory and secure stockholders, they circulated job applications as far as the Midwest. The Bobby Kennedy Memorial Fund provided Model Valley with an intern, Brady Deaton, who was a Kennedy intern and economist, who later taught at Virginia Tech and was provost at the University of Missouri. He and his family spent a year helping develop the venture. Ethel Kennedy came for the factory dedication.

The Clairfield Pallet Factory hired fifteen workers, but the problems they faced were too great for their resources and the enterprise closed after three years.

Through the Pallet Factory failure, Marie witnessed firsthand the overwhelming burden placed by bureaucracies on small economic development projects:

I worked with the Model Valley Development Corporation between 1968 and 1972 and experienced with them the strangling reality of three major bureaucratic structures the community had to engage with to make the factory possible. I experienced the . . . rejection of requests for ten acres of land from the seven major land companies who owned over eighty percent of the Clearfork Valley. We completed the research required from the bureaucracies in order to seek stockholders and to get a government loan. The market was secure; the hardwood was there. Our manager and marketers were getting good training. . . . The plant went bankrupt for several reasons. The . . . bureaucratic red tape created by an overdeveloped nation was central to the downfall of the factory. The leadership of the Model Valley Development Corporation came from the community of Clairfield and Hamblintown. To get a small business loan the community was required to create another corporation—a local development corporation. There were rules about percentages of board members that could be on both boards. Then, to create the for-profit corporation with stockholders, we needed yet more people. It was difficult to find enough leadership and equally difficult to remember who was responsible for what and what hat you were wearing with what issue. All of this was required to start a business employing fifteen people.

Other problems included regular trips to Knoxville seventy miles away to sharpen the saw, competing pallet factories, and failure to be accurate about withholding taxes. The major external problems included denial of access to timber resources from major [absentee] landholding companies and the failure of a firm in Cleveland to purchase our product as it had promised.

As a leader in the project, Shelby felt a personal responsibility for not overseeing the operation more actively: "[L]ike a lot of others, [I just said] those people that wanted to run the factory, let them run it. But maybe if I had . . . kept a little closer watch on it [it would not have failed]. Because it had the potential of being a solid sound business. But we didn't find out [it was failing] until it was too late."[14]

Marie said of the loss: "For some people [the failure] was like a closed book. . . . But you know my attitude is, 'Well, look, if you hadn't tried to start a factory you never would have gotten that forty acres, and if you hadn't gotten those forty acres you'd never have this village square, you'd never have twenty homes built.'"

When the pallet factory failed, the Model Valley finally had land to work with. They were able to use it for a number of purposes including a permanent health clinic, offices for legal services, and housing for the crafts cooperative. In time the crafts group moved out and was replaced by a thrift shop. Still later a wood shop was added. A post office, public library, and the water utility brought the valley closer to getting government investment in the area. The county welfare department and the United States Department of Agriculture also made use of the Model Valley space.

Model Valley made land available for private housing. Shelby described how they stumbled into developing subdivisions:

We didn't take federal money because it was too much red tape. The way we do things, there isn't any way that these government agents would let us do it. First thing they would do, they would tell you, "It's not suitable what you're wanting to do; . . . it won't meet our criteria." Well, my thing was, that's all the land we got, we have to use it. And for two hundred years people had been up here and it was supporting houses. . . .

There was a nice little holler and a little place where you could do some homes. The board told me, "Well, you could go up there and survey two or three pieces, see if anybody likes it. We don't think anybody will buy it but you go ahead." So I got my surveyor and he come up and he surveyed this block out, . . . and we spent the whole day. I believe it was five or six lots that we got surveyed and laid out.

We were coming back down off the hill, it was late and we could hear people talking. We found a whole bunch of guys and they were all staking out their piece of land! They were all picking out the piece of land they wanted to build a house on! . . . Every lot was sold by the time we got to the last ones. . . .We could have sold that many more if I had had them. . . .

But that first subdivided area was one of the breakthroughs for us, because we were proving to people that you can do this, you can build a house there. . . .

So it's made homes available to people who never would have been able to have a home or a piece of land, and they're very independent, they're very protective of that land. They don't want you to infringe on an inch of it.[15]

Shelby recalled that once people started building on Model Valley land, there was a ripple effect. "We had people around who had heard, . . . you can't build houses back there; . . . that's a jungle. . . . After the first home was built I heard this man say, 'If they can build on that there I can build one down here.' The first thing you know, it's just like peas popping up! They began building all along the road. People think, 'Well, if they can do it we can do it.' And it made people put a little effort out to make things happen for themselves."[16]

Even getting financing was a struggle, but Model Valley with their usual creativeness found ways to help people fund their new homes. Shelby recalled encouraging many to set up mobile homes, when banks would not loan them money to build houses:

To do a house up here the banks just would not talk to them about making a home loan. We got one loan through the Farmers Home Loan; they did finally come through with one loan.[17] We did one . . . with a homeowner furnishing all of his materials . . . and then we did his house with CETA labor. Then another house we contracted . . . for fourteen thousand dollars—that was labor and materials— and we did that house on grants. . . .

My thing was if I can get a person on that piece of property in a mobile home they're going to pay it off. So I told them, . . . let's go with . . . mobile homes. So that's what we did. . . . I said, "Let them at least have a dry, decent place to live because some of them are being flooded every time it rains, you know." See, at the time you couldn't get a loan to build a house but they could get a trailer financed and set up on their lot. It didn't make sense to me, but that was the deal.[18]

The philosophy of Model Valley housing development has been to help people own their own lots and homes. After years of living in company-run coal camps where there was no land available to buy, people wanted a place of their own.

Shelby and the Model Valley Board have worked to help people be independent and in control. Shelby looked back over their labor of transformation:

That's been part of our thing here is to try to get people to do for themselves, and not be obligated to nobody but themselves. I've wished a lot of times that my dad and my stepmother could see the change that took place in this valley in the past twenty-five years, ... because in their last years of their lives all they saw was deterioration in the valley. They saw all the young people leave practically. . . . They saw mining camps come down and disappear. . . . it was a real down feeling for them.

You take thirty, forty years ago people would never have dreamed that there would have been a public water system in this valley. I mean they would have laughed at you. But the water system is here and that's something.

There's a whole lot of things out there in the future we're looking at. We're looking at land development up here, more houses. We're even hoping to get some kind of light industry. If we can get that, get some people a little employment that'll be a lot of help.

How much longer I'm going to continue to come up here [to the Model Valley office] I don't know. I don't want to accept retirement . . . but it's been a sort of enjoyable thing.[19]

In both Virginia and Tennessee some of the economic development efforts did not survive, but important lessons were learned. In both Dungannon sewing factories they learned that it was difficult to have concern for the workers and operate a competitive business in a cutthroat industry. They did not have enough capital to make a mistake. They also lacked sufficient management and marketing skills and other resources to survive in the competitive marketplace. They were outside the mainstream economy and without political power to influence the development policies—not only within their county but in the larger global economy where they were operating.

In the Clairfield pallet factory and Big Stone Gap Bread and Chicken co-op, they had similar problems of management and could not find skilled managers with the education and training to operate community-based economic development projects well. Both had some help from outside economists, but only in the short term. In both situations outside competition helped close them out. In Big Stone Gap, Kentucky Fried Chicken moved in, and in Clairfield they were isolated from necessary services and did not have sufficient infrastructure. In later economic development that occurred in other rural communities, the focus has been on providing services and production for less competitive niches. In Clairfield they also found that the generic, bureaucratic, organizational requirements for incorporation and operation did not fit their rural situation, and the rules prevented their use of local leadership and resources. After the pallet factory experience, Model Valley refused later government funding for their housing development to avoid the unsuitable regulations. They worked outside the mainstream economy and depended on foundations, churches, and friends to fund their projects.

Despite the creativity, vigor, and social capital that these rural communities can provide, they all discovered that major changes in development policies were needed before rural communities could really develop economic security and substantially improve their income and economic well-being.

Chapter 13

ADVOCACY, SOCIAL ACTION, AND EMPOWERMENT OF WOMEN

I made the commitment to help the next generation clean up the messes.

By being friends and visitors with the poor, Glenmary Sisters became advocates for the individual families they visited. Yet they were hindered from larger community work by the rules of their order, which prevented them from attending secular meetings or participating fully in the social movements that were emerging in the region. As secular community participants, however, they were drawn into these movements; some became leaders in these efforts to correct or prevent the destruction of the communities that had become their homes.

Working in collaboration with Vanderbilt University students and concerned citizens, the FOCIS members in Tennessee helped organize Save Our Cumberland Mountains (SOCM)—one of the strongest citizen organizations in the region with 1,500 members—which continues to work with communities to protect the area's natural resources. Like many of the organizations and programs FOCIS women helped develop, SOCM, an outgrowth of the health fairs, began with listening, asking questions, research, and then action. Some SOCM activities, especially anti–strip mining protests, made members targets of violence; attempts were made to run them out of the region. But most of their work is less confrontational and continues their pattern of creating and implementing alternative community development services. Woodland Community Land Trust, a major project of Marie Cirillo's in Tennessee, strives to return corporate-owned land to local residents to help develop sustainable communities. Combined with this is development of a Community Learning Center to create a space for education, reflection, and assessment. The Woodland Land Trust project represents one of the most ambitious and visionary projects dealing with what many define as the root causes of the poverty and lack of development in the Appalachian Region: corporate ownership and control of the land and resources and a lack of voice or power by members of the community. By securing land and working to develop an education base, the community will have both power and resources in the future.

Individually, FOCIS women may write letters to the editor or give support to other groups, but typically they work as part of a team with members of the community—most often, a group of fellow women residents. They became friends and teachers to many women in the community and in that process mentored, educated, and empowered many women leaders.

They worked in the community with the marginalized, and "sided with the poor" as they had been instructed to do as Catholic Sisters. The organization they formed, FOCIS, can be seen as an act of resistence and an alternative to the institutional church. When Glenmary Sisters took the call of Vatican II "to be in the world, acting on behalf of justice and participating in our world's transformation,"[1] the theology behind this commitment transformed their idea of ministry. It led them to work for systemic change and to make an "option for the poor" fundamental to their work. It further led them into the social justice movements of the last half of the twentieth century. In turn their experience on mission and in these movements impacted them and transformed how they worked with health care, education, and other community issues. In the same way their commitment to the call led them to resist the patriarchal hierarchy of the church and, ultimately, leave their order. As they sought to reform the church, they reached an impasse: a breakdown of communication, the inability to right a situation. But from what seemed like disintegration came transformation to a more creative form of ministry.

FOCIS is still true to its roots in religious life. In the booklet "Spirituality, Social Justice, and the Glenmary Tradition," Father Matthew Fox writes about the role of religious orders as a "resistance unit" in the history of the church and society. He characterizes the Desert Fathers as resisting the marriage of the church and the Roman Empire: "Christians of social conscience and deep spirituality who resisted such collusion (among other things it meant Christians could now be conscripted to fight in the military) went into the desert." He goes on to describe the resistance of Benedict through the formation of the monastic life and that of Francis and Dominic through their return to Gospel living in the midst of privilege.[2] FOCIS women reserved this pattern of resistance as they moved from the religious order to poor communities where they were freed from the restrictions of the order to become more active participants. They moved from passive resistance to active resistance.

FOCIS members moved naturally between social service work, advocacy, and social action, and often combined all three. Their early mission work with families quickly led them into social activism. Monica Appleby recalled the Sisters' work with welfare rights as one of their earliest roles as "activists":

[As Glenmary Sisters] we were at odds with the welfare people. We would always be coming to the office with someone from the community who seemed to be in need of services they weren't receiving, so we were a thorn in their sides. They didn't like it that we interfered in their work, and that is how we got involved in welfare reform, because the people started to organize themselves into welfare rights groups. Sometimes we could help with transportation. We didn't plan to be activists; it grew out of our relationships with people and helping them get through the systems that would supposedly help them. In turn, they were rejected, and people lived in terrible, terrible conditions. So when we tried to change those systems is when we became active that way.

The 1960s and 1970s in the Appalachian Mountains were a time of change and social movements, including the anti–strip mining and black-lung movements, union reform, Civil Rights, school desegregation, and many other community action groups developed by the OEO War on Poverty programs. The type of involvement and the groups with which Glenmary and FOCIS members worked varied according to the community and the issues and problems confronting people there. In east Tennessee, strip mining became a central concern. In southwest Virginia, a fight for welfare rights galvanized a major social movement in Dickenson County, while black-lung groups organized in Wise County. Later on, FOCIS members living and working in different communities found themselves caught up in other causes: the anti-war and peace movement, including Central America solidarity groups; environmental issues involving timbering practices, power company actions, and pollution; mine safety and coal taxation issues; and school consolidation.

In 1971 Bill Dow, Marie Cirillo, and the Vanderbilt students who were working to develop health services began researching land ownership and the mineral tax structure to find out why there was no money for health care and other social needs in the area. Their activity drew the ire of some powerful entities and inspired Marie and others to organize a community watchdog group:

The Vanderbilt students did the land tenure study in five counties. When it was finished they returned to each community with the results. The study made it clear that coal companies were not paying their fair share of taxes on what they produced. We were informed that the state had a law, which required everything to be taxed fairly. The strategy was to form a five-county organization [Save Our Cumberland Mountains] with at least one representative from each county. I became a charter member. The Campbell and Claiborne representatives came from the Clearfork Valley. Our first activity was to get a lawyer and bring the state to task for not taxing coal. I remember some of the first SOCM research consisted of researchers going to many states to see how they did it because our state people said they did not know how. We told them how. What is sad to me is that even after we won our case and got the counties to be more fair in their assessments, we had to be a continual watchdog—monitoring our government—it just doesn't seem right.

John Gaventa, one of the students who worked on the study, recalled the legal and social barriers that plagued the group's efforts to uncover the corporate improprieties, which were occurring at Appalachia's expense:

I was a student at Vanderbilt, and in the summer of 1971, the summer I was leaving college, three of us went to Clairfield . . . to work on a project with the Student Health Coalition: to look at the question of who owns the land and who paid the taxes, with the idea of understanding why there was no tax revenue to use for health care. And so we were this secret part of the health coalition, and we slipped into courthouses and did the research on who owned the land in five counties in upper east Tennessee. And out of that eighteen citizens came together and filed a lawsuit—we had two to three from each of the five counties and those eighteen became SOCM—Save Our Cumberland Mountains.

That's when I first met Marie Cirillo. . . . She became one of the original SOCM people and . . . one of the original people to take action on the land issues. During the research she became concerned about the American Association . . . the British company that owned all the land around Clairfield. And Marie put me in touch with several other people and asked if I could look into that company since I was leaving to go to England [on a Rhodes Scholarship at Oxford University].

That got me involved in the long saga of working with the community of Clairfield, with the community group but very much at Marie's leadership, quietly documenting the impact of that company's ownership in east Tennessee and trying to discover in England who the real owners were. . . . [B]efore I left I had been elected to the Board of Trustees of Vanderbilt so they had to fly me back for meetings twice a year. I would come back on Cecil Rhodes's[3] and Vanderbilt's money and go up to Marie's and spend a few weeks at a time helping the community document the land issues. Then I took almost a year off, really working with that community to document the impact of that one land company and to see if some actions could be taken. That is when the Granada television group came from England and we worked very closely with Marie and the group there to make the film called "The Stripping of Appalachia," which exposed the Lord Mayor of London's sins and was shown nationally in Britain. [The Lord Mayor was a major stockholder in the company.]

That led to a lot of violence . . . against people who had been speaking out. My car had the brake lines cut and Marie's house was shot into. A number of other people were threatened. We decided that we had done as much as we could do at that time. I went back to England and was encouraged to write it up into the book.[4]

Violence directed at the students gained them the sympathy of Shelby York's father. One particular attack, Shelby recalled, forced his dad to reevaluate his impressions of the students and their work in the region:

[T]hey were both old, my dad and stepmother. My dad, he'd say: "The holler's getting full of hippies, there's hippies everywhere you look." The students had set up an office down on the side of the road. . . . A lot of them were doing research work. But I mentioned something or other about that building and my dad said, "There's a bunch of hippies taking over."

Those are the words my daddy used. Well, one night about two o'clock in the morning, somebody burned that building down. Well, my dad got real upset about it because he knew there were ten, fifteen, students there at that time, a whole group of them. But two o'clock in the morning everybody's asleep and you burn a house down, you're going to burn everybody up; and that's what upset him. . . . "You know," he said, "whoever that was they could have burnt them kids up!" They were no longer hippies; they were just kids. "Could have burnt them kids up!" From then on, he didn't have any more comments.[5]

The land study was shining light on how a few companies had controlled most of the resources in the valley but managed to pay few taxes. Marie explained how SOCM used the new video technology to mobilize Tennesseans against the powerful companies:

Because Clearfork had some video equipment, SOCM borrowed it from time to time to demonstrate wrongdoings. Once they caught a company "layer loading," that is, they put the higher grade coal in the center of the truck, where they knew TVA would test it for quality. This got on the local news and caused quite a bit of excitement. Naturally some SOCM people were threatened.

When John Gaventa went to Oxford and chose to do his dissertation on the British land company that owned most of the valley, he found a filmmaker who agreed to do a documentary about the American Association's operations in the Clearfork Valley. When that was produced we got a copy. John helped us organize small groups throughout the state whom we showed the film to. The idea was to get support . . . throughout the state when SOCM was ready to move on legislative initiatives. What we did when we showed the film to a prestigious group was to video their reaction to the film that showed the environmental devastation caused by strip mining. We would add these small group reactions to the showing. It was my first experience at mobilizing at a state level.

The experience was also her first at working against the grain of public opinion. Marie, who had won community approval for her work on the health clinic issue, now had to contend with neighbors' hostility and suspicion:

When Jean left and somebody found me the house in Roses Creek, I moved from where I was to Roses Creek. At that time, Roses Creek was the biggest producer of moonshine. So when I moved here people thought I was an undercover FBI or whoever it is that follows the moonshiners, so I was suspect on that count. Then we got into organizing SOCM and having concerns about strip mining, so then I was suspect by the companies.

I do remember when we took on the issue of some of the strip-mine legislation and the coal miners really mobilized to try to stop that legislation for reclaiming [strip-mined land], some of the people here were genuinely confused about my role. Because . . . those who were my friends saw me doing these things to help them; but then, for me to be getting into something where they might lose their job, it was difficult for them to understand. People were confused, and I know when I would go up to Clairfield where the clinic and the development corporation were, even my friends would be afraid to say hello to me. . . .

The other thing, though, that happened was a couple of men who were strip miners and who were privy to all of this terrible stuff so many were saying about me came to me. I remember one man that wanted to tell me about how he felt about strip mining. This was the time when [people] wanted to run me out of town because they thought I was responsible for these environmental laws. And it was so strange, because he had something he had to tell me. And he said, "Come with me, Marie."

So I go with him, and we go way up into the mountains. And I began to get a little nervous about, you know, what *is* this? But . . . who could have heard us I don't know. It was almost like he had to be sure he was giving me this secret where nobody, nobody would hear it. He couldn't tell me down here, we had to go way into the mountains and then he told me how he felt about strip mining. I remember him saying to me how it pained him to be tearing up the lands, but he knew he had no other choice if he wanted to feed his family. But he said, "For every time I made a cut in the mountains, I knew I was losing the future for my children." I think him telling me that made it worth all of the harassment that I went through for those couple of years. I'll always remember that. That man is dead now, but I can just visually still see the secrets in the forest.

Marie's support of anti–strip mining legislation made her the object of attack by coal company "hit men." An organized attempt to run her out of town took the form of telephone harassment, dynamite blasts in her front yard, and threats on her life. Marie recalled that three-week nightmare: "We were shot at—the holes are still in the house. Our windows

Marie Cirillo speaking at CORE Appalachian Ministries meeting in Georgia. Glenmary Home Missioners photo, 1971.

were broken. A car with a loud speaker drove by one night with the speaker threatening to burn us out and rape us. A volunteer driving my car suddenly had the steering mechanism fail and the car ran off the mountain."[6]

Despite the attacks against her, Marie bears no ill-will, choosing instead to focus on her work and goals for the future: "The threats to me brought out the worst and the best in the community. I have forgotten the worst, but the best stays with me. . . . I made a commitment to help the next generation clean up the messes."[7]

Maureen Linneman wrote the song "This Land is Home to Me" at a gathering of grassroots community leaders at the Highlander Center in Tennessee. It became a song sung at many meetings dealing with the strip mining and destruction of communities. She shared the experience of writing it:

Having lived in the mountains for a while, I had become familiar with both the beauty and pain of the area and people. When I asked a group of mountain people about their lives, their words and emotions flowed so naturally. Family ties and mountainsides, children, roots, home, economic justice, and the desire to have freedom to live their lives and values, their way of life. I was inspired, took their words and composed a song that I was able to sing to them that weekend. Their response was extremely positive and encouraged me to name [it] "This Land is Home to Me."

> ...This land means more to me
> Than all the races and the places in the world around
> This land of mountains and valleys and streams . . .
> But people come and go . . .
> But though they now are gone
> Their hearts still live on
> In the mother sighs, the family ties, the mountain sides. . . .

For the FOCIS women in cities the issues were not about land as much as housing, education, and health services. During the 1960s and 1970s Elizabeth Roth Turner was involved with a number of social movements in Chicago, initially as part of FOCIS. She met her future husband, social activist Dan Turner, in Chicago shortly after the infamous '68 Democratic Convention.

Besides FOCIS's presence in the neighborhood, there were many other groups and agencies doing community work. . . . Most groups recognized FOCIS for its ability to relate to the people of the neighborhood. We were often approached to work on projects with them. We cooperated with a lead poisoning detection and prevention program. We found places for young men to live while the agency that sponsored their coming to Chicago found them jobs. Sometimes we felt used by these groups for their political purposes and kept a watchful eye that we not betray the confidence placed in us.

There was so much going on in Chicago and in the nation that groups wanted to organize Appalachian involvement [for]: Civil Rights related issues, War on Poverty, anti–Vietnam war protests, 1968 Democratic Convention, urban renewal. The mainstream media was also in the neighborhood blowing fuses as they filmed the inside of our apartments and asked about whether we were still nuns. The movie *Medium Cool* was being filmed in Uptown with live scenes of Chicago police beating up protesters in Grant Park during the 1968 Democratic Convention. Families and their children whom we knew were often approached to be in movies or documentaries. We were asked for advice about the purpose and trustworthiness of the filmmakers. . . .

The Model Cities program set up an office in Uptown. I was recruited by Bob Dunne, a staff member and former Jesuit, to be a community representative on the Model Cities Council. The appointment came from Richard J. Daley, Chicago mayor at the time. I attended meetings in the evenings. Agendas dealt with the schools, the proposed junior college, the need for more mental health services, housing, urban renewal. It was through Model Cities that I met leaders from the Native American groups in Uptown and with them became a strong voice on the Council. When a Chicago Board of Health center was proposed for Uptown, I served on the community planning council which was consulted on architectural design, kinds of services to be provided and the hiring of the first administrator. Relating to Model Cities with its urban renewal emphasis became a major focus and I recruited Appalachians to speak at committee meetings.[8]

At a gathering in 1991, FOCIS members listed the social movements they had been part of. These included many of the religious, environmental, educational, health, civil rights, poverty-welfare, and peace and justice movements in the country.

Catherine Rumschlag has long been a faithful letter-writer and participant in picket lines and vigils in southwest Virginia around issues relating to peace, Central American solidarity, the environment, and welfare. Father John Rausch writes a column in Catholic newspapers about issues such as economic justice, capital punishment, housing, and welfare reform. Linda and Bill Mashburn have worked with groups in Nicaragua and are active in opposing the U.S. Army's notorious School of the Americas. Mary Herr has been an advocate for children and families in the legal and agency systems in western North Carolina. Patrick Ronan, who organized the early anti–strip mining and land ownership movements in southwest Virginia, currently advocates for health services for Vietnam veterans. Now an environmental theologian, Dick Austin had helped lead the fight in West Virginia for surface-mining regulations in the 1960s and, in the 1980s, helped the Virginia community of Brumley Gap win their battle against a power company that wanted to destroy a valley with a pump storage facility. After buying Chestnut Ridge Farm, Dick assisted in the development of groups involved in organic farming and sustainable development. In the late '80s he and The River Farm residents became involved in tense skirmishing over pollution issues surrounding the Louisiana Pacific wafer-board plant in Dungannon. In North Carolina Maureen Linneman has worked with centers for abused women around issues of domestic violence. In 1972, after the horrific failure of a poorly constructed Pittston Company sludge pond dam caused a flood that killed 125 people in West Virginia,[9] Anne Leibig, who owned Pittston stock as a result of her research on coal issues, accompanied Buffalo Creek survivors to the Pittston stockholders' meeting in Richmond, where at the survivors' request she made a statement on their behalf.

In the 1980s Monica and Michael Appleby spent six years working with the National Council of Churches of Christ U.S.A. as regional representatives for southern Africa. From their base in Gaborone, Botswana, they became involved with anti-apartheid groups and South African exiles. They were living in Gaborone when South African military forces raided the city in June 1985 and murdered sixteen people in their homes. Four of the victims had worked in Arts and Resistance projects with the Applebys. After returning from southern Africa, Michael joined with student groups in Blacksburg to push Virginia Tech to divest holdings in U.S. corporations profiting from the apartheid state. Later, Monica worked for Planned Parenthood on a special grant to monitor the political activities of extreme right religious groups. She was drawn into the abortion/choice debate when she became public affairs coordinator for Planned Parenthood in Virginia's New River Valley. In 1996 she made the news in the valley, speaking out in an article entitled, "Can Faith Affirm Right to Abortion?"

In the article Monica was quoted as saying: [The Catholic Church has] "consistently taught that individual conscience is primary. After prayer, reflection and study, conscience is the ultimate arbiter of decision making." While acknowledging the church's official position that abortion is a serious sin, Monica pointed out that "individual Catholics often have to make choices between church policy and personal conviction. People think Catholics are all of one mind, that we walk in lockstep, but we're very heterogeneous and diverse." She said she would describe herself as "pro-choice rather than pro-abortion."[10]

Although FOCIS members have been involved in many social action responses to established injustice, they have consistently concentrated on creating alternative systems, organizations, and development models like the CDCs and FOCIS itself. In one of their first publications, they described themselves as "a counter-community in a society which is fragmented rather than integrated, which mistrusts dedication to any cause and which encourages self-seeking and profit-making rather than service. The members of FOCIS do among themselves what they envision for society."[11]

For the past twenty years Marie Cirillo has been working to return land to the community from corporate owners and help people obtain space for living and community development. But she has also sought to build a community relationship with the land that is cooperative and sustainable. With a long-standing commitment to an idea, Marie worked to organize people and land in the Clearfork Valley into a community land trust. She recalled how the original concept developed:

When Monica was in Boston she heard a lecture by Bob Swann,[12] which she thought provided some answer for central Appalachia. She came home and told us about Bob and his idea of a community land trust. The heart of this movement would be to put land back in the hands of a local community. In our society where corporate control threatens small efforts, this had to be a collective effort. [The] land trust would be a local corporation that would buy land and redistribute it under protective covenants. Some would be allocated to agricultural production, some for public spaces, some for preservation and restoration, etc. But most would remain for housing settlement.

When the Woodland Community Land Trust first organized we could not get non-profit, tax-exempt status. It was such a new concept that the IRS was not sure how to deal with it. How could a land-based organization be a non-profit? . . . For a long time the . . . Trust had to depend on loans to acquire land. I could see the value to this. If the group built itself not depending on grants, then the movement could grow on its own internal strength. Stephen Wile and his wife gave Woodland its first loan. Its only grant of seven thousand dollars came from the Daughters of Charity. It has been a hard way to go. Started in 1977, Woodland finally got its tax-exempt status in 1991.

With support from many churches and individuals, Woodland acquired 101 acres of land on Roses Creek Hollow, and created a development corporation to assist families wanting to settle on trust lands. By 1998 the Land Trust had a land base of 320 acres and a people base of eighteen families (fifty-five people), a dedicated board and committed staff. The land is divided into twenty-four house sites, six acres of cultivated garden . . . a picnic and theater area and a three-acre campsite. The Land Trust community includes an emergency shelter, three mobile homes for transitional housing, gardens, a Christmas tree stand, and the Living Learning Center. Two hundred seventy-five acres . . . are dedicated to sustainable forestry. All land is dedicated to ecologically and socially sound development.[13]

A separate Woodland Community Development Corporation was created in 1988 to administer the housing and small-business aspects of the land trust. One of the small businesses was a portable sawmill that provided wood for the homes built on the land. Another project was the native materials house building with a special training program for local people of Native American descent to learn to build houses at the Land Trust's woodworking shop. Since the native materials homes do not meet government standards, they were not eligible for government funding. Instead they were built for approximately five thousand dollars of church and private donations.[14] In 1989 the United Nations awarded the Land Trust first prize on World Habitat Day in recognition of "a significant contribution to the provision of adequate shelter to the poorer segments of the community."[15]

Egan Mountain, the newest part of the Trust, became the scene for Earth Day Celebration 2000. A metal sculpture by Margaret Gregg, a symbol of the Earth, was placed on its summit. "Local people, friends and partners made a pilgrimage walk to the top of Egan Mountain to celebrate freeing the land from a $50,000 debt and dedicating community efforts to restoring the land."[16]

In the process of living and working in communities and working with local groups on such problems as land ownership and strip mining, there is a symbiotic relationship in which both local community members and the FOCIS organizer/community worker are empowered. Monica described how a good relationship between organizer/community worker and community member leads to empowerment: "We were able to empower ourselves and others, especially the women we worked with side-by-side. We did this through creating relationships as friends and co-workers. In communities and within organizations, we have had many roles—neighbor, friend, citizen, worker, and participant. Also mentor, catalyst, organizer, entrepreneur, and trainer. The most enduring and the most present even now is that of friend."

Years before Anne Leibig became her mentor, Teri Vautrin recalls that she was a trusted friend:

I've known Anne Leibig since I was yay high to a grasshopper because we were one of the Catholic families in Dante. So when Anne and Monica and them would come down in the summertime to do Bible school and stuff, they would come to our house and Anne would grab me and we'd go canvassing up and down the hollers. She'd come back year after year after year, and when I graduated from high school, she'd already made the break with Glenmary. They took me up there when I was fourteen so one of the Sisters could explain the facts of life to me.[17]

As an adult in Dungannon, Teri was a student in the Depot education program and worked with Anne at the DDC. Anne encouraged and helped her to develop another organization, Appalachian Women Empowered (AWE), to provide training and support for women.

Nancy Robinson remembered how Anne, as mentor, trainer, and friend, accompanied her on her journey to become a community leader:

Anne was the one that saw the potential in me. Anne saw something in me that I didn't know existed. She taught me how to be and work with community. And I always have a soft spot for Anne in my heart because she's really a good leader; she's a good organizer.

I was real shy. We started working together [after] I'd been here for maybe a year. When she'd ask me to call certain people, I'd need her to leave the room. Let me tell you how she introduced me to public speaking. I had never spoken; I was the kind of person who gets up in front of a crowd and would literally pass out. I mean boom, I'm gone. 'Cause I'd forget to breathe I'd get so scared. So Anne would take me with her to different functions to talk about DDC, and I had to learn myself. She'd just give me different portions to talk about. And then as time went on, she'd give me a little more. One day she called and said, "I have this other engagement and you're going to have to do this by yourself."

That's how it began. That's good leadership, teaching others, helping others grow. She's helped me grow a lot. I don't know if other people that come into the community see the community's vision or their vision of what the community should be. I think Anne knew that it had to come from the community. But we just didn't have the organizational skills, so Anne gave me the encouragement. And she taught me how to help others. There are mostly women here [at DDC]. It's like you take a little flower, a little bud—you know how flowers eventually just open, open—pretty soon they just blossom out into a beautiful flower. And I've seen that happen so many times in this community.[18]

Leadership development of rural women has been an informal by-product of working in communities with women. Providing mentoring and support to women led to empowerment. Scott County activist Teri Vautrin grew up knowing the Sisters and their work and witnessed the evolution in their ministry as they became FOCIS:

As human beings they were terrific and as women they were terrific, but they were also different . . . in that there seemed to be an energy and a sense of questioning that wasn't present in other religious folks that were coming through. And there was just this amount of energy, energy, energy, and they were trying to hold themselves back from just taking the ball and going. There was a real sense of dissatisfaction, and that sense never came across as dissatisfaction with the mountains, or with the people, but always with the institution, the church. But it was never vocalized.

[When they became FOCIS] it was the same kind of work that they were doing but it was different. It seemed that those chains had been broken, and it was just like the whole world was possible. . . .[19]

What happened in Dungannon was that the DDC was a model for how community organizing can do it. Some folks who come into communities to help don't understand what empowerment is about and a dependence develops between communities and resource people. And when resource people don't understand that you have to share skills, not keep them, the community will always be dependent. To get a community independent, you need to let go of those skills. FOCIS had the correct definition of what empowerment is. They also realized they cannot be the God, saviors of everything that's going on, but can hook into places where an impact can be made.[20]

In 1985 the Women's Task Force of the Catholic Committee of Appalachia began to communicate with other women about the possibility of holding a region wide celebratory women's gathering. The Task Force also began recording the life stories of ordinary women in the mountains, which they published as a collection in 1988.[21] A Women's Round Table, based in southwest Virginia, grew from these interests. "The Round Table wanted to gather women from a wide range of backgrounds to share their stories, draw strength from their cultural experience and celebrate the rising of women's spirit."[22] FOCIS was involved with Anne Leibig, Monica Appleby, and Catherine Rumschlag as members of the original Round Table. The gathering, with its theme "In Praise of Mountain Women," was attended by 160 women in May 1991. Many of the women were connected through the Catholic Sister network. Others were born and bred in the mountains, some leaving home, children, and spouse for the first time to journey on their own behalf. Women who couldn't afford to pay were given scholarships.

On that weekend in Virginia five women shared difficult personal stories with the entire group; then participants broke into smaller groups called "home circles" where people were encouraged to share their own stories and affirm the experiences of others. "Women took risks to tell stories of pain, struggle, oppression and healing. Women danced the dance of anger. They also danced the dance of empowerment. . . . The weekend together created dangerous memories and formed a unique community where women's gifts were shared and respected."[23]

Afterwards Teri Vautrin described the gathering in prose and in a poem: "It was a way for women to come together and say, 'Look, we survived so far, let's celebrate our struggles, let's celebrate that we're here, let's look at who we are, and see what the issues are, and let's move on, but first, let's just celebrate.' It was a terrific weekend."[24]

We journeyed
from hollers, cities, towns of these mountains
leaving homes,
family,
friends,

some bringing children,
to come together
to create new homes
a home circle
to create new family
with new friends
to claim and raise OUR flag
to create a safe place
to share, learn
to join in our claiming ourselves
to celebrate. . . .[25]

Even before the weekend was over, energized participants were already asking when the next one would happen. Four additional gatherings have now taken place: in 1993, 1995, 1997, and 1999, with a sixth celebration scheduled for October 2004 in Abingdon, Virginia.

The touch of FOCIS members has been everywhere in shaping and sustaining these transformative events. Anne Leibig helped design and lead the rituals. Catherine Rumschlag served as Round Table treasurer to oversee support funds that flowed through FOCIS books. In 1991 Maureen Linneman produced a songbook and wrote a special song for the gathering, while Margaret Gregg served as event artist, designing a flag, logo, and brochures and supplying props for group art.

Margaret encouraged each circle of women to create wreaths to commemorate their experience at the Round Table:

The "props" aspect of my work focused on wreaths for all the home circles. The wreaths would be assembled on the floor in the center of the circles. A significant part of many cultural traditions, wreaths are used to honor the living and the dead and special occasions. Coiled, twisted, entwined. Participants were encouraged to bring natural materials and all sorts of decorations and found objects. I brought some barbed wire, peacock feathers, cotton balls, greens and twigs. Sweet, sharp, soft. The wreaths in each home circle continued to be reconfigured as the gathering progressed. On the last day they spontaneously merged.[26]

Margaret offered some insights from philosopher Heide Göttner-Abendroth that illuminate her artistic approach and understanding of the power of ritual in women's gatherings: "Matriarchal art is not a thing, a commodity, or a fetish but an energetic process."

These observations help clarify the power of the gatherings for the women who have attended. A participant in the first two events penned

Anne Leibig leads Sunday morning processing at In Praise of Mountain Women gathering, May 1993.

reflections that underscore their lasting impact. After the first celebration in 1993, Gayle Combs of Anneville, Kentucky, wrote:

Being a mountain woman from rural Kentucky, I face the same obstacles as each of you. I suffer from depression, anxiety, medical problems due to obesity, children with learning disabilities, a handicapped child. I live on the edge of poverty. My husband and I rarely talk, because our paths cross only when time allows.

The traditional values and beliefs I grew up with in my childhood are harder and harder to deal with. . . . We each have to do what it takes to survive. . . .

I have tried many times to move forward, only to be struck down in defeat. But I recently graduated from Sue Bennett College with an associate degree in psychology. I am now enrolled in the Human Services program, hoping to achieve my bachelor's degree by May 1995. I work as a volunteer with a life skills class of fifth graders. In spring I will teach the adult class. . . .

For many women, this gathering is the first step to realizing life can offer more. . . . Maureen Linneman's song, "In Praise of Mountain Women," offers courage, and our colorful flag should always be held high to remind us we can overcome our burdens and reach solidarity.[27]

In 1999 the In Praise of Mountain Women Round Table published *Our Book*, a report on the first four gatherings and a manual of how the events are organized. Copies can be obtained for ten dollars each from the Appalachian Office of Justice and Peace, P.O. Box 660, Saint Paul, VA 24283.

PART 4

Honoring and Trespassing Boundaries

Chapter 14

FOCIS AS CHURCH

God, the Earthworm! I can be like an earthworm. I can participate in the transformation, the creation, and the redemption.

Although FOCIS women are no longer women religious, they continue to be religious women. Yet they have changed so much, spiritually and in their religious practices. Some have even transferred their religious affiliation from the Catholic Church to Presbyterian, Quaker, and other Protestant groups. Some remain Catholic and speak of how they have worked to "forgive the church." Some remain faithful communicants in the Catholic Church but also participate in an alternative women's church. Most find their deepest religious experiences within FOCIS and in the rural communities where they live and work.

The women were taught to give up their individuality when they entered the convent. They have reclaimed it and treasure and nurture it in themselves and each other. No longer rote, their prayers are now creative expressions. They now find God not in quiet cloister but in the daily experiences of their lives. As a gardener, Monica can find God in the creation work of earthworms in compost. They have bravely taken over the liturgy, rebuilt ties to their families, developed new families, and cared for families and each other.

As an alternative to the convent and to the institutional church, FOCIS has provided the support and setting for their creative religious expressions. FOCIS became church; through FOCIS they have developed creative liturgies, celebrations drawn from their life experiences. Through their friendships and relationships in the communities and the support of the FOCIS network, they developed a theology of friendship and community.

From 1989 through 1993, the Festival of Friends members, in a study group, made an intense and deliberate effort to understand and express their own theology as well as their community theology. In the process, they were developing their own local theology based on their experiences in community, in relationships with God and each other, and their personal life experiences. Monica said: "To restate Aquinas we were people of faith seeking understanding in community."

They also grew in feminine consciousness. When they confronted the patri-
archal church they did not have much sense of being "revolutionary women."
Today they see that they were "feminists" and see themselves not only as feminists
but as feminist theologians expressing a theology of friendship and community.

An outline of their personal change and growth would look like the string
figure known as a cat's cradle: They moved from missionary zeal to partner-
ship and participation; from romantic idealism to critical analysis and trans-
formation; from obedience to understanding powerlessness and using power
on the margins; from acceptance of patriarchy to women's consciousness; and
from dependence through marginalization to creating alternatives.

Ritual and ceremony were important parts of life in the convent that
were continued in FOCIS. However, the ceremonies became more experimental and participatory. Their liturgies evolved to include much more
about community, the environment, their experiences, and friends. From
their formation as a group, FOCIS members have held a special service at
each of their meetings, and Anne Leibig has been the primary celebrant,
leading the rituals and planning celebrations. Her poems "I Want to Be a
Celebrant" and "I Am a Celebrant" express her long-held desire to fulfill
this role and how she does it. In the following excerpts from an article in
Now and Then, Anne wrote of her aspiration to become a celebrant and
the way her life brought her to that door.

"I Want to Be a Celebrant"

I want to be a celebrant.
I want to gather people
   to set aside time and space
   for song and story

I want to be a celebrant
I want to gather elements
   to name the meaning
   to bless and break

I want to be a celebrant
I want to gather with friends
   to rest and re-create
   to taste and see

I had to find my own way
I had to hear my own voice

Diagram of Personal Change and Growth of Glenmary Sisters

From Covenant to Community

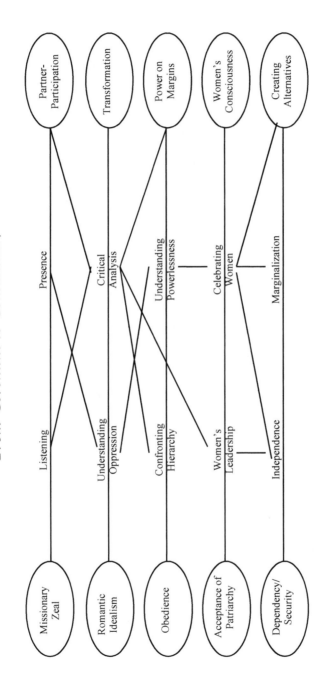

My growing-up world did not call
a woman to be a celebrant. . . .

This has been my journey to make up my own mind. Living in central Appalachia since 1963 has provided a context for me to listen to my call to be a celebrant.
This call includes valuing celebration, noticing when celebrations are happening,
being alert to opportunities for celebration and open to the range of expression.

I attended my first Council of Southern Mountains meeting in 1968 at Fontana
Dam, a large celebration of over a thousand people from all over Appalachia. I
began to see a new kind of celebration that was inclusive; it was not as tightly
structured as the Roman Catholic liturgy. . . . People sang songs, stories were
told, young and old wanted to make the world better for all people. After this I
wanted to travel to every meeting. I liked the meetings because there were a range
of people sharing visions and strategies for a participatory world. The music, the
sharing of food, the good stories, all of this was celebration; and as a participant I
was a celebrant. The last meeting I remember was at Pipestem, West Virginia (I
think in 1973), where I helped Helen Lewis roast a pig. . . .

Gatherings at the River Farm [in the early days] while homes were being built
and gardening and farming were attempted, were a time of celebration. I learned
new ways to celebrate. Usually after a work project there was a great meal, music,
stories and the river nearby for summer immersion. I remember at these times I
would often want things to be more structured, but celebrations would come out
of what I thought was chaos. I learned to rest in this chaos and trust the process.
Helen, with her anthropological sensitivity, talent for good food and generosity of
spirit, encouraged me anytime I expressed a need for ritual and celebration. I
would have a sense of the importance from my growing up and Helen would have
the resource from her study of culture; and sometimes we would make up a ritual,
using cornmeal, spring flowers or some other available element. . . .

Growing up Catholic, morning Mass and feast day processions awakened the
sense of symbol and mystery in celebration. Living in Appalachia has helped me to
make up my own mind, work with others for a better world, trust the process,
value food, song and stories. . . . But being a celebrant is something that cannot
be done alone; it is a role that requires mutuality and inclusiveness, it happens in
the interhuman space. The present actors with me as celebrants are the women
and men of FOCIS, the women of Dungannon and Appalachia. In recent years
they have confirmed me through asking that I create with them celebrations of
graduation, croning [a ritual initiation by elder women that welcomes other women
into old age and into becoming a wise woman elder], divorce, praise, prayer and
friendship.

"I Am a Celebrant!"

I have traveled from my birthplace.
I cannot swallow the wafer whole

in this new place
I have had to chew and
Make up my own mind!

I am a celebrant
I live in Dungannon
I gather with
FOCIS and the Women of the Mountains
Celebrating
Naming meaning,
Respectfully and with joy.[1]

Glenmary priest, economist, and FOCIS member John Rausch has lived and worked in the region since the early 1970s. Participation in many projects and gatherings with FOCIS people has altered his vision of himself and his role as priest and celebrant:

I became a member of FOCIS after being their Rent-A-Priest for a couple of years. Throughout its history FOCIS gathered people for significant events with songs and symbols, and the Catholic liturgy played a central role during weekend meetings. So, when Sunday came, they wanted a priest for Mass. Since I worked in social ministries, I did not have a parish and could schedule FOCIS for a Sunday morning. They actually paid me a stipend, which was the accustomed thing.

After saying Mass for them a time, they asked me to join. In order to do good liturgy you really have to be part of the group. FOCIS taught me that.

In the early 1970s Anne Leibig was in Dungannon and I was the pastor in Saint Paul. When Dick and Anne married, it was not officially an RC, Inc., wedding. I had no problems with that. In fact, I went to the wedding. But officially, the Bishop of Wheeling was really uptight, because Anne had worked for him some years before.

Then Anne came around with this understanding that she had always wanted to be a celebrant. She'd never had the opportunity to really express herself, but she thought FOCIS could be the community to test her calling. I welcomed her playing a larger part in the liturgy; after all, FOCIS membership was overwhelmingly women.

Rather than rushing into the liturgy, Anne would get people to center with breathing exercises, and then lead them in some sort of guided meditation. From there we continued with the Liturgy of the Word. The readings were usually taken from something that was very important to somebody that weekend—a poem or passage from some book—but the Gospel for the day was always included. The dialogued homily deepened the previous discussions or weekend theme by filtering the ideas through a faith perspective. The treatment of the topic came from the experience of the people. It represented authentic liturgy.

When I prayed parts of the Mass, I would interject references to what people had said during the meeting. Words just rolled out of my mouth as I mentioned somebody's child was in trouble or somebody's mother was sick, or maybe somebody was happy for a nice event in their life.

So all of a sudden it was through the FOCIS community—that process—that I learned to work with Anne as a co-celebrant, and I appreciated liturgy as a celebration of life lived by a certain people. . . .

I have a healthier and more wholesome interaction with women as a result of FOCIS. Relationships continue to challenge me, but I see them in a better political dimension. I represent the oppressors! I'm a White, male, American, Roman Catholic priest—ordained. . . . And I think what FOCIS does is constantly challenge me to push the institutions or structures that I'm part of.[2]

FOCIS as a group had not emphasized theological study or reflection on their own theology. When Monica returned in 1987 from six years in southern Africa, she spearheaded the formation of a FOCIS theology group. She had learned about contextual theology, an African expression of liberation.[3]

My idea was to get FOCIS people to do something different because I thought we were getting caught where you just level off—on a plateau. I came back from Africa with new energy and I thought, "I would like to study theology with this group!" I had learned about local theology and contextual theology, an African expression of liberation theology. I thought that we, as Glenmary and FOCIS, had actually done local theology . . . but we didn't have a name for it, like we were doing community development and we didn't have a name for it. A lot of the things we did were more intuitive. We didn't have names or theory behind it. . . . But when I went to Africa, I learned names for what we had done so I thought we needed to tell our story. I wanted to make telling our story my theology project. These three things I wanted: storytelling, negotiation-mediation, and feminist theology. These would be my three studies.

Thirteen FOCIS members joined Monica in forming a theology study group, which explored several possible ways of proceeding. One option was taking a seminary course or enrolling in a degree program. Don Freeman from Lancaster Theology Seminary in Gettysburg, Pennsylvania, spent a weekend with the group and helped lead a workshop and discussion of their goals and objectives.

At the retreat, the women verbalized their growing perception of FOCIS as church. Linda Mashburn recalled the significance of that realization and the empowerment it gave them:

At the Lancaster workshop several FOCIS members identified FOCIS as their church. As a Protestant I feel comfortable saying that FOCIS is my church, but I understand it is difficult for people brought up in the Catholic Church to label it as church. Yet for me it has always epitomized the best of what church is: the Body of Christ. It is wonderful that other FOCIS members could name it that way. . . .

One of the remarkable things that came out of the workshop was a list of the organizations and programs which have come from the work of these five FOCIS members (Catherine, Marie, Monica, Anne, and myself). We put on the board all the different organizations that had come from our work . . . and there were over fifty organizations, programs, and corporations. It was phenomenal that five women had given birth to that much creative effort. I mean here in Statesville, where I live, I helped organize Hospice, a soup kitchen, and Habitat, and I was president of the Crisis Intervention Ministries, through which I started at least one new program.

I can remember a wonderful drawing that Catherine did of herself in the middle of a parade. She said: "I see myself encouraging everybody. I am not leading the parade, but I'm a cheerleader in the midst of the movement encouraging everyone on." And I thought that was very perceptive of the style of leadership she has given. She also admitted, "I haven't always known what direction FOCIS is going, so I couldn't be out front!"

At the workshop Don Freeman was the only ordained person, and he did none of the liturgy on the last day. Catherine said the words of consecration over the bread and wine, and nobody looked in Don's direction and nobody made any attempt to give him a leadership role. Catherine and Anne organized that liturgy, and we celebrated.

While I was living in Berea, in the early days of FOCIS, they had some meetings in which they tried to evaluate what kind of an organization they were becoming, and where they were going. I participated, and said I felt much like Paul might have felt in the early days of the church when he traveled around and visited some of the young churches around Asia Minor. When I visited a FOCIS household I felt I was visiting a wonderful young new church. I experienced the fellowship, and there was so much in common in how we perceived problems, possibilities and shared the hope, the work, everything. I felt totally at home.

The members of the group decided they did not want to meet the college theology course requirement for the Lancaster program. Instead, Catherine Rumschlag, Kathy Hutson, and Lenore Mullarney entered the Loyola Institute of Ministry Extension (LIMEX) program that offered a master's degree or certificate in pastoral ministry. Lenore had to drop out for health reasons, but Catherine and Kathy graduated in 1997 after completing the ten-course requirement.

The theology study group continued to meet and pursue their interests in University Without Walls fashion. They began to incorporate a theology focus into FOCIS's annual meetings. At the first meeting in January 1989, they discussed the book *Dangerous Memories: House Churches and Our American Story*, by Bernard J. Lee and Michael Cowan[4] and explored the dangerous memory of intentional communities.

Lee and Cowan quote Johann Baptist Metz from his book *Faith in History and Society*: "There are dangerous memories, memories which make demands on us. These are memories in which earlier experiences break through to the centre-point of our lives and reveal new and dangerous insights for the present. . . . They break through the canon of prevailing structures of plausibility and have certain subversive features. Such memories are like dangerous and incalculable visitations from the past. They are memories, as it were, with a future content." This sentiment expressed FOCIS members' motivation and hope for the theology study group: They wanted to explore their dangerous memories. They were asked to reflect on what new and dangerous insights their past experiences reveal for the present and what they demand of them today.

At the 1990 meeting Anne Leibig presented a review of the book *Fierce Tenderness* by Mary Hunt, who described friendship as a theological experience:

> As I read the book I found myself saying so often, "Oh, yes, this is my experience in FOCIS!" I thought of our summer and winter gatherings as being theologizing experiences; "the organic and communal process of sharing insights, stories and reflection on questions of ultimate meaning" (61).
>
> Hunt's definition of friendship is, "Those voluntary relationships that are entered into by people who intend one another's well being and who intend that their love relationship is part of a justice seeking community" (29). FOCIS has been the context for my learning of friendship and that the love I have shared with you has been part of our communities in service.[5]

At the same 1990 meeting an evocative banner created by Margaret Gregg inspired them to begin a theological pilgrimage into their past. The banner held "stars, papers, footprints, travels and shadows."[6] Monica said, "This process [became] a recognition and a celebration of places and people that have formed and sustained us individually and as a community. We [decided to make some pilgrimages and] visit Big Stone, Clairfield, Knoxville, Cherokee, and the beach. At the weekend beach retreat we explored feminist theology."[7]

In November 1990 when they met at Marie Cirillo's house on Roses Creek (near Clairfield), they focused on community theology. The invitation explained: "We value our history of connectedness and rootedness in community. And we want to construct our theology from this experience. We want to learn what theological method and reflection are in our particular situation. And we want to discover ways to express our faith by discoursing with the community of Roses Creek, FOCIS people and resource theologians."[8] They met with Clairfield residents and two feminist theologians, Mary Anne Hinsdale from Holy Cross College and Marianne Sawicki from Louisville, Kentucky. And in her call to her neighbors Marie wrote: "I have to believe that my total life is a prayer and that community is my church. I have to believe that God is here, with us and among us, because this is where my spirit finds nurture, and who but God is giver of all gifts. So we need time to celebrate this from time to time."[9]

For the workshop everyone was asked to consider the question, "Where do I feel close to God?" They were to bring their way of expressing the answer through music, scripture, poetry, art, storytelling.[10] Participants drew a picture of the God "present with us this day, in this place, at this time, and the pictures became IKONS—Holy Pictures." They studied each other's icons and their interpretations increased and expanded as time passed.[11]

Monica set down these thoughts about her experience:

As I was sitting with the others as we beheld our icons, gazed at them and said what we saw, I saw what I did in a new way. Those bright colored waves, they were earthworms, they were glowworms, no, earthworms. And then it struck. God the earthworm! I can be like an earthworm. I can participate in the transformation, the creation and the redemption. Someone afterward said they thought what I drew was a broken rainbow. The church, the broken rainbow. I . . . read [an article by Rosemary Reuther and] I can see from it that the work of community is a redemptive work, a participation in the transformation, the in and out, the going forward and then back, the journey, the turning, the revolution, the upheaval in personal and family life, the fears and jealousy, . . . sin and forgiveness. Earthworm work: what goes in comes out different, renewed.

God the Earthworm. The one who takes in and lets out. The one who loosens and enriches the soil. The ground. The one who passes through while we pass over. You are a gift to the soil and to the fruits that grow in its goodness. We meet you in the garden earth.[12]

Marie later wrote her reflections for the group in the form of a poem:

We started our journey with a sharing of OUR EXPERIENCE OF GOD. We listened to ourselves and each other, experiencing the God contained within that one room:

> God is breath, protector, in my ability to lead a dance,
> community, music,
> which way do I go, where I am bound,
> garden growing wild,
> exhaustion, part of creation, oneness,
> clearing out extra baggage, nature,
> let it go.
> I have been forgiven, symbols on altar, performance,
> in touch, extremes,
> let's go,
> why old live and young die,
> so many contradictions,
> child-taskmaster, driven,
> let go,
> leaves drop, sun sets,
> morning together, night alone,
> daytime lost in activity,
> know self/naked, give self away,
> love,
> bringing people together, via telephone, writing,
> coming home,
> when walls come down, experiencing what is different,
> delighting in diversity, in that way all the same,
> all delightful, all beautiful, the joy and pain,
> the bright side and the shadowy side,
> growth has something to do with accepting it—
> I SHALL BE WITH YOU, SUCH AS I AM,
> our culture—as we are.[13]

The theology group continued to develop exercises and discussion topics for programs at the FOCIS annual meetings. For the January 1991 meeting they asked members to bring a picture of their home place. Participants could ask the people they lived with to help draw the picture. Monica explained: "One of the important parts of our theology study methodology is that we bring something from our life experience to our gatherings."[14]

At the January 1992 annual meeting, in preparation for their twenty-fifth anniversary celebration, they developed a "Wall of Friends," and people brought names and remembrances. Anne Leibig recalled the spiritual and commemorative experience of that ritual:

[W]hen we began studying feminist theology, we read this book about God as friend,[15] and that women having friends and being friends is one of the gifts that Mary Hunt [discerns], and that to reflect on that is a way of meeting God. So . . . we thought for this weekend "friends" would be an opening theme, and that we'd bring the friends' names that we'd like to celebrate twenty-five years with. So . . . this morning when we were thinking about putting our Wall of Friends up, we remembered that the Vietnam Wall is the place where names were put of people who had given their lives. So that gave us a context of a symbol, or a ritual, how when we put our names up we are remembering and naming and calling on these people as part of who we are.

Mary Herr's religious experiences include both Cherokee and Christian rituals, which have been combined in the sweat lodge experience. In 1992 Mary Herr and the theology group invited the FOCIS members to experience a sweat lodge. Approximately fifteen took part. Mary explained how Cherokee practices have expanded her sense of the spiritual:

In the 1980s there was a renewed interest among some of the Cherokee people (especially those with college degrees) to learn more about the traditional ways. I was invited to participate in the Cherokee stomp dance in Oklahoma, and the sweat lodge and talking circle in Cherokee. I was delighted to find that there are many similarities between the traditional Cherokee ceremonies, the sweat lodge, and the Catholic liturgy. Participating in these ceremonies brought me closer to the Creator and to all of creation.

The intimacy and sharing of the sweat lodge and talking circle enabled me to pray with others from different faiths, races, and backgrounds in a way I never would have thought was possible. My spiritual life was expanded to limits that it is difficult to describe. Sitting on Mother Earth in the sweat lodge, listening to the rocks sing and talk, feeling the sometimes intense heat from the water poured over the hot rocks, smoking the Sacred Pipe, and praying with my sisters from far and near all brought me closer to the Creator and to those with whom I shared these experiences. I feel I have grown, not through the church but through sweat ceremonies. There is more of a sense of community and family than at the church. I feel like I have the best of two worlds: the traditional Catholic Church and the sweat ceremonies.[16]

The present day Glenmary Sisters and Fathers celebrated their fiftieth anniversary in 1991 with a symposium. Some FOCIS members attended, and the FOCIS group later decided they would celebrate their twenty-fifth anniversary with a festival and a big reunion called a Festival of Friends. Monica commented on this decision at the Highlander workshop: "We may not know how to do symposiums, or do doctorates, or write books, but we knew we could do a celebration! So that's kind of the history of how we've come from a master's in theology to a party."[17]

The FOCIS twenty-fifth anniversary Festival of Friends, held in June 1993 at Cumberland Falls State Park in Kentucky, became the culmination of the FOCIS theological process to that moment. FOCIS members and cherished companions from stages of their life journey gathered for a weekend of "recycling and recircling" to: "revisit, redirect, respond, relax, restore, reinforce, renew, revision, remember, revise, review, restructure, relate, rejoice, revolt, release."[18]

The celebration emerged from four years of spiritual journey and nine months of detailed planning. FOCIS artist Margaret Gregg coordinated the festival and structured its events.

A major theme of the festival was "bones," as in, "Dem bones gonna rise again."[19] The physical "bones" were twenty-five emblematic words—one for each year, five for each half-decade, of the history of FOCIS—that Margaret painted onto wooden bone-shapes which she installed along a nature trail in the park. (Margaret had initially tried real bones, but discovered she couldn't boil them clean enough.) She winnowed this remnant from an aggregate of hundreds of words and phrases encapsulating the five periods, which FOCIS members had suggested earlier.

Groups or individuals could wander the trail, which ended at a waterfall, any time during the festival weekend, reflecting upon these bones of their shared past. FOCIS member Kathleen Mavournin knitted skeleton and flesh around the bones in an extraordinary poem for the occasion:

"Age of Discovery"

Reaching for risk, for work in the world, we are climbing the
    whirlwind,
confused and expanding, feeling our ways into outer commitments—
making homes, making marriages, schools and communities—
Activists turning our gifts into love into tools and the struggle
for change is changing the struggle: riding the wind of discovery.
Branching and blooming, birthing new families, some of us leaving
or living alone—community stretched by dispersal, kept strong

by memory, faith and reunion; now there are men in our midst
sharing diversity, energy, love—maturation evolves
out of questions and visions; hope and necessity mother discovery.

Don't make it look easy or bury the anger, grinding frustration,
the bad times, the fear—some of us lonely or badly beleaguered
by life's expectations; families grow and grow older—now deaths
intersperse with the births—we reorient, rallying, building
new ways to be women, to work, to resist, and to relish discovery.

Some of us parenting, all of us pouring out love on the people
around us—we're nurturing lives, feeding souls, sharing trials and
        dreaming
up livelihoods, healing—however we can: we're in service to this
Holy world and each other—craving connections to keep ourselves
        going,
surviving and growing, each bringing all her discovery.

Croning, now older and deeper and broader, more loving—and odder;
taking our liturgy back to our hearts and theology
out of the classroom, back to the land—and community
more than a name, is the dream and remembering, framework and
        catapult:
weeping and singing, we've come quarter century still on the way to
        discovery.[20]

Margaret Gregg developed a mixture of symbolic activities that were
interspersed with discussions and fun and games. In addition, the festival
featured a spiral cakewalk (the spiral or maze symbolizing both the past
and the external and internal universe); recycling bags (collections of tal-
ismanic objects randomly redistributed); an overnight pig-roast (a man
thing); the tying together of the Friendship Quilt developed by Jane
McElroy; a banquet; discussion groups (Shared History, Images, Visions);
a reading by poet-playwright Jo Carson; dance, song, and music; and a
Sunday ritual.[21]

The friendship quilt was developed by Jane McElroy to celebrate
twenty-five years of FOCIS, the blocks representing the members of
FOCIS, framed by a border with the names of many friends and extended
family who have participated so richly in diverse ways over the years. She
explains the design:

The individual blocks are in the Log Cabin pattern. Anne Leibig suggested this pattern, having read in Elaine Showalter's article, "Piecing and Writing," that this is considered the most archetypal quilt design. It has been recognized as combining the male and female, representing the union of opposites and safe passage from one world to another. According to American tradition, the center square of each block represents hearth and home. Moving in toward, or out from that block (depending on your perspective), are the "logs," laid alternately on either adjacent or opposite sides. . . .

Standing back, you can see that the "logs" framing each block create a chain that connects them all and unites them into a greater overall pattern.[22]

Since the Festival of Friends, the quilt continues to be used at meetings, ceremonies, funerals, and sometimes bedtime in people's homes. Monica explains: "It is a connection to community and helps us remember the 'high' times when we are together and when we are apart, dispersed into the places we live our life and death."

In their October 1998 workshop, as FOCIS members reflected on their organization's life, they discussed FOCIS theology and the group's relationship to church. Linda Mashburn, John Rausch, Kathy Hutson, and Dene Peterson were the major participants in the conversations that followed:

LINDA MASHBURN: What I really learned through FOCIS is that faith is not a set of doctrines, it's not a set of religious beliefs—it's that willingness to risk and to step out, and hope that if you're doing your part, God's doing God's part—Her part, yes—and that you'll end up on the right side of the struggle. . . . And I watched FOCIS members doing it repeatedly in those early years. . . . As I've learned from Central American friends, they've got a nice Spanish phrase that says basically, "Jesus Christ is a verb, not a noun."

KATHY HUTSON: I think FOCIS is primarily a religious organization. . . . There's a spiritual bonding. Here is an intense group that really loves each other. And there's been a lot of pain and there's been a lot of suffering and there's also been a lot of forgiveness. It's that picture of church. And then to celebrate it in a kind of fullness of our being together, and an acknowledgment of how it fits in the world picture—it's not just our little group. . . .

JOHN RAUSCH: [W]hen it comes to theology and spirituality . . . I think FOCIS has much to teach the American church. I really did learn liturgy from the FOCIS gatherings. I had a three-hour course in liturgy in seminary. And I learned what the *epiklesis* was, the *anamnesis* is, and all these other wonderful things, which you know, if you met them on the street you'd like to beat them with a stick. But in terms of what is liturgy, I learned experientially from the FOCIS gathering. I came as someone who was a representative of the orthodox church. And I was stretched. And by stretching me, I've taken what I have learned from FOCIS into other communities. And people really do affirm the way I do Mass, because of this. So it's not lifeless at all; it's more life-giving. Through our experiences, we can show concrete expressions of what it means to be church. And that will bleed across denominational lines. And that will bleed across wonderfully, nicely worded theological statements. And the institutions [would be] free not to have a wonderful, pure, defined dogma.

In this group I've been given the permission to be someone who is a seeker of "How do I express theology from my experience and from what I've seen?"

We ought to do much more reflecting on what we really believe as FOCIS, because I think that FOCIS has something to help the American Catholic Church. And it will bring down the house; the folks who are the high priests of theology will rebel; they will negate us. . . .

LINDA: And what I want to also say, as a Protestant, is that it is extremely liberating to us in our boxes when we see Catholics break [out]. . . . Even before I ran into FOCIS when I was with some Maryknoll seminarians who took communion from a Protestant minister, you know suddenly that broke down all kinds of barriers for me. Because then when I celebrated communion with them without any priest or minister, it was OK. . . . I mean, we all need liberation, is what I'm saying.

JOHN: Right. Well, ecumenism is another whole area. When RC, Inc., talks about ecumenism, they're talking about tea and crumpets. And "Let's have a proposition and let's have a debate about whether Jesus is present in the Eucharist," or something. That's the way theologians debate the thing. We live it. I have to be reminded who isn't a card-carrying Catholic person.

LINDA: The differences between what FOCIS is and what institutionalized religion in the United States has become, is that it is that safe place: people that nurture my calling. Because as a Protestant, there is no group of religious; for a woman to have a calling back in the '50s when women weren't even ordained, you either became a missionary or a director of Christian education—those were the two options. . . . Yet when I found FOCIS members, I felt immediately that I shared that common calling. To development work in Appalachia, to a certain lifestyle, toward values, toward what I do with my life.

In any of our gatherings, the worship emerges out of the meeting, and the themes and things that are discussed. So that when we get to the worship near the end of the gathering, everybody is in part contributing to that and it grows out of the whole experience. I mean even though it's planned by a core group of people, everybody gets a chance to participate when the actual liturgy is done.

DENE: We look at all service as ministry, it seems to me, which is a theological concept. And I think if the ministry weren't theology, I'd be in a hard way to come to the celebrations. Because then what am I celebrating? I mean, I'm not getting juiced to go out and give. I've already gone out and given; now I'm celebrating.

LINDA: Right. It's what we do in the world that we bring to worship to celebrate, or what happens in the world.

DENE: Well God depends on us to do his action. Who else is gonna do it? Other than other humans?

LINDA: Our theology is our work and our mission and our activities, and sometimes they seem very mundane and routine when we talk about nonprofits and organizing, and this, that, and the other. But the fact of the matter remains, that every member of the original Glenmary/FOCIS members, felt a real vocation and calling. That this was their ministry in life. This was their lifelong calling. And I don't think that any of the original members abandoned that calling in moving out into FOCIS and into their activities. And I think those of us who were not a part of that had felt a similar calling.

When I try to describe to my own local church one of the big differences between FOCIS and that congregation—and it's a small congregation that is basically supportive, and that when there's a crisis in a family, does do a reasonable job of rallying—but they never, ever, on a Sunday or any other time, sit around in a circle, or in a face-to-face way, and share. The way this group does at annual meetings or at other times, in terms of what's going on with us personally. . . . But it's incredible how much I didn't know about the other people, because we never spent that time sharing with one another.

MARIE: That's true in this little church in Jellico; there's mostly hardly twenty people there. And we welcome someone new into the church and, "This is so-and-so." And I thought, you know, "Is there going to be an opportunity to get to know them?" And I've been going there for thirty-two years, and I still don't know anything about the lives of the people I sit in church with.

DENE: Vatican II said, "The people are the church." This community is the church.

MARIE: So we're gonna claim that. As we did right from the beginning (laughter).[23]

Even though the theology group is no longer actively meeting, the theology work of FOCIS continues. Recently Monica wrote, "The book itself [*Mountain Sisters*] is an expression of what I said I wanted my theology study to be . . . storytelling, feminist theology, and negotiation/mediation. . . . And the FOCIS meetings [have taken on] these elements of reflection, community support, study and celebration. Theology is faith seeking understanding (Thomas Aquinas). And I heard a woman theologian add that theology is faith seeking understanding in community. That is the FOCIS theology.[24]

Theologian Elizabeth Bounds perceived an intuitive feminism in Glenmary/ FOCIS theology and actions that was ahead of its time:

[The Glenmary Sisters understood intuitively] that spirit couldn't be lived out in the institution of the church as women in the church, and . . . they realized that at some level they had to live out that same spirit outside the institutional church. They really are living out in some ways the true church. . . . When it comes to some very fundamental issues concerning women, birth control being one, ordination being another, there has been no move [by the institutional church].

God is not envisioned as an utterly transcendent old White man. Certainly common [to feminist theology] is to break down this old image of God. The implication of that, besides how you view God, is a very different understanding of power, and that means a very different understanding of the God/human relation, and that means a very different understanding of power within the church. Because you say that God is not an utterly transcendent being, but is of us, among us, and present in relationships among people. So when there is a dynamic relation, work for change, God is present in those human relationships. I would say the [FOCIS women] are very much doing feminist theological work. They were really remarkably ahead in terms of that understanding.[25]

Chapter 15

JOURNEY NOT ARRIVAL[1]

Most of us were against organized anything that would hamper the spirit.

They left holy space as courageous young women; they had to redefine poverty, chastity, and obedience. They had to discover what commitment meant in a dispersed community. They redefined, they improvised, they learned as they journeyed. Intuitively, they developed a pedagogy similar to the approach and theory of Paulo Freire, detailed in his book Pedagogy of the Oppressed.[2] *Some things they learned through education and training: the Appalachian Training Program in Chicago, Monica's experiences at Harvard Community Education Program, and the workshops at Highlander Center. Much was gleaned through evaluation and reflection on their own experience.*

Reflecting on their journey, they recognized that they were prophetic voices and leaders in the Catholic women's liberation movement. They have provided models for future Sisters and friends and colleagues. They developed an organization of resistance (FOCIS) and helped communities create alternative organizations connected to each other. They created an organization suited to a mobile, dispersed community, based on what Walter Brueggemann calls a prophetic ministry, "a ministry offering an alternative perception of reality [which lets] people see their own history in the light of God's freedom and his will for justice."[3]

As many are now facing retirement and aging, their current project is developing an innovative, ecumenical retirement community, which will meet the spiritual as well as physical needs of its members. Again they are developing an alternative that not only meets their needs but also provides a model for the larger community. The dispersed community is now regathering to care for one another; it is the joining of people from different places who want to live a community life and practice "aging with spirit."

Have they changed the church? Or is it so sexist, patriarchal, and hierarchical that it cannot learn from the present-day Sisters who are asking for greater

*participation and recognition or from former Sisters such as the FOCIS women?
There have been many changes in the ways in which Catholic Sisters live and
work. Many of the experiments which the Glenmary Sisters and other orders
carried out in the 1960s are now customary for current Sisters, but there are
still struggles with the church hierarchy for full participation. In the epilogue,
former mother superior Catherine Rumschlag responds to comments by Sister
Nancy Sylvester, former president of the Leadership Conference of Women Religious, who feels present-day Sisters have reached an impasse in negotiations
with the church. When the Glenmary Sisters reached such an impasse, Mother
Superior Catherine challenged them to "walk on water." Sister Nancy invites
current Sisters to "go to the desert to see with our heart the next steps."*

*FOCIS may not provide an acceptable model for women religious today,
but it does stand as an example of how a group of Sisters moved as a community of resistance to a community of support and friendship. Along with the
freedom and independence they gained, there were also losses, pain, and grieving. But for this group of women to remain true to their commitment, they
had to move from being women religious to religious women. They have been
resilient—like the people in rural communities where they have lived and
worked—because they have each other. In addition to their ties to one another,
they have been sustained by music and cultural arts, meaningful work, celebration, faith, and stories.*

At the time the women left Glenmary and formed FOCIS, their actions
were not seen—by themselves or others—as a feminist revolt of Catholic
Sisters. Yet they chose to continue as a community of women, a community they had first joined to become "women of power" like the nuns they
knew as teachers.

Maureen Linneman recalled how Glenmary nurtured their potential:

It's almost like there's a sociological path [in our history], where there has
been an underground stirring for identity and meaningful work life among women.
And in going into Glenmary, I think there was a new kind of dedication that we
saw later in various movements in our country, and eventually the women's movement. It seems like historically, it was an underground river that was stirring that
we were also part of. I feel there was a progressive life. That my life now is still
attached to where I was going or what I was feeling as a very young woman.[4]

Although governed by and often serving men, the convent was a
woman-run world. Geraldine Peterson noted: "Social researchers say that
women who attend all-women colleges are more likely to end up in leadership positions. The convent was certainly an 'all girls' school and my

institution of higher learning. It was perfect for me to be the strong decisive woman I am."

Over time, Jean Luce observed an evolution in the women's perception of their 1967 actions:

I don't remember a conversation along the lines of, "We are growing as women, we are taking a stand contrary to the patriarchal church." We didn't put it in those terms, but that is what it was. As we got further away from it and developed the language of the women's movement, we began to see our own experience in the light of the women's movement.

When I moved to Somerville, I was selected by a group of women to run [a women's shelter]. Which was really ludicrous because I had never been married, and I hadn't been battered as a child, but somehow they saw me as somebody who was able to relate to other women. I think at an intuitive level women were gravitating to women who had gone through an experience of saying no to authority or convention. "No, I don't have to behave the way you want me to behave, I don't have to live the life that you dictate to me; I will choose my own. We will choose our own." I think our doing that was a tremendous step toward women's identity; it was a feminist kind of action.

Today FOCIS women appraise their past in feminist terms:

MONICA APPLEBY: I think it was a real confrontation with men who are the hierarchy of the church, who didn't have the same experience we had. I mean they didn't have to wear funny clothes when they visited people. . . . [The] men had more access to the place where decisions were made; they were in it. . . . Wanting to make our own decisions was threatening. As a woman in the church you can't be an adult, you always have to be a child, and that is not how I want to interact in the church. I am an adult woman. . . .

ANNE LEIBIG: I sense that we have been women who want to create what we believe in, rather than confront and change the other. For me, looking at all the corporations I have helped form says I would rather create than confront and change others. We left Glenmary and created a new organization rather than confront and change.

The process of building their own organization produced a new sense of power, a power they were able to share. Monica Appleby reflected on FOCIS members' positive influence on other women in the communities they served.

Becoming a Glenmary Sister was an experience of personal development and finding out about the institutional church from the inside. We were given the opportunity to do things we had never done before, never even dreamed of do-ing. Through experiencing our own personal power we came at odds with the institution of the church and left to "create something new." . . .

I think that is one of the contributions we made in communities: we helped other women create their own organizations so that they could do what they wanted to do in their community. We had to create our own organization. When I first came here there were no community organizations. There was the family and the church. There were no grassroots community organizations. Now there are organizations with names like Appalachian Women Empowered, Black Lung Movement. Community and regional organizations were mainly started by women. . . . The people who actually do the work are women. Sometimes you will find men who seem to be elected to the boards. But the glue and hard work is always women.[5]

Marie Cirillo explained why the group so often found women to be the glue that sustained community effort:

One of the major things is that I think women understand the connectedness of one thing to another better. . . . So I think that's one of the major pieces: that women understand relationships better. And I think, because of that, they're more in tune with process than product. So they are better nurturers. I think it could be obviously something beyond what you've been trained or taught. Women are more patient: many of them stick to things longer; they are more enduring when things get discouraging. That's good for continuity in terms of non-profits, and trying to keep it alive. And they network, and that's part of the connectedness. They talk more.

Marie did not begin to think of women's issues as separate from other social change issues until about 1980, when she attended a meeting of Rural American Women in Washington, D.C.:

I was so amazed that I was with a group of people who not only shared the same interests, but put those things in the same priority. My experience in the past had been that if I were with rural people my agenda would be pretty much the same, but when it got into what's most important it was generally other things, [because] men set those priorities. [But] these were all women, they had the rural agenda and they had the priorities that I did, so I thought there must be some-thing about rural women!

So I drove home. And I was so excited about what happened at that meeting [that] I called some of the non-profits in the area that I knew were run by women. And we had never thought to get them to meet each other, or what could happen if they got together. So we all got five or six of our women from our groups and we went down to Crazy Quilt, the quilt crafts center. And . . . I mean, the energy! It was just one day; but the talk, the level of dialogue there—you could hardly hear yourself think, it was just going so fast. And it was just high, high energy. And that's the group that eventually created Mountain Women's Exchange.

The women evolved their ways of working in community. In a progression whose linearity may be oversimplified, they moved from missionary work (offering charity and compassion) to social service (providing food, clothes, housing, and transportation) to advocacy (speaking for and with, questioning institutions and agencies, serving as ombudswomen) to action for social change (leading campaigns for welfare rights, black-lung benefits, strip-mining regulation, and community organizing). Their activities evolved from visiting the poor and oppressed, organizing Bible schools, and meeting material needs, to assisting as advocates and finally joining the poor in social movements and working in communities to provide empowering services like legal aid and education; to develop needed infrastructure like water, health, and housing; and to strategically plan and move toward more sustainable, controlled development.

Some specific community-based development projects instituted in the region with FOCIS involvement were: the Model Valley CDC, the pallet factory, and Woodland Community Land Trust in Clairfield; the tomato-growing co-op, Bread and Chicken Co-op, and Appalachian Family Ministries in Big Stone Gap; the building co-op, Mountain People's Manor housing, and Appalachia Community Development Corporation in Appalachia; and the Dungannon Development Commission, sewing co-op, sewing factory, community laundry, and housing project in Dungannon. In all of these there was an evolutionary progression from earlier activities. The Glenmary Bible schools and family visiting were the "earthworm work" which resulted in a methodology and pedagogy for community-based development. Monica once said the arts programs and health fairs were just Bible school without the Bible.

When asked at the 1998 Highlander workshop to describe their methodology of community development, members found it difficult to articulate:

MARIE CIRILLO: What I remember is our struggle to get from running around doing Bible school here, here, here and here; to be working more in the communities. And that's when we created this ministry and we got the bishops to support it, right?

ANNE LEIBIG: The question is, how do we spell out the methodology? And one thought that comes out of my psychology is that there's a holding space for growth and healing. Being a therapist, it's like, sometimes I don't know what's happened in the interaction with a client, but I'm getting more of a sense of just having a safe holding space that supports the energy of healing. And that somehow, coming to Glenmary Sisters felt like a safe holding space for me. And other people were there that had creative energies to not only be safe and holding, but grow and express. . . . I think the holding place of Glenmary Sisters was generative; and FOCIS came out of that generativity. And there's a continuity; and then now I think all of us, when we gather, we do that. We support each other and feel safe. But then that gives us the possibility to go to where we are, and carry that holding space. One of the methodologies would be, experiencing among ourselves a holding space of safety and generativity, and then being able to take that to the places where we support. . . .

MONICA APPLEBY: I think that's the place where relationships can grow. It's different than confrontation or community organizing, which is viewed as not creating a safe place, but a battleground. . . .

MAUREEN LINNEMAN: You know, probably a lot of it developed as a reaction to the institutional church that Glenmary was up against. It influenced us to create something different. Because if that wasn't working, we've got to find something different. We know hierarchy is what we feel oppressed by, so we've got to come up with something that's more circular than hierarchical. . . .

MONICA: I think that in the beginning in Big Stone [Gap], it was really just following your gut; and doing what seemed needed to be done, relating with people more than programs. But when I went to Chicago, that's when things became more articulated. And I do think research, planning, action, and evaluation became more action and research—the research didn't come first. . . . or the kind of research was action research. . . .[6] Which was more getting in there.

The arts program was a concrete expression of what we learned in Chicago. Dr. [Martin] Corcoran called [the arts projects] "cultural caravans"; and we put that together in a community action proposal that we brought down to our local community action program. The methodology was spelled out in the community action program. And we did that largely influenced by what we were learning with Corcoran and by his language. . . .

MARIE: I don't think I thought of it as research, but in the listening process there was this basic intuition, to listen to see where that person's passion was. When I found five or ten people that had that same passion, I'd bring them together. And then we'd start the planning, and then they'd get into their action. I think part of that listening process was that we knew from Bible schools and from the culture, that we could hear more about the values and passions of people through some of their art and music, than by sitting down doing formal research.

So that's where I think our artistic and Bible school experiences came together with Corcoran's methodology. It was listening and hearing people's passions and then we mobilized around that.[7]

The women who created FOCIS were conflicted and ambivalent not just about established social institutions but even at times about the dynamics of their own organization. Marie commented:

Most of us were so against organized anything that would hamper the spirit that it took years to decide the right way to re-socialize. Some of us rejected how the church structure killed our spirit, but we had some sense of organizing and wanted to be with the mountain people in starting a process together. We became the community developers, the founders of local non-profit organizations, the strategists, the ones reflecting on the ways of FOCIS. We believed it was easier to change the world by creating alternative institutions rather than reforming the existing ones. . . .

At the 1998 workshop Donna Haig Friedman, a FOCIS member who works on community health issues in Massachusetts, lauded Catherine's combination of quiet leadership and bold vision:

Catherine, you were a tremendous model of a different way of leadership, non-hierarchical. Of letting go of a leadership role, of sharing it. It felt like a fluid leadership. . . . And that was such an inspiration. And I really feel like I have carried that as a kind of constant. In the places where I have worked, and the communities that I'm building where I am. Along with that energy and vitality, and a different way of being a woman than was usual for then. I think of this as sort of a way. . . . of knowing that you can break out of boxes. There's no box that can't be broken ("FOCIS Workshop 10/24/98 Transcription," 55).

Marie continued the conversation, saying, "Father Bishop did not want the Sisters to work in institutions: We had Bible stories under the trees, we carried them around from place to place. But the little parishes couldn't support us and we had to find work. . . . Some of us had to go into institutions and we inserted new programs within those institutions. Others of us tried to keep connected to the church and do rural development. And then when we went into the communities some of us tried to create alternative institutions. We moved into this process of change and falling apart so we can come together in new ways."

At the 1998 workshop Marie elaborated further on the ties between the women's ministry work and the church:

Working for the church: . . . that was one of our ways of trying to move the church into a new ministry. That's how I perceived it, and I guess the way I perceive it now. And I think with all the years that I have retained [my development job with the Diocese of Nashville], that I haven't gotten support from the church, other than financial support. 'Cause they don't know any more today about what the ministry could be.

And I also know that if the church hadn't supported it, I never would have been able to stay in any community 25, 28–32 years actually, to do it (50–51).

Participants at the workshop considered FOCIS's relationship to their work as individuals. Many FOCIS members have problems knowing whether to consider their work personal work or FOCIS work. They wonder, is it legitimate to credit FOCIS for work done alone or with people in the community who never even hear of FOCIS? Who is accountable? These were some of the questions that triggered a lively conversation:

CATHERINE RUMSCHLAG: Well I think FOCIS is the organization or the overall connection that allows us to receive the support and assistance that we need to be and to do the things that we do. I don't attribute the emergency shelter to FOCIS. I don't expect FOCIS to bail me out if I mess up. I'm just stuck with it. If I incur so many expenses I can't pay them, I'll have to go bankrupt. FOCIS . . . doesn't presume to provide financial backing for whatever people decide to do. So I think it's more a network and support system. And . . . a non-profit corporation, tax-exempt, which can be used for the purposes of directing funds, grants, etc. . . . I don't think FOCIS does works, as FOCIS.

ANNE LEIBIG: I think FOCIS is when we gather as a FOCIS group, like this weekend or the annual meeting in January; somehow to me that's when FOCIS happens. As a holding space to nurture. And then when I go out and do my own work, I have that in myself to help me feel supported and energized. But my own work is my own work. . . . I feel FOCIS is a support place. And it's also a network of friends, where we can gossip and stay connected to each other. So in our gossiping FOCIS exists. . . .

DONNA HAIG FRIEDMAN: In addition . . . I think there's a certain set of values, a way of looking at the world, and a way of looking at our work, that we hold in common. And I think this tension between "when am I a FOCIS member and when am I myself" is sort of built in to being a loosely knit organization. It used to bother me, now it doesn't bother me. And it feels good to have a holding place and a place for different types of nurturance and support and reaffirmation of the values and reconnection. And then go off and do stuff, feeling connected, but maybe not as geographically. . . . I think some of that tension is inherent in having chosen a loosely connected organization.

KATHLEEN MAUVORNIN: I'm thinking in terms of plants and roots. That FOCIS is like the soil in which a plant roots and from which we receive nurturance; but the soil and the plant are not the same thing. . . . What really feels right to me is this atmosphere of people who care, who are emotionally and socially involved with their communities and their people, where they live; and who come together to share that kind of commitment. That's what I feel rooted about here. And it's very much the same kind of rootedness that I have with my family of origin. It's that sense of commitment to living in this world to make it a better place (67–68).

The group talked about the work they had done and how they felt about leaving programs, moving on or passing it on to others. As founders it was sometimes hard to give up control and difficult when a cherished project did not survive or moved in a direction they felt was not the best way. Linda Mashburn spoke with both pride and regret about leaving programs one has begun:

Because there have been . . . many creative wonderful institutions created through FOCIS, they have also been like children: some growing in different directions; some don't make it past infancy. . . . There have been some that have died or that lasted ten wonderful years and weren't needed anymore, and just passed out of existence. And some—you know I think of my own child in some of this, in the Hot Springs health program. And . . . I was really very distraught about their decision not to accept federal money. And to *ditch the sliding scale*! Which, in my mind, was part of the heart of the program, so that now, poor people in Madison County can't get health—well they can go, but they have to swallow their pride and deal with their enormous debt to the program. And most mountain people, as you all know, don't do that. They just go without care. They don't go begging when they've got a huge debt to a doctor. So I frequently said that Madison County needs a free clinic, or a new program with a sliding scale. But all I'm saying is, institutions change, and it takes a tremendous amount of struggle all the time to keep even ones we birth . . . in the right. . . .

ANNE: Well . . . all this stuff in Appalachia and Big Stone Gap—it's gone. . . . We've had energy to create things, but we've also needed to know they don't have to live forever. Maybe what's missing is some of the real grieving; that there's the losses, too. . . .

JOAN WEINGARTNER: Or recognition that it's OK that things don't last forever. You know, that's not a sign necessarily of failure. . . .

LINDA: And sometimes you have to turn adult children loose, and let them make their own mistakes and go their own way (42).

The FOCIS ring has been an important symbolic link between their sisterhood and community partnership. The ring was designed by Margaret Gregg in 1967 and is worn by members, has been passed on to spouses, was given up at marriage and then reclaimed. It symbolized the relationships developed between people and their connection to communities which continually move and change. Monica described it this way:

It is silver, with connecting circles, and one circle has a cross and sometimes it looks like the sun and sometimes it looks like a constellation. What I think FOCIS has evolved into is a ring of relationships. Not one community that is closed but the connecting of several communities: FOCIS as one of several, where individual people entered (like entering the convent), bringing their experiences of birth family and place, of Glenmary women's religious Catholic community, personal visions and qualities and habits (not a gray, uniform habit). People entered the same geographical community and worked and lived there differently: e.g., Marie and Mary Jo in Clairfield, Kathy and Catherine in Big Stone Gap, Anne and I in Dungannon. People entered projects and programs and played different roles and then let go, stayed or moved in and out.

The September 2000 FOCIS gathering placed special emphasis on both the members' involvement in developing a new kind of retirement community, and also on the FOCIS children who were there. Donna Haig Friedman's daughter Sarah later wrote about her September experience and the role of FOCIS in her life:

Why did I come? I think it is for a family I don't have where I want one: Catherine and Kathy Hutson danced together this morning like a proper couple. They have their own bedrooms in their new house but they are a couple for life, retiring together, and loving each other as partners. Catherine wears her hair in a braid wrapped round her head. She is quick witted and tranquil. She had brownies in the tupperware for those of us who came to visit their house, a jumbo jar of peanuts, soda and beer. Unlike my grandmother, Catherine let the brownies sit in the middle of the coffee table and poured herself a beer into a tall clear glass as her guests made themselves at home. . . .

Catherine started up a Bread and Chicken House [in Big Stone Gap]. . . . I picture a flurry of chicken feathers and flour, and Catherine standing serenely in the middle of it all. . . . She is a presence. Sagelike and playful. . . . As the group disperses, Catherine cuts the last of her bread into half slices, leaving the jams and butter and tomatoes for travelers to grab on their way. . . . When she hugs me, she chuckles and tells me, "Be good." She tells Nellie [Appleby], "Be careful in New York City."

Marie Cirillo waits for us with her little notebook. She is fine with the fact that last year I was an artist, the year before a newspaper writer, and this year a school reformer. She wants Nellie's and my email addresses so when next she comes to New York, she can convene a group of us of the second generation of artists, writers, and reformers. Yesterday, Marie listened to my explanation of my job over breakfast and pushed me to consider whether or not such reform furthers the movement to instill entrepreneurial values in our public schools. In fact, I'm sure she is right. "Marie is amazing, always thinking," said my mother as we straggled out and down the hill after breakfast. Does she live alone, I wonder? I have never talked to Marie about her life. . . . Her ideas move too fast to stop for that kind of historical background.

At times, FOCIS feels like a meeting of the country's last remaining revolutionary thinkers who are still conscious of their power. "Unintentional feminists," says Marge Gregg, quoting an article written about the group.[8] "Not bad words, but there's no need to dwell on them." She brought a broken mirror to the meeting. It sits in a semicircle around the low-to-the-ground altar. The mirror symbolizes how our brokenness means that we can see more, she says.

Anne Leibig always leads the liturgy. After Marge explains the mirror, Anne asks Catherine to tell the story of the bread. Catherine says, "Well, first we grew the wheat ourselves out back. . . ." She receives hearty laughter. Anne cries during liturgy, usually when she reads from scripture. This year she asks us to think about faces. . . . I still don't know all the faces in the circle. Jean Luce I know now. She made herself a part of my weekend this year, taking every chance to look me in the face and tell me, "I am so glad you came." I don't know how many people said those words with a hug during the sign of peace. I could say to everyone, "So glad you are here." Maybe I have come simply for that.[9]

FOCIS members—especially those who have officially retired—spend precious little time these days basking in the sun. Instead they are hard at work birthing a new model for retirement living: a planned, intentional community that addresses the spiritual as well as the physical needs of its members.

The idea and leadership for building this community has come from Geraldine ("Dene") Peterson. She borrowed the notion from philosopher and medical doctor Drew Leder, who became interested in aging in the 1980s and developed a model for late-life spiritual communities, which he eventually described in his book *Spiritual Passages: Embracing Life's Sacred Journeys* (Putnam, 1997). Dene was living in Ann Arbor and working at the Newman Center on the University of Michigan campus when she first presented her vision to FOCIS around 1991. No one was interested. But she is nothing if not persistent, and when she repackaged the concept for a FOCIS gathering in 1994, her enthusiasm spurred the creation of the FOCIS Futures Committee to develop the idea.

Dene recalled that the idea began with an awareness of the aging women's need for housing: "The idea was to take care of each other till we die and be affordable. . . . I think the first notion that was brought was housing. Jean [Luce] had this stuff about co-housing and I'd never heard of co-housing but it sounded like a good idea. So we kind of explored and learned more about co-housing first."[10]

Dene's initial dream was to have multiple community sites "in places you'd like to go, like one in Hawaii, one in Denver, one in Florida, one in the mountains, . . . [with] water and mountains and beauty wherever you go."[11] As a practical matter, the Futures Committee settled on a first location somewhere in Appalachia. In search of the right location, they visited Georgia, Tennessee, and even a biosphere community in North Carolina. Finally the committee settled on Abingdon, Virginia, after Anne Leibig and Dick Austin hosted a weekend visit there in 1997.

After retiring herself, Dene moved first to Gatlinburg and later to Abingdon in May 1998, "with the idea of looking for land."

> I would go roaming a neighborhood and look at empty land I thought would be . . . suitable and then I would go to the County Courthouse and look up the plots and see what they were [valued] at. Then I would write people a letter and say what we wanted to do and then I would call them a week later. Finally we found four acres of land that was actually for sale. It was what we wanted: to be walkable to town was one of the criteria. . . . [It] just seemed perfect. And the guy was willing to sell it at almost half the market value. And so it is just like a miracle. I mean, God takes care of her children is all I got to say.[12]

Their gently rolling property in a racially mixed neighborhood abuts the beautiful Virginia Creeper Trail, a thirty-four-mile rails-to-trails route for hikers, bikers, and joggers. When it is completed in 2004, the planned retirement community, to be named "The ElderSpirit Community," will be near the town center and convenient to the public library, hospital, churches, restaurants, and shops.

The women took the community's name from Drew Leder, who encourages his readers to "Imagine a center that would provide a spiritual setting for older adults . . . an ElderSpirit Center resonating with traditional leadership, dignity, and ritual."[13]

Futures Committee member Kathy Hutson explained the goals of the ElderSpirit Community:

The main idea is that the group is interested in a kind of spiritual and philo-sophical life as they get older, and so that would be one aspect. And another would be to assist each other. . . . Another aspect of it is to be involved with the community. We all have a long history of being active where we are. [Since] we are located in a Black neighborhood . . . maybe we'll be diverse racially and cer-tainly in terms of different religious backgrounds.[14]

ElderSpirit residency won't be limited to FOCIS or members of par-ticular faiths. In a recent prospectus the committee wrote: "[The community's] spirituality is not denomination-based; rather it is one's own spiritual path to live beyond the material. We struggle to have a spirituality that is broad enough to be inclusive and yet not so watered down it has little meaning."[15] The Mission Statement reads:

ElderSpirit communities are organized to offer members opportunities for in-tegration with God, themselves, and all creation in their later years, including times of incapacity and death. Members lead lives of service to one another and to the larger community, using time, talents and resources in a loving, wise and responsible way.[16]

Dene described their plan for the community's makeup and living arrangements:

In order to provide service to each other we are asking people to join the community when they retire between [ages] fifty and seventy. This will provide an age span of at least twenty to thirty years in the community, which should give us enough caregivers. The community will be twenty to thirty houses in a co-housing model and a land trust. Co-housing has individual households clustered around a common house with shared facilities such as dining room and an area for work-shop, laundries, etc. Each home is self-sufficient with a complete kitchen. The common house will be an ecumenical center. It will have a chapel or prayer place, besides a laundry. Laundry and prayer make the world go round.[17]

Dene noted that while she is working in her own interest to actualize her vision, the community also has the potential to help many others:

If it works for me and FOCIS, I think it could work for a lot of people who are low income, which we are. . . . Middle income people are also having more trouble finding ways to retire. They find it is terribly expensive, not very rewarding, but no other alternatives. [With communities like this society could also] eliminate a lot of people who are in nursing homes just because they can't function independently but don't really need nursing care. And then there are so many single women [who] . . . are trying to run a household and they don't have enough money. . . . So really, this model could be replicable. If it would work it could really have an effect. There are so many Baby Boomers coming into old age now. . . . So FOCIS just keeps on facing and creating new challenges and new models. It's great.[18]

The Retirement Research Foundation has awarded FOCIS a three-year development grant to create a replicable model community. In April 2000 Kathy Hutson investigated co-housing facilities in Denmark. Reporting on the various arrangements she visited, Kathy wrote: "The main message (and the constant in the groups): Meet weekly for six months to know each other and to know if you want to live with each other for the rest of your life!!"[19]

The ElderSpirit group has formed Trailview Development Corporation to assume oversight and fiscal responsibility for the project. The corporation has contracted for development, financing, packaging, and management and has hired an architectural firm and engineers.

Now with a board of directors, local advisory board, and membership of 42, the ElderSpirit Community issues a quarterly newsletter and periodic mailings with updates on developments. The group of potential residents and supporters gathers monthly for discussion and planning. Groundbreaking is scheduled for March 2003, and completion in fall 2004.

Jean-Marie Luce, ElderSpirit Community coordinator, recently taught a six-week course at the College for Older Adults in Abingdon on spiritual issues related to aging. Anne Leibig, who has worked in Abingdon for almost twenty years as a Gestalt therapist, is developing a course on Mutual Support Skills for the college. "In mutual support of one another in our later years, we need skills to care for the other (i.e., parent, child, spouse, friend) and ourselves. Often people can feel overwhelmed while caring for the other and forget themselves. Or at times when they do care for themselves, they may feel they are abandoning the other: Mutuality means the ability to do both."[20]

Friends visit and write and take an interest in the community. Joan Weingartner's friend and new FOCIS member Jean Gibb recently wrote:

Many years ago I read about a community of medieval women artists, musicians and writers called a *beguinage* and was intrigued with the concept of independent women living together in a mutually supportive housing group. When Joan told me about the FOCIS ElderSpirit project, it felt like serendipity. . . .

It is a rich experience to be in the midst of a genuinely loving and generous community. The liturgy is always moving and beautiful and the spirit is very much alive. And besides, y'all are a lot of fun.[21]

A core group of seven FOCIS members now live in the Abingdon area. They are already extending care to one another when needs arise, celebrating special occasions, and meeting for reflection, discussion, prayer, and work. Dene Peterson wrote in a recent ElderSpirit newsletter:

In response to the immediate needs of one of our members, Lenore Mullarney, ElderSpirit has been given the opportunity to develop a model for mutual care. Lenore is eighty-three and lives with Catherine Rumschlag and Kathy Hutson. She fell in late September and added four compression fractures to her already hurting spine. About two weeks later, she was hospitalized due to an irregular heartbeat. The three days of hospitalization alerted us to the need for multiple caregivers. She is now home and five of us have formed a Care Team to work out ways for Lenore to get needed care and to support one another in the process. Local ElderSpirit members and FOCIS friends have been great in making sure that someone is always in the house with Lenore. There is a wonderful young woman whom Lenore hires to be there when none of us is available. The plan is working and Lenore is responding well to all her visitors and she can now get around the house some on her own.[22]

Lenore died in February 2002, and FOCIS celebrated her life at the annual meeting in Knoxville. Many Knoxville friends joined the FOCIS members to remember her life and work. Lenore had left instructions in her will to provided the wine and Irish whiskey for her wake. Catherine and Anne accompanied the body to her family home in Messina, New York.

As FOCIS members are reaching this new stage in their lives, they are choosing different ways and different places to retire. Marie Cirillo reflects on her thirty years in the Clearfork Valley:

By living here I certainly get an experience of maturing in a way that I feel all right about. I have yet to feel like this is not a place to grow and I've never felt like I'm drying up here or I'm burned out. Which means there's enough coming into my life to keep me growing.

I'm sure part of the positioning is feeling that I'm still open to learning from the people and the land. Too few people choose to learn this way. . . . so I think as long as I stay open to learning from where I'm living that people are satisfied that they're giving me something and then those that keep with me are open to learning something from me! . . .

I don't think about leaving. I think about how to remove myself from pieces of the work that are critical pieces; . . . and I don't want people to become dependent on me because I'm not going to be around forever. It used to be pretty easy with the earlier groups that got started. There was a point when a Model Valley group or a clinic group or a craft group or whatever got to where they had their tasks and they got the system set up and they didn't need me any more. . . .

If my health holds up and everything else, the thing I need to do is create that setting where people really can reflect back and learn what this paradigm shift is that we're in the process of. So that instead of doing these things intuitively, which we are doing, we can articulate what we stand for. I think that's part of why getting in the dialogues with the oral history, getting in dialogue with these students doing summer projects [is important].

Mary Jo Leygraaf is content to stay in Clairfield. "There's little pressure here. . . . I like it because the pace is so much slower. . . . I'm just lucky I landed here! When I left home I never knew this is where I'd end up. But it's just how it happened. There's a lot of nice people, a lot of people with good ol' wholesome values."

Monica thinks about returning someday to live on The River Farm in Dungannon. She has continued her membership and attends the monthly work weekends with her son, Max. Michael, her husband, has Alzheimer's disease and is in an Alzheimer's Care facility in Blacksburg, Virginia.

Helen Lewis has sold her house on The River Farm (which Monica might occupy) and moved to Georgia to be near her sister. Lecturing, committee work, and visiting community-based projects around the world leave Helen little time to warm the seat of the rocking chair on her back porch overlooking bluebird houses along a mountain meadow.

Anne Leibig and Dick Austin continue to live on Chestnut Ridge Farm and are actively participating in the planning of ElderSpirit. They will have a house in the new community and keep the farm; some of the land will be given to the Nature Conservancy.

Margaret Gregg says that she will stay in her nineteenth-century grist mill studio-home in Tennessee as long as she can go up and down the stairs. Afterward, she will move to ElderSpirit, which seems to be fast becoming the new Motherhouse and FOCIS center.

A number of FOCIS members are entering their sixties. To celebrate the occasion their January 2001 meeting in Knoxville featured a "Sixty-Year Extravaganza" planned by Margaret Gregg. Her invitation began:

Now gifted with 60 years
Many FOCIS people are celebrating
The sacred and sexy sixties
What more boundaries to be honored
And trespassed![23]

How do we judge the contribution of the Glenmary Sisters/FOCIS members? Perhaps history will be the judge. This book contributes to the written history and gathering of recollections and documents. Monica adds these thoughts to close the project:

We did stay in or near Appalachia, rural America, no-priest land, which is becoming more no-priest land. Now Sisters are the pastors of many rural parishes. Missionaries are still coming into the area, and there is an Asian priest from San Francisco in McDowell County. There is a growing number of mountain Sisters who have come into the region but not as missionaries.

We made contributions on the regional and local level as we became players with others in church and social change circles. We also created a sustaining-type organization that recognizes the value of the individual person and her particular gifts and connections in the community. We created a low-maintenance type organization. I see FOCIS as a transitional organization during a transitional time in history. Hopefully, the church, the Roman Catholic Church in particular, will change its hierarchical male-dominated power elite government. Hopefully, women will have equal rights and responsibilities in society, in general. I think FOCIS as an organization will end with the founders and their friends. We did stay. And we did go away and come back.

EPILOGUE

Religious Women Continue the Struggle

The Glenmary Sisters were prophetic voices in the 1960s when they took the decrees of Vatican II seriously. Early in the process Pope Pius XII voiced the conviction that "sisters could be a powerful force for the healing of the world if they shed the accretions that had left them an anomaly in current times."[1] The Glenmary Sisters sought to make their work and the Catholic Church relevant to modern life. They confronted the hierarchy of the church and lost that battle, but they continued to build a way of working in community and established their own community of friends who support and love each other.

Even though they left the church organizationally, FOCIS women remain part of the faith community and are connected in solidarity with their sisters still struggling on the inside and the outside to renew and transform the church.

The Glenmary Sisters continue and are now based in the diocese of Owensboro, Kentucky. Sister Rosemary (Esterkamp) celebrated her fiftieth anniversary in the community in 1998. Recently she reflected on her own experience of changing habits: "One of the great differences between the early days and the present is being a Catholic Sister in a habit. . . . Were I in a habit today I think it would affect relationships and how people perceive Catholic Sisters."[2] Within the decade following the FOCIS exodus, Glenmary women—like all U.S. religious—were able to modify or discard habits, renew their work and prayer life, and adapt to changing times.

Yet for women religious in the church an enduring impasse remains: the conflict with the hierarchy around women's gifts and roles. Kathy McCarthy (formerly Sister Mary Patrick), who has struggled with that impasse since leaving Glenmary, recently found a way to bypass the *lex Romana*. On June 11, 2000, in Palm Desert, California, she was ordained a priest in the Old Ecumenical Catholic Church, which is not part of the Roman Church. Kathy wrote a letter to FOCIS, thanking members for their gift of a stole and their emotional and spiritual support:

I loved your response to my invitation to my ordination. I wear that gorgeous stole a lot and feel your hands and shoulders somewhere there. I have always, since leaving Glenmary, been very involved in forming liturgy experiences that come close to the reality of joy and celebration and foretaste of the Kingdom/ Queendom of God that liturgy is supposed to be. . . . I started the pining after priesthood and felt all the agony of closed doors for many years. . . . The fact of being 68 now and the fact of the present Vatican situation combined to make a decision to find a place that would be as close to the Roman tradition as possible and would accept women as priests. The Old Ecumenical Catholic Church clearly stated that they ordain women. . . . The Board of that Church accepted my up-coming Doctorate in Ministry from the University of Creation Spirituality. I passed all the psychological tests, my background and experiences fit, so, I was deemed acceptable. . . .

I feel wonderfully free of a lot of hiding out in the Roman way, yet not adher-ing to the Roman laws. . . . I love to say the Mass and I love to preach. . . . Katie, my two-year-old granddaughter, sees me saying Mass and "knows" that is every woman's place, if they choose. How normal and how healing may my choice become for many little girls and grown women, too.[3]

Monica noted that close ties still bind the women who left Glenmary to form FOCIS with those who stayed in the order or left to pursue other interests:

We in FOCIS remember and miss the women who left the Glenmary Sisters in the upheaval of the 1960s and continued their lives in service to their community. Recently we had the opportunity to reconnect with several. Ellen Browne (Sister Juliana) has helped tremendously with her contacts in the field of "conscious aging" in the planning and resource development for ElderSpirit. Stephanie and Joseph Hemelings helped with the care of Lenore Mullarney, who became critically ill and died February 23, 2002. The group in Cincinnati still gets together several times a year for potluck celebrations. Each FOCIS annual meeting and newsletter brings news from the dispersed community. These continuing connections are strong and stronger still it seems as people experience serious illness and death and tragedy. Glenmary Sisters Martha and Catherine attended the memorial service for Lenore which FOCIS held in Knoxville at their 2002 March meeting.

We are grateful and proud of the groups of Sisters from diverse orders who have entered Appalachian communities since the 1970s and have stayed. They are a faithful witness to the tradition of women in community. There are so many volunteers who still pour in to this region and who leave but take an important life experience with them. The difference now is that local communities are organizing and benefitting from their work.

Through the writing of this book we realize how close a bond we have with the women who remained as Glenmary Sisters and other American communities of women religious and volunteers. New forms of service and partnership are in the process of creation through their efforts.

In her presidential address to the 2000 Assembly of the Leadership Conference of Women Religious (LCWR), Sister Nancy Sylvester spoke of the renewal journey of women religious over the latter half of the twentieth century and the nature of the relationship with the church they inhabit today. She spoke of how their response to the call of Vatican II to be in the world and participate in its transformation has led women to unexpected places of ministry. She said, "We have come to trust our experience and to claim it as a legitimate authority in our lives. We have come to profoundly deeper understandings regarding creation, Incarnation, the beauty of our bodies and our sexuality. This leads us to extend God's loving care to all of creation and to extend our commitment to action on behalf of justice to the whole earth community."[4]

She spoke of their problems with Vatican officials who do not validate women's experience as "authentic religious life" and who still insist on commitment to a corporate and institutional apostolate under a patriarchal clerical culture. She noted that "this understanding of authentic religious life does fit securely into the prevailing [patriarchal] worldview. . . . But we dare to say that we beg to differ with it" (Nancy Sylvester, "Presidential Address," 3). She related how in questioning the patriarchal perspective, women have sought to dialogue with Vatican officials; participate in decisions that affect them; change unjust structures and laws; and develop open and accountable processes, in a context of mutuality and right relationships. She recounted religious women's reactions of frustration, anger, and deep sadness to the hierarchy's responses "that seem authoritarian, punitive, disrespectful of our legitimate authority as elected leaders and . . . our capacity to be moral agents" (4).

She then challenged her Sisters "to embrace the impasse or dark night" where they find themselves in their quest and thus "free the Spirit to push us in the direction of intuition, imagination, contemplative reflection and ongoing discernment." She invited them "now to go to the desert to see with our heart the next steps on our public journey as women religious in our church" (11–12).

Sister Nancy's message triggered painful flashbacks as FOCIS members relived their own experiences from thirty-three years before. Women religious still face the same impasse which Mother Mary Catherine articulated in her telephone conversation with Monsignor McCarthy in 1965. Glenmary Sisters were another casualty of the system along with those named by LCWR's president in her litany of groups and individuals who were marginalized or silenced in their attempts to reform the church. FOCIS can wholeheartedly partake of her conclusion that in attempting to confine women within a lesser universe, the church has lost a resource without price: "the gift of women committed to action on behalf of justice and transformation of the world" (8).

Catherine Rumschlag was moved to respond:

Dear Sister Nancy Sylvester:

I have read your Presidential Address to the Leadership Conference of Women Religious, given August 18, 2000, which happened to be my 74th birthday.

I want to thank you for presenting this brave and insightful statement to the LCWR Assembly. As superior of the Glenmary Sisters during Vatican II and until 1967, I felt many of the tensions which you describe. There seemed to be no way to carry out the directives for renewal of our congregation, as called for by the Bishops of the General Council and profoundly desired by most Glenmary Sisters, while remaining in the structure of canonical religious life. Therefore nearly half of this young congregation (established officially 1952) elected to receive dispensation from vows and continue our work as a lay organization, Federation of Communities in Service.

I have witnessed many changes in the lives and apostolate of religious communities, and rejoiced that they could accomplish these things and continue as religious congregations. I have known some small part of the difficulties Sisters have had in relation to officials in the Church. I am sure you understand these problems much more completely.

Your description of the situation as an "impasse," a term which you define, clarifies for me the situation of Glenmary Sisters in 1966. The conclusion of our community leaders was that we needed to follow the path of renewal as discerned by our members. The alternative seemed to be complete disintegration of our young community.

There is certainly much at stake in the prayer and discernment phase that you are calling for. I pray with you that the Spirit of God will bring a resurrection experience from these difficulties, and that for all concerned "sorrow will be turned into joy." (John 16:20, RSV, Zondervan Bible Publishers)

Reflecting on how FOCIS emerged from their impasse, Monica wonders whether the group has provided lessons for future generations of women religious and other community-minded activists:

The Federation of Communities in Service has become an informal self-organizing system—a Federation of Friends. Since we are not formally connected, we don't need to worry about our organizational relationship with the church. That's a big relief.

It feels freeing on one hand to be able to create your own life in a particular place with the help of a nurturing community to call on for help at times or to celebrate with. On the other hand, there is the need for courage and personal responsibility to find the "right" way to continue the work of justice and love and to live a prayerful life. Some basic training may be needed—after all, making and enjoying community over a weekend is an art form!

Sometimes I wonder about who will continue this work after us? What about the next generation? Then I say to myself, that Max and Nellie will create their own organization to express their values and hope for society and the earth. And if they ask how, I will tell them about my experience in FOCIS (and other organizations) and remind them about this book.

IN MEMORY OF
LENORE MULLARNEY

In memory of Lenore Mullarney. Photo by André Abecassis.

Lenore Mullarney died February 23, 2002, at the age of eighty-four.

In her interview for the FOCIS book she said, "FOCIS members live full lives. They are involved in the community where they live." Lenore came to the Glenmary Sisters in her mid-thirties, unlike most of the teenagers in her postulant group. She had an adult life before joining the Home Mission Sisters of America and was a model of a grown woman who continued to do new things. Lenore was the treasurer and secretary of FOCIS and in many ways kept the organization official. Her files made the FOCIS book compilers' work easier. Thank you, Lenore, for your faithful, full, and gracious life. We will live fully and be involved in the community where we live. That is "Our great hope in common."

VOICES

FOCIS meeting 2000, Abingdon, Virginia. Photo by Nellie Appleby.

*Dates in parentheses denote when entered Glenmary; the names are listed in alphabetical order.

MONICA (KELLY) APPLEBY: (1955) *Sister Mary Monica.* Born in Chicago, Illinois, as "Pat" Kelly, Monica was on mission in Big Stone Gap, Virginia, from 1959 to 1970 with Glenmary and FOCIS. She was elected the first president of FOCIS. She is married to Michael Appleby and has two children, Max and Nellie. She lives on Bitter Ridge outside of Blacksburg, Virginia.

RICHARD AUSTIN: Born in Cleveland, Ohio, in 1934. Dick is a Presbyterian Minister and has been married to Anne Leibig since 1974. They met when they were both in ministry in West Virginia. Dick joined FOCIS in the early 1970s. Dick and Anne live on Chestnut Ridge Farm near Dungannon, Virginia.

KAY (KAERCHER) BARNETT: (1953) *Sister Mary Magdalene.* Born in Sioux Falls, South Dakota, Kay was one of the Sisters who participated in *Lumen Vitae* in 1959–1960. While in Glenmary, she taught school in Russellville, Kentucky, did parish work in Statesboro, Georgia, and assisted at the novitiate in Fayetteville. After leaving Glenmary, she continued to teach special education to learning disabled students, first in Kimball, West Virginia, and then in Minnesota and Indiana. Kay and her husband, Jack, live in Terre Haute, Indiana.

MARIE CIRILLO: (1948) *Sister Marie of Fatima.* Born in Brooklyn, New York, Marie was a member of the Glenmary General Council. She opened the mission in Pond Creek, Ohio. While in school at Loyola University, Marie inspired the Training Program in Chicago. She has lived in the Clearfork Valley in Tennessee since 1967.

DONNA (HAIG) FRIEDMAN: (1964) *Sister Mary Donna.* Born in Illinois, Donna spent one semester at Marquette University and asked to be transferred to Big Stone Gap. She is the director of the Center for Social Policy at the McCormack Institute for Public Affairs at the University of Massachusetts in Boston.

STEPHANIE (FAGAN) HEMELINGS: (1951) *Sister Mary Stephen/Sister Stephanie.* Born in Wilmington, Delaware, Stephanie was in charge of the Public Relations Office of the Glenmary Sisters and was elected vicaress general. Stephanie lives in Alexandria, Virginia, with her husband, Joseph Hemelings. After working for several years in the field of mental retardation and as a coordinator of volunteer visitors for homebound elderly in Washington, D.C., she continues to work, on her own, as an informal caregiver to seniors and handicapped persons.

MARGARET GREGG: (1959) *Sister Mary Ruth.* Born in Chicago, Illinois, Margaret, an artist, created many important images for Glenmary. When on mission in Big Stone Gap she worked with community women to help them produce and market their crafts as a source of income. After leaving the order, she worked with the Epworth ecumenical group in

Knoxville and in the Clear Creek Valley. Today Margaret lives and works in an 1869 grist mill (that she continues to restore) in Limestone, Tennessee.

MARY HERR: Born in Springfield, Illinois, Mary grew up on a farm sixty miles south of there. A former VISTA volunteer with a secretarial and insurance background, Mary met FOCIS members in Knoxville and began volunteering in Clairfield. Mary later moved to Clairfield, helping establish the legal services program there and training numerous paralegals throughout the region. Since 1978 Mary has lived in Cherokee, North Carolina, where she has helped found many social services programs. She presently has two part-time jobs as multicultural parish worker in Cherokee and as regional faith formation consultant for the Charlotte, North Carolina, Diocese.

KATHY HUTSON: Born in South Bend, Indiana, Kathy spent the summer of 1963 as a Glenmary Volunteer in Big Stone Gap and has been friends with people in FOCIS ever since. She joined FOCIS in 1968 and lived at the FOCIS house in Big Stone Gap. She is a speech pathologist and has worked in public schools in Appalachia for the past thirty years. For the past twenty years she has lived with Catherine Rumschlag and helped run the emergency shelter at Christ Hill, until she moved to Abingdon in 1999.

ANNE LEIBIG: (1959) *Sister Mary Phillip/Sister Anne.* Born in Corning, New York, Anne was missioned in Big Stone Gap and Appalachia, Virginia (1963–1967), while still a Sister. Since leaving Glenmary and forming FOCIS, Anne has helped found many other organizations. Anne is married to Dick Austin. She currently lives in Dungannon and works as a Gestalt Therapist at the Abingdon Center for Psychiatry, Counseling, and Education, which she owns with two other women. In 1990 Anne was asked to become the official FOCIS celebrant.

HELEN LEWIS: Born in Nicholson, Georgia, Helen is a sociologist and activist. Helen, Monica and Michael Appleby, and Anne Leibig co-founded The River Farm, Clinch River Educational Co-operative, and the University Without Walls. One of the founders of Appalachian Studies, Helen has been involved in many of the social justice movements in the region. She has worked at the Highlander Center, Berea College, Appalachian State University, and Appalshop. Helen lives in Morganton, Georgia, and is semi-retired. She continues to write, consult, and do workshops and occasional teaching. Helen is the major writer and compiler of this book.

MARY JO LEYGRAAF: (1957) *Sister Mary Jacinta/Sister Mary Jo*. Born in Little Chute, Wisconsin, Mary Jo was on mission in Georgetown, Ohio, during the "troubles." After leaving the order, Mary Jo joined Marie Cirillo and Jean Luce in Clairfield, Tennessee, where she worked with youth and taught pottery. Except for the three years spent getting her degree at the University of Tennessee, Mary Jo has lived in Clairfield for the past thirty years. She works as the bookkeeper and secretary for the Model Valley Economic Development Corporation and the Clearfork Utility District.

MAUREEN LINNEMAN: (1962) *Sister Mary Eileen*. Born in Cincinnati, Ohio, Maureen was one of the first Sisters to wear the experimental habit and to be self-employed outside of Glenmary. She worked as a VISTA Appalachian Volunteer in Artesian Well, near Big Stone Gap. Always drawn to music, Maureen taught herself the guitar and started using it in her work. She wrote "This Land is Home to Me" at an Appalachian networking workshop at the Highlander Center. Today Maureen works as a family and child therapist. She has three children, David, Patrick, and Michael, and has recently moved from Hendersonville to Asheville, North Carolina.

JEAN M. LUCE: (1959) *Sister Jean Marie*. Born in Chicago, Illinois, Jean joined Marie Cirillo in east Tennessee after leaving the order and became the director of the Clairfield Community Center funded by the Office of Equal Opportunity. She was the dean of admission and financial aid at Emory and Henry College for seven years. She lives in Asheville, North Carolina, and works with Geraldine Peterson to develop the ElderSpirit Community.

LINDA (OCKER) MASHBURN: Born in Saint Louis, Missouri, Linda came to Appalachia, after doing nursing in India, to coordinate health fairs for the United Presbyterian Church and the Council of Southern Mountains. After meeting FOCIS members early on, she was inspired to collaborate with them on health fairs throughout the region and to join the group. She founded the Hot Springs Health Program in Hot Springs, North Carolina, with the help of Rae Ann Gasiorowski, another FOCIS member, and ran it for many years. Today she is "retired" in Brevard,

North Carolina, and she and her husband, Bill Mashburn, do volunteer work in Central America.

KATHLEEN MAUVORNIN: Born in Minneapolis, Minnesota, Kathleen was involved in the Epworth Urban Ministry, where she met FOCIS members. Eventually it just seemed natural to join the group. She still lives in Knoxville, retired now from her profession as geneticist. She is married to Bob Richmond, a physician. She works part time as a storyteller.

LENORE MULLARNEY: (1952) *Sister Mary Lenore.* Born in Massena, New York, Lenore was superior at the Eaton Mission, the secretary at the Motherhouse, and the treasurer for the Communications Office. After leaving Glenmary, she moved to Knoxville, where she served as the FOCIS treasurer from 1968 to 1997 and worked for the Commission on Religion in Appalachia (CORA) and the Knox County Association for Retarded Citizens. Lenore retired in 1987. In 1999 she sold her house in Knoxville and moved to Abingdon, Virginia. She died on February 23, 2002, at the age of eighty-four.

SUE (BLAND) MURPHY (1962) *Sister Mary Susan.* Born in Lebanon, Kentucky, Sue was stationed in Fayetteville, Cincinnati, at the Motherhouse, and for a short time in Saint Paul, Virginia. She was a member of Cincinnati FOCIS. She is a special education teacher and lives with her partner, Sherri, in the Cincinnati area.

KAREN NAGEL (1964) *Sister Mary Karen.* Born in Beach, North Dakota, Karen was stationed in Fayetteville and in Milwaukee. Karen was a member of Cincinnati FOCIS. She teaches special education in Cincinnati.

GERALDINE ("DENE") PETERSON: (1947) *Sister Mary Gerald/Sister Geraldine.* Born in Loretto, Kentucky, Dene was a member of the General Council, superior at the new mission in Georgetown, and cook in the seminary kitchen. Dene joined FOCIS in 1996. She initiated the FOCIS Futures Committee responsible for developing the ElderSpirit Community in Abingdon, Virginia.

JOHN RAUSCH: Born in Philadelphia, John is a Glenmary Priest. He became a member of FOCIS in 1988 and is the coordinator for peace and justice with the Diocese of Lexington, Kentucky.

GINNY REMEDI-BROWN (1965) *Sister Mary Carmen*. Born in Chicago, Illinois, and raised on a farm on the city outskirts, Ginny moved to Big Stone Gap immediately after the FOCIS Leave-taking ceremony. Ginny was a founding member of the Christ Hill Community and lived there until 1981, when she moved to Boston. With her partner, Fern Brown, Ginny is the mother of Antonetta Remedi-Brown, born January 27, 2000. The three live in Malden, Massachusetts.

BETH (BUSAN) RONAN: (1964) *Sister Mary Beth*. Born in Cincinnati, Ohio, Beth came to Big Stone Gap as a Glenmary Volunteer in 1963 and joined the order in 1964. After leaving the order, she married Patrick Ronan, a former Glenmary Brother and the first man to join FOCIS. A nurse practitioner, Beth started the Home Health Services for the Appalachian Regional Hospital in Wise, Virginia, and was nursing supervisor in the Mount Rodgers Public Health District in southwest Virginia. She and Patrick have four children and live in Crystal River, Florida.

CATHERINE RUMSCHLAG: (1944) *Mother Mary Catherine*. Born in Decatur, Indiana, Catherine was the eighth candidate to join the newly formed Home Mission Sisters of America. She served as Glenmary's mother general from the order's first profession of vows in 1952 to 1967, when a group of Sisters left to form the Federation of Communities in Service (FOCIS). In January 1969, Catherine moved to Big Stone Gap, where she founded the Bread and Chicken Co-op and operated an emergency shelter for eighteen years. In 1999, she retired and moved to Abingdon, Virginia, where she shares a home with Kathy Hutson.

MARY SCHWEITZER: (1954) *Sister Mary Paul*. Born in Dayton, Ohio, Mary was missioned in Ohio, Georgia, and Virginia. While in Georgia, Mary took classes at Georgia Southern as part of the effort to integrate universities, and she also received her bachelor's degree from there. She joined FOCIS in 1978. Mary has a son, Hans, and is retired from teaching at Winthrop University in South Carolina after twenty-three years.

KATHY (McCRADY) SIMONSE (1963) *Sister Mary Sheila*. Born in Fort Wayne, Indiana, Kathy was sent after profession to Alverno College in Milwaukee for a degree in music education. Kathy arrived in Welch, West Virginia, in the fall of 1968 and taught music in the McDowell County schools for two years. She left for the Washington, D.C., area in 1970 and married Arnie Simonse, a theology professor turned social worker. They have five children. Since 1999, Kathy and Arnie have worked as full-time volunteers with the Passionist Volunteer community in Pineville, West Virginia, just fourteen miles from Welch. Arnie was the coordinator of the Glenmary Co-Missioners. They plan to retire in the mountains one way or another.

MARY (McCANN) THAMANN: (1950) *Sister Margaret Mary*. Born in Gilford, Indiana, Mary served on the missions in Eaton and West Portsmouth Ohio as a Glenmary Sister and at the Motherhouse and training centers. Mary currently lives in Cincinnati with her husband, Harold Thamann.

ELIZABETH (ROTH) TURNER (1955) *Sister Mary Joan*. The Roth family lived across the road from the Glenmary Sisters in Pond Creek, Ohio. They were helpful neighbors and friends. "Betty"—as she was called early on—joined the Sisters after a year in college and a year of work. She served in Saint Paul, Virginia; in Fayetteville at the training center; and in Chicago. She stayed in the Uptown neighborhood, where she was an active citizen, until 1980. She and her husband, Dan Turner, have been active on peace and justice issues supporting El Salvador and have traveled there several times. Dan and Elizabeth moved to Oakland at the invitation of Matthew Fox, where Dan became the editor of *Creation Spirituality* magazine. Elizabeth and Dan participated in the Peace Pilgrimage, walking community to community from Auschwitz, Germany, to Hiroshima, Japan. Elizabeth is currently working in the Oakland unified school district as a substitute teacher and as a volunteer with Saint Mary's Center for the homeless.

JOAN WEINGARTNER: (1964) *Sister Joan Marie*. Born in Cincinnati, Ohio, Joan moved to Welch, West Virginia, after leaving the order and joining FOCIS. After two years she returned to Cincinnati and worked with the FOCIS group in Cincinnati FOCIS ARTS, eventually returning to school and becoming the city manager for Crestview Hills, Kentucky. Joan has a son, Jonathan. She lives in Abingdon, Virginia.

EVELYN (EATON) WHITEHEAD: (1956) *Sister Mary Evelyn*. Born in New Orleans, Louisiana, Evelyn helped Marie and Geraldine start the

Glenmary Ministry to Appalachian Community in Chicago after getting her masters in philosophy at Saint Louis University. Evelyn helped develop and administer the training program in Chicago. She holds a doctorate from the University of Chicago in philosophy. She currently lives in South Bend, Indiana, with her husband, Jim, a pastoral theologian. They work together as authors and lecturers in adult development and spirituality.

Appendix B

GLOSSARY[1]

Apostolic. Of or relating to a succession of spiritual authority from the New Testament apostles.

Apostolic Orders. Another term for *active orders*—those engaged in ministries that answer a need in society. Prior to the 1960s, apostolic communities for women commonly interpreted their mission as education or health care.

Bishop. Most frequently, the pastoral leader of a diocese. Only ordained priests can be consecrated bishops.

Brothers. Members of a congregation of men who are in ministry but not in or preparing for holy orders.

Canon Law. Body of laws that govern the church. Revised most recently in 1983.

Canonical Status. Recognition that a religious community has official standing in the Roman Catholic Church.

Catechetics. Oral or written religious instruction.

Celebrant. The person who is officiating at the Eucharist.

Celibacy. Unmarried state required of Roman Catholic priests and women and men who are members of vowed religious communities; also, abstention from sexual intercourse.

Celibate. One who practices celibacy.

Chancery. The archdiocesan administrative branch that creates and manages official documents.

Chapter of Faults. A monthly event when everyone in the house/community met and confessed the rules they might have broken. The superior then gave a penance.

Charism. Gifts or graces given by God to individuals or groups for the good of the community. From Greek for *gift*, the word has its roots in Paul (I Corinthians 12:4–11). A charism given to the foundress or founder of a religious community is passed on from one generation to the next, although it may need to be updated or refocused.

Cloister. Areas of a convent or monastery reserved exclusively for members of the religious community.

Community. Colloquially, and in the context of this book, a generic term used to describe members of a religious group or the group itself. Living "in community" no longer necessarily means living in the same geographic place but does imply other commitments to the group. Official distinctions designate the kind of vows, charter, and governance a particular community might have and whether it is technically a congregation or an order.

Contemplative Life. In the strict sense, a life dedicated to work and prayer in a cloistered community. Since Vatican II, the term has been explored in a broader context; many women religious who are not cloistered nuns feel that they too are called to be contemplative women.

Convent. Officially, a residence for women religious. The term has most frequently been used to describe the rather large buildings where sisters who taught in parish schools lived. Today two or three nuns living together might call their inner-city walk-up apartment a "convent."

Desert Experience. The desert not only is a physical reality but also carries symbolic meaning. In spiritual imagery, the desert is the place where solitude and community confront each other, where the human and the divine meet.

Diocese. Geographic Catholic community under the pastoral care of a bishop.

Eucharist. From Greek for *thanksgiving.* Sacramental celebration of the death and resurrection of Christ. Often referred to as the Mass.

Formation. Program each religious community designs to train its prospective members. See "novice."

General Council. A religious order's equivalent of a senior management team.

Habit. Distinctive clothing worn by religious communities.

Hebdomadarian. Leadership position in reciting the divine office, rotated weekly. Cantor—leader in singing the Psalms (part of the office).

Hierarchy. Technically, the clergy, including bishops, priests, and deacons. In general usage, the term often refers to those in positions of authority in the institutional church—bishops, cardinals, and the pope.

Liturgy. Public and official prayers and rites of the church. Colloquially, the term is often used to refer to the Mass.

Mother Superior; Mother General. Titles given in some religious orders to the woman in charge. Today, many communities prefer to use the title *president.* Others have a collegial style of management, with no designated superior.

Motherhouse. This may be the place where the religious community originated. It also means the community's headquarters or base of operations—where the mother general or president lives, where the novitiate is, and where chapter meetings are held. Increasingly, it is the site of infirmaries and residences for elderly sisters.

Novice. Woman preparing to profess vows in a religious community. Canon law requires that every novice must have at least one full year and a day of *canonical novitiate,* during which the candidate studies scripture, theology, and the history of the religious group she is joining. Many communities require additional time. The life of novices and the content of formation programs have changed radically since Vatican II; they also differ greatly from one religious community to another. In most cases, however, a novice's spiritual formation is still supervised by a mistress of novices.

Novitiate. Place where or period of time (usually two years for Sisters) during which a novice is trained. After the canonical year (a year and a day) sisters engage in "professional work" after professing their vows. Priests studied in seminary the second year.

Orders. Religious communities of women founded before 1752, often in connection with orders of men. (For example, the Dominicans, Benedictines, Franciscans, and Carmelites are orders of both men and women.) The distinction between *order* and *congregation* is technical and not frequently used now.

Postulant. One who is admitted to a religious order as a probationary candidate before entering the novitiate.

Profession. Pronouncement of vows. Usually a formal ceremony that members of the religious community, family, and friends attend. To *profess vows* or to be a *professed* means to make a declaration of intent to live a life of poverty, chastity, and obedience for a given period of time (temporary vows) or forever (final vows).

Second Vatican Council, Vatican II. Convened in 1962 by Pope John XXIII to open the church to the modern world, Vatican II was an ecumenical council, an assembly of official representatives from the worldwide Roman Catholic Church. John XXIII also invited observers and auditors; Protestants, Jews, and Catholic laymen and laywomen—including some nuns—were among the groups permitted to view the sessions, though not to participate.

Sister. Specifically, a woman who is a member of a religious congregation, not a cloistered order. However, the term is used interchangeably with *nun* and *woman religious.*

Spiritual Direction. Process of trying to understand one's relationship with God, with the help of a trained director.

Spirituality. Lived expression of one's ultimate beliefs.

Venias. An action of lying prostrate on the floor as a symbol of humiliation to elicit pardons or indulgences for "insignificant" sins.

Vocation. From Latin *vocare*, to call. Inclination toward a particular way of life which Christians see as a call from God. Since Vatican II, no one vocation, specifically to religious life as opposed to married or single life, is seen as superior to any other.

Vows. Most generally, solemn promises made to God. More specifically, public promises made by members of religious communities. These are most frequently the vows of poverty, chastity, and obedience. Some communities take additional vows. (The Benedictines, for example, take a fourth vow, of stability—emphasizing their rootedness in their particular monastery.)

Woman Religious. Member of a religious community. Used as an alternative—and often preferred—term for *nun* or *sister*.

NOTES

Preface

1. Monica Kelly Appleby, "A Baptism by Immersion in Big Stone Gap: From South Side Chicago to Southern Appalachia," in *Christianity in Appalachia: Profiles in Regional Pluralism*, ed. Bill J. Leonard (Knoxville: Univ. of Tennessee Press, 1999), 278–297; Monica Kelly Appleby, "Women and Revolutionary Relations: Community-Building in Appalachia," in *Neither Separate Nor Equal: Women, Race and Class in the South*, ed. Barbara Ellen Smith (Philadelphia: Temple Univ. Press, 1999).

2. Marie Tedesco, "The Women of Glenmary and FOCIS: A Modern-Day Version of 'Fotched-On' Women" (paper presented at the Conference for the Study of Gender and Ethnicity in Appalachia, Marshall University, Huntington, W. Va., March 2000).

3. Chris Valley to Helen Lewis, email, 25 July 2000, Personal Papers of Chris Valley, Atlanta, Ga.

Introduction

1. The term "religious" refers to a Catholic woman or man who belongs to a religious order (i.e., nuns, Brothers, and certain priests).

2. Carol K. Coburn and Martha Smith, *Spirited Lives, How Nuns Shaped Catholic Culture and American Life* (Chapel Hill: The Univ. of North Carolina Press, 1999), 300.

3. Lisa W. Foderaro, "A Diminishing Sisterhood in the Market for Recruits," *New York Times*, 16 Jan. 2000.

4. Coleman McCarthy, "The Revolutionary Mary," *Washington Post*, 25 Dec. 1996.

5. Appleby, "Baptism by Immersion," 278–297.

Prologue

1. Mother Mary Catherine Rumschlag, press release, 26 July 1967, East Tennessee State Univ. Archives, Johnson City, Tenn.

2. Art Winter, "Glenmary Down to 15; 50 Leave for Lay Work," *The National Catholic Reporter*, July 1967, East Tennessee State Univ. Archives.

Chapter 1

1. Father William Howard Bishop, *Glenmary Sisters Constitution*, n.p., n.d., Chapter 1, Article 1, Notre Dame Univ. Archives, South Bend, Ind.

2. Luigi Liguitti, *The Glenmary Challenge* (Cincinnati: Glenmary Home Missioners, Autumn 1953), 11.

3. The Glenmary women were not officially recognized as a religious community until 1952.

4. Tedesco, "Women of Glenmary and FOCIS."

5. Mary Philip Trauth, "A New American Catholic History: The Hidden History," in *U.S. Catholic Historian*, vol. 8, no. 3 (New York: United States Catholic Historical Society, 1989), 180.

Chapter 2

1. Carole Garibaldi Rogers, *Poverty, Chastity, and Change* (New York: Twayne, 1996), xiv.

2. Ibid., xv.

3. Sister Mary Philip Ryan, "Glenmary and Adrian Paper," Glenmary papers, East Tennessee State Univ. Archives, 3.

4. See Chapter 12 for a description of the cooperative and its history.

5. The Adrian Dominicans, headquartered in Adrian, Michigan, are a branch of Dominican nuns different from the Ohio Dominicans mentioned earlier.

6. Ryan, "Glenmary and Adrian," 3.

7. In their initial stage of formation, candidates for membership are called "postulants."

8. Ryan, "Glenmary and Adrian," 17.

9. Sister Kevin, and later Sister John Joseph. A Superior is the person in charge of a location where religious are housed or of their work or training.

10. Ryan, "Glenmary and Adrian," 19.

11. Hebdomadarian—leadership position in reciting the divine office, rotated weekly. Cantor—leader in singing the Psalms (part of the office).

12. Ryan, "Glenmary and Adrian," 20.

13. For many centuries women and men entering Catholic religious orders chose a new name as part of the entering ceremony, to signify the putting aside of the old self and their new life of dedication to God. Typically the name was that of a New Testament figure or saint. The practice is now largely discontinued in the

United States. Monica, drawn to Saint Augustine for his preconversion wildness, named herself after his mother.

Chapter 3

1. Lucy Kaylin, *For the Love of God, The Faith and Future of the American Nun* (New York: William Morrow, 2000), 34.

2. Anne Leibig, "Appalachia Converts Sisters," *Sisters Today*, April 1968.

3. This Appalachia, plus the one in the quote from Geraldine Peterson that follows, is a town in Wise County, Virginia.

4. Sister Joan is Sister Mary Joan, who later became Sister Elizabeth and is now Elizabeth Roth Turner.

5. According to a reliable source, Saint Mary's Church and Convent was on Broadway, not Kenmore.

6. Dr. Martin Corcoran, with doctorates from Loyola in both psychology and sociology, was experienced as a consulting psychologist, research director, and professor. He played important roles with Glenmary, both as executive director of the Appalachian Field Study Center and as a source of advice in the community's struggle to shape its future.

7. Sister Anna is Shirley Gallahon. She left Glenmary early on and returned to her birthplace of Cincinnati, where she became a longtime community activist.

8. *Community Bulletin*, April 1966, East Tennessee State Univ. Archives, 2.

9. Kathleen Kaercher Barnett, Extract from talk given at weekend women's retreat, April 1996 (East Tennessee State Univ. Archives, copy of typescript), 2.

10. The Council of Southern Mountains (CSM), originally the Council of Southern Mountain Workers and made up of missionary workers in the mountains, was funded by Office of Economic Opportunity (OEO) to develop poverty programs in the 1960s. It expanded to became an active people's organization addressing problems of strip mining, welfare rights, community development, and workers' and union reform. Federal funding was funneled to CSM because it was the only regional organization in the mountains in the early days of the War on Poverty.

11. "The Appalachian Volunteers were a special group of VISTA volunteers trained and supported in the region. The first contract with VISTA was through the Council of Southern Mountains then later the AVs, as we called them, formed their own organization." (Monica Appleby, e-mail to editor, 2001).

12. At that time southwest Virginia was part of the Diocese of Wheeling.

13. Clinch Valley College in Wise, Virginia, is now called the University of Virginia College at Wise.

14. Anne Leibig, "Excerpts from Interview Material on Religion in Appalachia," n.d., East Tennessee State Univ. Archives, 1. The tapes and transcriptions for the Religious Survey are in the Berea College Archives, Berea, Ky.

15. Anne Leibig, "Appalachia Converts Sisters," in *Sisters Today*, April 1968.

16. "New nuns" was a catchphrase among Catholics at this time to indicate orders that were changing dramatically in response to the challenge of Vatican II.

17. Michael Novak, "The New Nuns," *Saturday Evening Post*, July 1966.

Chapter 4

1. Sister Evelyn (Evelyn Eaton Whitehead), interview by Studs Terkel, in *Division Street: America* (New York: Discus Books/Avon, 1967), 143.

2. In a March 1966 letter to the archbishop, she humbly said: "Your Grace has indicated, though in no precise words, that you do not consider me as qualified for the position I hold. I certainly agree with this, and I have lived with this conviction these thirteen years. Yet when I accepted the position I saw it as God's plan, difficult as it was to understand. I still see it that way, but I would be pleased to give up the position tomorrow if Your Grace should indicate that this would be for the good of the community and the Church" (23 March 1966, Univ. of Notre Dame Archives).

3. [Mother Mary Catherine Rumschlag], "An Account of Relationships Between Glenmary Sisters and Cincinnati Hierarchy September 1965 to September 1966," Glenmary papers, Univ. of Notre Dame Archives.

4. "Apostolic Delegate" to Archbishop Alter, 11 Aug. 1966, Univ. of Notre Dame Archives.

5. "Archbishop Curbs Glenmary Sisters," *National Catholic Reporter*, 21 Sept. 1966, 1.

6. Kathleen Kaercher Barnett, Extract from talk given at weekend women's retreat, April 1996 (East Tennessee State Univ. Archives, copy of typescript), 3.

7. "Archbishop Curbs Glenmary Sisters."

8. The General Council was the order's equivalent of a senior management team.

9. Mother Catherine to Glenmary Sisters, 30 May 1961, East Tennessee State Univ. Archives.

10. Monsignor Edward McCarthy to Mother Catherine, 13 Oct. 1965, Univ. of Notre Dame Archives.

11. The delegation of decision-making to people who encounter the problem directly at the local level.

12. Art Winter, *National Catholic Reporter*, 21 Feb. 1992.

13. Archbishop Alter to Mother Catherine, 18 Sept. 1965, East Tennessee State Univ. Archives.

14. Ninety-Seven Glenmary Sisters to Archbishop Alter, 26 Aug. 1966, Historical Archives of the Chancery, Archdiocese of Cincinnati. For a description of the Special Chapter, see the pages that follow.

15. "Statement Concerning the Goals of the Glenmary Sisters Community," 26 Aug. 1966, Historical Archives of the Chancery, Archdiocese of Cincinnati.

16. Anne Leibig, journal entry, 27 Aug. 1966, Personal Papers of Anne Leibig, Dungannon, Va.

17. Report of telephone conversation between Secretary McCarthy and Mother Mary Catherine, 3 Nov. 1966, Private Papers of Catherine Rumschlag, Abingdon, Va.

18. See for example, the Letters to Editor section, *National Catholic Reporter*, 26 Sept. 1966, 4.

19. Mother Catherine to Glenmary Sisters, 7 Oct. 1966, East Tennessee State Univ. Archives.

20. Sister Stephanie to Glenmary Sisters, 21 May 1966, East Tennessee State Univ. Archives.

21. Mother Mary Catherine to Glenmary Sisters, 14 Nov. 1966, East Tennessee State Univ. Archives.

22. Mother Mary Catherine to the Glenmary Sisters, 25 Dec. 1966, East Tennessee State Univ. Archives.

23. "Purpose of Glenmary Sisters and Policies Related to the Purpose," 1967, Univ. of Notre Dame Archives.

24. J. Cardinal Antoniutti, "Decree," 15 March 1967, East Tennessee State Univ. Archives.

Chapter 5

1. Sister Mary Catherine Rumschlag, "Report of Administration," East Tennessee State Univ. Archives, 3; "The Register of the Reverend Mother General," entries for 13, 16, 17, and 18 April under heading "1967," n.p., n.d., Univ. of Notre Dame Archives.

2. One form they considered and rejected, on the advice of a canon lawyer, was a secular institute (a specific type of organization connected to the church). The lawyer said it would be "the wrong move, because the secular institute was canonically under the same congregation as the vowed religious . . . . And we were marked women. So we would have no more leeway in that role as we did in this one." (Evelyn Eaton Whitehead, interview by Jean Luce, South Bend, Indiana, 1990.

3. Kathleen Kaercher Barnett, Extract from talk given at weekend women's retreat, April 1996 (East Tennessee State Univ. Archives, copy of typescript), 4.

4. Maureen O'Connor to Glemary Sisters, 4 April 1967, University of Notre Dame Archives.

5. Maureen O'Connor to Glenmary Sisters, 4 April 1967, University of Notre Dame Archives. In August 1972, five years after leaving, O'Connor said in an interview in the *Chicago Sun-Times*:

"'I was 18 years old when I entered the Glenmary order in Cincinnati in 1956. We wanted to create home missionaries who would work with Appalachian whites. It was a good concept but it got bogged down right away by all the rules of the church and the battles over internal structure.

'The church should be a vast source for good. Instead, we see the church and state in collaboration. . . . One of the things I really treasure is a letter from Dan Berrigan in which he told me that he admired what our order was doing and wished he had the courage to do the same. Can you imagine Dan Berrigan worrying about courage?

'You know, just before the end, four of us from Glenmary went to Baltimore to visit Dan Berrigan's church. We wanted to go in there and work in his parish with the poor. But it became apparent the Catholic church was not going to let us work within the structure and so 20 of us resigned from the order all at once.'" See Tom Fitzpatrick, "Maureen Goes with What She's Got," *Chicago Sun-Times*, 16 Aug. 1972, Univ. of Notre Dame Archives.

6. This beautiful property, originally used as the Order's Motherhouse, was sold to the Glenmary Fathers and became the site of their present headquarters.

7. Catherine Rumschlag, letter of resignation, July 1967, East Tennessee State Univ. Archives.

8. The chancery is the archdiocesan administrative branch that creates and manages official documents.

9. Throughout the book, quotations from FOCIS members that do not have citations are from the extensive oral history interviews conducted by Jean Luce and others in the early 1990s. Transcripts are located in the archives of East Tennessee State Univ.

10. Rumschlag, letter of resignation.

11. Barnett, Extract, 4.

12. Elizabeth Bounds, interview by Rachel Goodman, transcription, Blacksburg, Va., 1992, East Tennessee State Univ. Archives.

13. Ibid.

Chapter 6

1. See Monica's pledge, Chapter 6.

2. The service was in the chapel of the Fayetteville center.

3. André L. Abecassis, "A Great Hope in Common," *Ave Maria*, [1967], 8–12.

4. Catherine Rumschlag, "Federation of Communities in Service," Appendix A, n.p., n.d. (East Tennessee State Univ. Archives, mimeograph).

5. "Charter of Incorporation," Article V, 1968, East Tennessee State Univ. Archives.

6. "Purpose and Objectives," n.p., n.d. (East Tennessee State Univ. Archives, mimeograph).

7. "FOCIS," n.p., n.d. (East Tennessee State Univ. Archives, mimeograph).

8. Rumschlag, "Federation," Appendix A, n.p.

9. Abecassis, "Great Hope," 2.

10. At this time the Diocese of Nashville included the entire state.

11. CORA, like the Council on Southern Mountains, played an important role in the support of progressive community-based organizations. June Rostan, executive director of the Southern Empowerment Project, offers a succinct definition: "CORA's major role . . . was as a conduit for funds from the major Protestant denominations to community development, direct service and organizing groups and a networking vehicle for people in various types of social and economic justice ministries in the region" (http://www.geocities.com/appalcora/Page_11x.html). Monica Appleby attended CORA's first board meeting in 1965.

12. "4 Nuns Leap 'Over the Wall,'" *Kingsport* (Tennessee) *Times-News*, n.p., n.d., East Tennessee State Univ. Archives.

13. Elizabeth Roth Turner (formerly Sister Mary Joan), "Chicago FOCIS," 22 Nov. 1998, (East Tennessee State Univ. Archives, computer generated), 1.

14. Monica Kelly, "President's Report," 1967, East Tennessee State Univ. Archives.

15. Abecassis, "Great Hope," 12.

16. Betty Bahl, "Light a New Torch of Service," *Extension*, Dec. 1967, East Tennessee State Univ. Archives.

Chapter 7

1. No one in FOCIS has been able to remember which of them coined this quote.

2. These may not resonate as major changes today, but they certainly were in the insular denominational environment of the 1960s.

3. Sisters who had taken permanent vows.

4. Annual Report 1968–1969, East Tennessee State Univ. Archives.

5. Some members like Lenore Mullarney opposed this change: "I fought against dissolving sharing finances. . . . I just knew that was basic to the whole concept. It [became] a different type of structure then, much more individualistic." See Lenore Mullarney, interview by Helen Lewis, transcript, Knoxville, Tenn., early 1990s, East Tennessee State University Archives. Catherine Rumschlag and Kathy Hutson continued the practice in their household at Christ Hill—using Kathy's salary as a speech therapist to subsidize Catherine's largely unpaid work in their ministry to the homeless—until their retirement in 1999. See FOCIS Workshop Transcription, New Market, Tenn., 24 Oct. 1998, East Tennessee State Univ. Archives, 29.

6. Turner, "Chicago FOCIS," 1.

7. Ibid, 2.

8. FOCIS Minutes, Aug. 1968, East Tennessee State Univ. Archives.

9. Turner, "Chicago FOCIS," 2.

10. Monica Kelly, "FOCIS—Catherine Rumschlag," in "Community: The Shape of the Future, Taped Interviews with 10 FOCIS Members," Attachment I, n.p., 1968 (East Tennessee State Univ. Archives, photocopy).

11. Ginny Remedi, interview by Fern Brown in "Interviews: Beginnings: Home Life and Growing Up; Convent/Community; Lesbians and Sense of Community," n.p., n.d., East Tennessee State Univ. Archives.

12. Executive Committee report, 1968, East Tennessee State Univ. Archives.

13. "Beginning Statement of FOCIS Process," [1969], East Tennessee State Univ. Archives.

14. Kathy Hutson, "Monica's Wedding," 1998 (East Tennessee State University Archives, computer generated).

15. FOCIS Workshop Transcription, 32.

16. Ibid., 30–31.

17. Monica Appleby to Marie Cirillo, 20 Sept. 1992, East Tennessee State Univ. Archives.

18. "Former Sister Continues Life of Service," *The Blacksburg Sun*, 5 Dec. 1979, East Tennessee State Univ. Archives.

Chapter 8

1. The activities of FOCIS ARTS are more fully documented in chapter 9.

2. Turner, "Chicago FOCIS," 9–10.

3. Ibid, 3–4.

4. Cincinnati Region Annual Report, 1969, East Tennessee State Univ. Archives.

5. FOCIS Workshop Transcription, 8–10, 31.

6. The former FOCIS Center house was sold in 1974.

7. Anne Leibig, "A Community Development Corporation" in *People's Appalachia*, Summer 1974, 47.

8. The story of the Bread and Chicken House is told in chapter 12.

9. Leibig, "Community Development," 48.

10. Ibid., 49. Paulo Freire (1921–1997) was an adult educator among the rural poor of Latin America whose work and thinking have greatly influenced education and community-based development in the U.S. Monica learned of his ideas when she went to Harvard (where he had taught) and introduced them to FOCIS.

11. In *Mountain Life and Work*, Jan. 1973.

12. Ibid.

13. Christ Hill is described in chapter 10. Intentional communities are small

groups of people who come together deliberately with a common commitment to one another and to Christian communities; they have goals of service and changing unjust structures.

14. Michael Appleby was a member of Vermont's famous troupe.

15. Possibly the most baroque rumor was that Helen—considered the mastermind—had amassed a secret regiment of tanks, presumably to be mobilized in the event that the decent citizens of Scott County decided to invade the farm.

16. County lines mean a great deal to Appalachians, perhaps in part because state governments have historically ignored their needs.

Chapter 9

1. Helen Lewis, "Fatalism or the Coal Industry" in *Appalachia: Social Context Past and Present*, ed. Bruce Ergood and Bruce E. Kuhre (Dubuque, Iowa: Kendall Hunt, 1976).

2. Some of the other foundations which also supported parts of the program were New York, Joint, and Johnson.

3. Robert Masden, "Discovery, Expression, Communication: An Arts Approach to the Problems of Appalachia," 1 Feb. 1969, Proposal, East Tennessee State Univ. Archives, 4.

4. Margaret Gregg, Exhibit D, "Appalachian Environment," in "Discovery, Expression, Communication Report 1969 Summer Projects," n.d., East Tennessee State Univ. Archives, 2–6.

5. "Dock Boggs [1898–1971, a Wise County native,] was one of the most distinctive and compelling of the old-time banjo pickers and singers in southern traditional music." See Mike Seeger, "Dock Boggs, Memories and Appreciations," in *old-time herald*, Winter 1998.

6. Ralph Stanley and Jean Ritchie are traditional Appalachian musicians who have achieved national stature; Mike Seeger, brother of Pete, is a Grammy-winning musician who employs traditional styles in his playing.

7. "Red dog" is the clinker product of spontaneous combustion in gob piles (the coal waste from mines). It is described as "a sharp-edged reddish rock used in some counties as a road base." See Lee Mueller and Lance Williams, "Power Plant to Use Coal Waste as Fuel Source," in *Lexington Herald-Leader*, 10 April 2000.

8. A slightly different version of this story appeared in Jack Wright's article, "Only Remembered for What He Has Done—Dock Boggs," in *old-time herald*, Fall 1998.

9. Musicians Rich Kirby and John McCutcheon performed together for a number of years. McCutcheon moved to Charlottesville in the 1980s, but Kirby still lives in Scott County on The River Farm. Wise County native Wright currently teaches at the University of Ohio Film School.

10. Nancy Herzberg, ed., *From Roots to Roses, The Autobiography of Tilda Kemplen* (Athens: Univ. of Georgia Press, 1992), 39.

Chapter 10

1. In the 1970s residents and organizers began calling Clear Fork Valley "Model Valley," a name used frequently in this book.

2. Shelby York, interview by Virginia Nickerson, tape recording, Clairfield, Tenn., fall 1996, East Tennessee State Univ. Archives.

3. The Highlander Research and Education Center (formerly the Highlander Folk School) has played an important role for FOCIS members since the 1960s. Founded in 1932 by Myles Horton, who believed in the power of education as a source of social change, Highlander began by offering adult education courses to poor Tennesseans. By the 1940s Highlander was working to build the southern labor movement across color lines and in the 1950s became involved in the nascent Civil Rights movement. In the 1970s and 1980s it was involved in research around environmental and economic injustice in Appalachia. The Center says, "Throughout our history, we have held to a central principle: For institutional change to be effective, it must begin with the people directly affected by the problems they are attempting to solve." See "Highlander Research and Education Center," in *The Capital Times*, 1 June 2001: http://www.captimes.com/freedom/weblog/newmarket/index.php, and the Highlander Web site: http://www.hrec.org/.

4. Elizabeth Hunter, "Hot Springs' Health Care Pioneers" in *Appalachia*, 30 (May–Aug. 1997): 18–19.

5. Shelby York interview.

6. Mary Herr, application to the University Without Walls (Roger Williams College), 1974, East Tennessee State Univ. Archives, 3.

7. Full-blooded Cherokee Richard (Yogi) Crowe later earned a master's degree in public health and became director of the American Indian recruiting program at the University of North Carolina School of Public Health.

8. Mary Herr, "Reflections on Working with Native Americans in Cherokee," n.p., n.d. (East Tennessee State Univ. Archives, typescript).

9. Father Paul Fredette, "Mary Herr, Minister Among the Cherokee" in *The Glenmary Challenge* (Winter 1994): 10.

10. Lisa L. Bocock to Nancy Susan Reynolds, Awards Advisory Panel, 26 May 1993, Attachment A, East Tennessee State Univ. Archives.

11. Herr, "Reflections on Working with Native Americans."

12. Kathleen Hutson, Appalachian Family Ministries newsletter, 1989–1990, East Tennessee State Univ. Archives.

13. In 1995 a Clinton-led Republican Congress set lifetime term limits for

most welfare recipients at five years but has yet to enact a similar restriction for the better-housed members on its own rolls.

14. Catherine Rumschlag, interview by Rachel Goodman, unattributed typescript copy, Big Stone Gap, Va., 1992, East Tennessee State Univ. Archives.

15. Woman-Church is an informal movement which began in the mid-1980s among largely Catholic and American women unhappy at the limitations of their roles and opportunities to use their gifts in the male-dominated formal church structure.

16. Catherine Rumschlag, *Appalachian Family Ministries Newsletter*, Christmas 1999, East Tennessee State Univ. Archives.

17. "County Chamber of Commerce Salutes Talented Local Citizens" in *Coalfield Progress*, 27 April 2000.

Chapter 11

1. "Institute for Cultural Exchange (a student experience program in Wise County, Virginia)," report of activities, Jan. 1969 (East Tennessee State Univ. Archives, copy of typescript).

2. Tufts University Lincoln Filene Center, "Appalachian Proposal," n.d. (East Tennessee State Univ. Archives, copy of typescript).

3. The students interviewed were in Helen Lewis's Urban Sociology class at Clinch Valley College.

4. The Union for Experimenting Colleges and Universities was originally formed in 1964 by ten institutions, including Bard, Antioch, Sarah Lawrence and Hofstra Universities. In 1970 funding from the U.S. Office of Education and the Ford and Carnegie Foundations helped the consortium establish the University Without Walls program described below.

5. Currently a fellow of the Institute of Development Studies in the United Kingdom, John Gaventa studies community participation and education methodologies. After studying the Clearfork Valley for years, in 1980 he published its history in *Power and Powerlessness: Quiescence and Rebellion in an Appalachian Valley* (Urbana-Champaign, Univ. of Illinois Press, 1980).

6. John Gaventa, interview by Helen Lewis, tape recording, Knoxville, Tenn., 1996, East Tennessee State Univ. Archives.

7. Fred Brown, *Knoxville News-Sentinel,* 31 Jan. 1973.

8. The new organization, Just Connections, involves community partners and the following colleges: Emory and Henry, Carson-Newman, Maryville, Tusculum, Union, Berea, SE Community College, and Ferrum, in West Virginia, Virginia, Tennessee, and Kentucky.

9. Marie Cirillo, "On a Ministry of Development," 20 April 1998, unpublished paper.

10. University Without Walls/Providence, "Packet VII: UWW Philosophy and Program Criteria," 1973, (single sheet), East Tennessee State Univ. Archives.

11. "General Information Brochure" of Appalachian University Without Walls, n.d., East Tennessee State Univ. Archives.

12. Ibid.

13. "Mountains are Campus for Scott County College," *Kingsport Times*, 30 June 1974.

14. Monica Appleby, "Towards a Rural College of Appalachia: An Experiment in Community-Based Education" (East Tennessee State Univ. Archives, copy of typescript), 4.

15. Ibid., 6–7.

16. Monica Appleby, Proposal to National Endowment for the Arts, Summer Arts Program, 1973, East Tennessee State Univ. Archives.

17. Helen M. Lewis et al., eds., *Picking Up the Pieces* (New Market, Tenn.: Highlander Center, 1986), 6–7. Poet Carol Honeycutt completed her associate of arts degree through the Depot classes and has continued to work with many women's empowerment projects including In Praise of Mountain Women (see chapter 13).

18. Helen Lewis and John Gaventa, *A Teacher's Guide to Community-Based Economics* (New Market, Tenn: Highlander Center, 1988).

19. Appalachian Field Study Center, "A Proposal for an Appalachian University Without Walls Degree Program to be Based in an Appalachian College," n.p., n.d. (East Tennessee State Univ. Archives, copy of typescript).

Chapter 12

1. In *Mountain Life and Work*, Jan. 1973.

2. "Bread and Chicken House to Close," *Big Stone Gap, Va. Post*, 8 June 1988, article in Virginia FOCIS scrapbook, East Tennessee State Univ. Archives.

3. Transcript paper, Personal Papers of John Rausch, Stanton, Ky.

4. Lewis *Picking Up the Pieces*, 28.

5. John Rausch, "The Legacy of Appalachian Cooperatives," typescript, John Rausch personal papers, Stanton, Ky.

6. Nancy Robinson, Bill Kenny, and Helen Lewis, "Dungannon Development Commission and Phoenix Industry, A Case Study Presented by Nancy Robinson, Bill Kenny, and Helen Lewis," n.d. (East Tennessee State Univ. Archives, computer-generated).

7. Ibid.

8. Ibid.

9. Ibid.

10. Nancy Robinson, interview by Edythe Ann Quinn, Dungannon, Va., 1990, quoted in Edythe Quinn, "Clinch River Health Services," transcript copy of University of Tennessee college class paper, East Tennessee State Univ. Archives, 33.

11. Shelby York, interview by Virginia Nickerson, recording and transcription, Clairfield, Tenn., 1997, East Tennessee State Univ. Archives.

12. Ibid.

13. Postmistress Louise Adams began organizing around water issues with other parents who had lost children in the epidemic.

14. York, interview.

15. Ibid.

16. Ibid.

17. Volunteer Trish Dillon spent the better part of a year persuading the Farmers Home Loan to work with the Model Valley group.

18. York, interview.

19. Ibid.

Chapter 13

1. Nancy Sylvester, "Presidential Address" to LCWR (Leadership Conference of Women Religious) Assembly 2000: "Risk the Sacred Journey," 18 Aug. 2000, (East Tennessee State Univ. Archives, photocopy of computer generated text), 2.

2. Matthew Fox, "Spirituality, Social Justice, and the Glenmary Tradition," Cincinnati Glenmary Home Missioners, 1978, East Tennessee State Univ. Archives, 6.

3. Cecil Rhodes, founder of the Rhodes Scholarships at Oxford, was an imperialist who became a virtual dictator of the Cape Colony (later the British colony of South Africa), made a huge fortune in diamonds through exploitation of native Africans, and founded the British colony of Rhodesia (now Zimbabwe).

4. John Gaventa, interview by Helen Lewis, tape recording, Knoxville, Tenn., 1996, East Tennessee State Univ. Archives. "The book," based on John's dissertation at Oxford, is *Power and Powerlessness: Quiescence and Rebellion in an Appalachian Valley* (Urbana-Champaign: Univ. of Illinois Press, 1980).

5. York, interview.

6. Mary Beth Dakoske Duffey, "Fidelity to a Promise of Service," *Catholic Rural Life*, April/May 1981, 23.

7. Mary Cirillo, Report to Bishop on Clairfield Activities, Sept. 1996, East Tennessee State Univ. Archives.

8. Turner, "Chicago FOCIS."

9. West Virginia State Archives, "Buffalo Creek," (http://www.wvculture.org/history/buffcreek/bctitle.html).

10. Cody Lowe, "Can Faith Affirm Right to Abortion?," *Roanoke Times and World News*, 12 March 1996.

11. *Stay With Us Don't Go 'Way*, report on FOCIS ARTS project, 1968, East Tennessee State Univ. Archives.

12. Activist Bob Swann, now 82, "is the father of [the land trust] movement.

It started during his civil rights work when he co-founded the first Community Land Trust in 1967 in Albany, Georgia with Slater King, a cousin of Martin Luther King, Jr. A group of concerned citizens bought 5,000 acres and leased it to small-scale African American farmers, who otherwise could not have afforded the land" (Tom Meier, "A Return to Community" in *Conscious Choice*, April 1999 [http://www.consciouschoice.com/issues/cc1204/schumacher.html]).

13. Woodland Community Land Trust brochure, n.d., East Tennessee State Univ. Archives.

14. For her seventieth birthday in 1999, Marie conveyed unhappy news in her invitation: "The past three years has brought a share of death and destruction. Six burnings have destroyed Woodlands major developments. Two homes, the saw that cut lumber for affordable homes, the woodshed that stored lumber for 2 houses, 4 camp cabins that house 16 volunteers over most of the summer and finally the beautiful little guest house that offered hospitality to many. All are gone from Woodland's property" ("These Are My Sentiments," 31 Oct. 1999, East Tennessee State Univ. Archives).

15. United Nations Centre for Human Settlements New York Office, "World Habitat Day Award," 2 Oct. 1989, (copy of certificate), East Tennessee State Univ. Archives.

16. Mary Cirillo, "Final Report for the Grant Agreement Between the Appalachian Regional Commission and the Federation of Communities in Service (FOCIS)," June 2000, East Tennessee State Univ. Archives, 8; Report for the Clearfork Community Institute: Planning and Organizational Development Grant, 2000, East Tennessee State Univ. Archives.

17. Teri Vautrin, interview by Rachel Goodman, tape recording, Dungannon, Va., 1992, East Tennessee State Univ. Archives.

18. Nancy Robinson, interview by Rachel Goodman, tape recording, Dungannon, Va., 1992, East Tennessee State Univ. Archives.

19. Vautrin, interview.

20. Ibid.

21. Beth Spence, *In Praise of Mountain Women* (Women's Task Force, Catholic Committee on Appalachia, 1988).

22. Jean Eason and Anne Leibig, "In Praise of Mountain Women: 1991 May 3–5 Abingdon, Va.," 1991 (East Tennessee State Univ. Archives, booklet), 1.

23. Jean Eason and Teri Vautrin, "In Praise of Mountain Women: Praise, Healing, Journey," Saint Paul, Va., 1995 (East Tennessee State Univ. Archives, booklet), 4. Dangerous memories refer to "memories which make demands on us . . . reveal[ing] new and dangerous insights for the present." Johann Baptist Metz, quoted in Bernard J. Lee and Michael Cowan's *Dangerous Memories: House Churches and Our American Story* (Kansas City, Mo.: Sheed & Ward, 1986). See discussion in chapter 14.

24. Jean Eason, "The Herstory of In Praise of Mountain Women," n.p., n.d. (East Tennessee State Univ. Archives, booklet).

25. Eason and Leibig, "In Praise of Mountain Women: 1991," 2.

26. Ibid., 19.

27. Eason and Vautrin, "In Praise of Mountain Women: Praise," 9–10.

Chapter 14

1. Except for the initial poem, this section is from Anne Leibig, "Becoming a Celebrant in Appalachia," *Now and Then* (Fall 1994): 33–35.

2. John Rausch, interview by Virginia Nickerson and Helen Lewis, tape recording, Berea, Ky., 16 March 1997, East Tennessee State Univ. Archives.

3. Contextual theology, liberation theology , and feminist theology are some of the new theological interpretations or transformative theologies which emerged in the 1960s and '70s. Liberation theology developed in the progressive church movements in South America in struggles for economic and social justice. Contextual theology emphasizes theology which relates to particular places and people with "a commitment to do justice and transform social reality as a fulfillment of the biblical message." In William K. Tabb, "Introduction: Transformative Theologies and the Commandment to do Justice," William K. Tabb, ed. *Churches in Struggle* (New York, N.Y.: Monthly Review Press, 1986), xiv.

4. Lee and Cowan, *Dangerous Memories.*

5. Anne Leibig, "A book review by Anne Leibig of *Fierce Tenderness, A Feminist Theology of Friendship*, Mary Hunt (New York: Crossroads, 1991) for FOCIS January gathering," n.p., n.d. (East Tennessee State Univ. Archives, photocopy of computer-generated text).

6. Monica Appleby to FOCIS members, 27 March 1990, East Tennessee State Univ. Archives.

7. Marie Cirillo, "You are Invited to Participate in a Community Theology Workshop in the Roses Creek Community at Marie Cirillo's Home," 1990 (East Tennessee State Univ. Archives, photocopy of invitation).

8. Feminist theologies developed to focus on the experiences, needs, and concerns of women, all emerging out of the common recognition of women's oppression. They critique patriarchy and emphasize the role of women's experience in the quest for justice and liberation. Donald K. McKim, *Westminster Dictionary of Theological Terms* (Louisville, Ky: Westminster John Knox Press, 1996), 104.

9. Unsigned form letter bearing handwritten notation, "To Community People," 3 Nov. 1990 (East Tennessee State Univ. Archives, photocopy).

10. Cirillo, "You are Invited."

11. Marie Cirillo, "Reflections and Sharings on Theology Weekend Nov. 1990 Roses Creek," n.d. (East Tennessee State Univ. Archives, photocopy of computer-generated text), 1.

12. Monica Appleby to Marie Cirillo and Anne Leibig, 24 Nov. 1990, East Tennessee State Univ. Archives; Monica Appleby, "God the Earthworm, . . ." 12 Nov. 1990, signed "Monica KAE," East Tennessee State Univ. Archives.

13.Cirillo, "Reflections."

14. Monica Appleby to FOCIS members, 23 Dec. 1990, East Tennessee State Univ. Archives.

15. For example, *Fierce Tenderness*.

16. Herr, "Reflections on Working with Native Americans."

17. Kathy Hutson, FOCIS meeting discussion, transcription, Knoxville, Tenn., 1992, East Tennessee State Univ. Archives.

18. Margaret Gregg, planning notes for 23 March 1993, East Tennessee State Univ. Archives.

19. From Ezekiel 37: "The hand of the Lord was upon me, and carried me out into the spirit of the Lord and set me down in the midst of the valley which was full of bones . . . and lo, they were very dry. And the Lord said unto me, Son of man, can these bones live? And I answered, O Lord God, thou knowest. Again the Lord said unto me, prophesy upon these bones: Behold I will cause breath to enter into you and ye shall live: And I will lay sinews upon you, and will bring up flesh upon you, and cover you with skin, and put breath into you, and ye shall live."

20. Festival of Friends brochure, East Tennessee State Univ. Archives.

21. Ibid.

22. Ibid.; Jane McElroy, "The Quilt," Festival of Friends brochure, 1993, East Tennessee State Univ. Archives. Jane was the quilt designer and project coordinator.

23. FOCIS Workshop Transcription, 8–10, 25, 31, 32, 59, 60–62, 67, 69. Parts also transcribed directly from audio tape of "Liturgy, Theology, and Spirituality" discussion group session at the workshop.

24. Monica Appleby to Suzanna O'Donnell, 19 Feb. 1999, East Tennessee State Univ. Archives.

25. Bounds, interview.

Chapter 15

1. Michel de Montaigne "The Journey Not the Arrival Matters" in *Essays*, translated by Charles Cotton (New York: Doubleday, 1947).

2. Paulo Freire, *Pedagogy of the Oppressed* (New York: Seabury Press, 1970).

3. Walter Brueggemann, *The Prophetic Imagination* (Philadelphia: Fortress Press, 1978), 110.

4. FOCIS Workshop Transcription, 34.

5. Appleby, "Women and Revolutionary Relations," 173, 175.

6. "Research, training, action, and evaluation" was the formula of successive steps Dr. Martin Corcoran had developed and instilled as the correct approach to community action/organizing.

7. FOCIS Workshop Transcription, 51–52, 54, 58–59.

8. Marie Tedesco, "The Women of Glenmary and FOCIS: A Modern-Day Version of 'Fotched-On' Women?" Paper presented to the Conference for the

Study of Gender and Ethnicity in Appalachia, Marshall Univ., West Virginia, March 5, 2000.

9. Sarah Friedman to Monica Appleby, Oct. 2000, typescript, East Tennessee State Univ. Archives.

10. Futures Committee Discussion at Highlander FOCIS Workshop, 25 Oct. 1998 (audio tape), East Tennessee State Univ. Archives.

11. Ibid.

12. Ibid.

13. Drew Leder, "A Spiritual Community in Later Life: A Modest Proposal," *Journal of Aging Studies* 10 (Summer 1996): 109.

14. Futures Committee Discussion.

15. "Monthly Meetings for Potential Residents," notice, 16 June 2000, East Tennessee State Univ. Archives.

16. Mission Statement, Brochure I, "An Ecumenical Neighborhood of Mutual Support," 16 June 2000, East Tennessee State Univ. Archives.

17. Futures Committee Discussion.

18. Ibid.

19. Kathleen Hutson, "Danish Co-Housing for Seniors Trip," *ElderSpirit Community News*, vol. 1, no. 4 (Fall 2000), East Tennessee State Univ. Archives.

20. *ElderSpirit Community News*, vol. 1, no. 4 (Fall 2000), East Tennessee Sate Univ. Archives.

21. FOCIS Newsletter, Fall 2000, East Tennessee Sate Univ. Archives.

22. *ElderSpirit Community News*, vol. 1, no. 1 (Fall 2000), East Tennessee Sate Univ. Archives, 3.

23. FOCIS Newsletter, Fall 2000, East Tennessee Sate Univ. Archives.

Epilogue

1. Lora Ann Quinonez and Mary Daniel Turner, *The Transformation of American Catholic Sisters* (Philadelphia: Temple Univ. Press, 1992), 18, quoted by Nancy Sylvester in "Presidential Address" to the Leadership Conference of Women Religious (LCWR) Assembly 2000, *Risk the Sacred Journey*, 18 Aug. 2000, 3.

2. Sister Rosemary Esterkamp, "50 Years of Service," *Kinship*, Spring 1998, 4–7.

3. Kathy McCarthy letter, FOCIS Newsletter, Fall/Winter 2000, 6.

4. Sylvester, "Presidential Address," 3.

Glossary

1. Some of the definitions come from Richard P. McBrien, ed., *The Harper Collins Encyclopedia of Catholicism* (New York: Harper Collins, 1995) in Rogers, *Poverty, Chastity, and Change*, 311–316. Others are from interviews with FOCIS women.

INDEX